Silvanu

Cornish Architec

Silvanus Trevail

Cornish Architect and Entrepreneur

Ronald Perry and Hazel Harradence

Francis
Boutle
Publishers

Frontispiece: Silvanus Trevail, President of the Society of Architects, Fellow of the Royal Institute of British Architects, County Councillor, Justice of the Peace, Mayor of Truro. Family papers

First published by Francis Boutle Publishers
272 Alexandra Park Road
London N22 7BG
Tel/Fax: (020) 8889 7744
Email: info@francisboutle.co.uk
www.francisboutle.co.uk

Silvanus Trevail: Cornish Architect and Entrepreneur
© Ronald Perry and Hazel Harradence, 2008

ISBN 978 1 903427 43 9

The authors

Hazel Harradence is a founder member and membership secretary of The Silvanus Trevail Society. The Society, formed in 1993, aims at increasing awareness of the historical significance of Trevail's architectural practice through research into his life and the preservation of his work. Hazel came to Cornwall bringing business and administrative skills that have been put to good use in connection with historical and environmental groups on whose committees she has served for many years. Researching various aspects of Cornish history has led to her lecturing across the county and producing articles on these subjects. She has spent a considerable amount of time working as a volunteer at Cornwall Record Office, assisting in cataloguing collections.

She is the sole author of the Silvanus Trevail *Register of Buildings*, the most comprehensive work of its kind ever produced for a British architect.

Ronald Perry B Sc, MA, Ph D, Dip Ed, is secretary of The Silvanus Trevail Society. He came to Cornwall in 1965, after administrative and academic experience in England, Germany and the Far East, to build up the Faculty of Management, Business and Professional Studies at Cornwall College. He has carried out numerous socio-economic surveys of the region for the British Social and Economic Research Development Group. More recently, he has published many historical studies, mainly dealing with the period when Silvanus Trevail lived, for the Institute of Cornish Studies of Exeter University, the Royal Institution of Cornwall, the Trevithick Society, the Cornwall Association of Local Historians, *An Baner Kernewek* and the China Clay History Society. For his contribution to the history of Cornwall, Dr Perry was created a Bard (*Scryfer Negis*) of the Cornish Gorsedd.

Contents

3		Foreword by Matthew Saunders MBE
5		Sources and acknowledgements
7		List of abbreviations
8		List of illustrations
13	One	An age of adventurers
20	Two	'Mr Trevail's landmarks'
29	Three	Competition, income and travel
41	Four	Triumphal arches, harbours of refuge and politics
53	Five	Trevail 'gets his knife' into some powerful men
62	Six	The 'Chancellor of the Exchequer' meets a setback
70	Seven	Grand plans for tourism
79	Eight	County Councillor, educational and health crusader
87	Nine	Railway hero, fisheries, housing the rich and poor
98	Ten	Resurrecting the tourist plan
105	Eleven	A crowded mayoral year
112	Twelve	Trevail in the world of commerce, banks and shops
124	Thirteen	Passmore Edwards and Silvanus Trevail
138	Fourteen	Seaside problems and Newquay riots
152	Fifteen	Public and private health problems
165	Sixteen	Presidential glories and personal tragedies
175	Seventeen	What drove Trevail to self-destruction?
185	Appendix	The buildings of Silvanus Trevail
220		Notes
233		Index

Foreword

Matthew Saunders MBE
Secretary, Ancient Monuments Society

Very few architects have societies set up in their name to keep the lamp of memory burning. Greek Thomson has one, so has Lutyens. But they are rare beasts. Rarer still are those capable of putting together a highly engaging and scholarly biography. Well, these authors have done just that, honouring and celebrating the work of their chosen subject, with insight coupled with honesty.

Silvanus (it seems natural to use the Christian name having felt so close to the man in these 17 chapters) emerges as complex but thoroughly of his time, the archetypal Victorian. This was manifested above all in sheer industry (he not only put up more structures than any other Cornish architect, he founded hotel companies, served as Mayor of Truro and became President of the Society of Architects). But his empathy with the spirit of that age emerged also in unflappability and social optimism (except in his declining months when he was given to profound personal pessimism). He was politically progressive, an astute and occasionally ruthless businessman, an inveterate traveller, argumentative and, yes, at times a pompous windbag. As with Pugin there is the air of the manic about his hyperactivity, burning out and early death. Samuel Smiles would have loved the strong element of rags to riches, made even more poignant by the Greek tragedy of the end — blowing his brains out in the toilet of a train on the way to a funeral.

The 18th and 19th centuries were the last great age of the provincial architect. Some so dominated their county or town that the names of the designer and locality became inseparable — Carr of York, Webster of Kendal, Harrison of Chester. By the 19th century such was the explosion in building that some names came to be associated with towns or cities alone — Watson Fothergill in Nottingham, the William Sugdens in Leek, William Watkins in Lincoln. James Hicks ruled the roost in Redruth and liked to think that Silvanus should be similarly corralled in Truro. If any town bears his stamp more than others it is indeed Truro, but the sheer energy, acumen and architectural imagination of the man soon led Silvanus to dominate the whole of his native county. Cornwall is Trevail country.

And the architecture is richly varied and inventive in both plan, elevation and style.

There is hardly any Cornish settlement of any pretension that lacks a chapel, hotel, school, library, bank or house, (newbuild or extension) by Silvanus. The language is normally inspired by the Renaissance but he was too eclectic to be pigeonholed even to that generous extent. There is a sheer love of materials, details and craftsmanship that leads occasionally to delightful perversity. There was an informal school of 'rogue' architects in the mid-nineteenth century and he too seems to have allowed sheer bravura to run away with him at times – thankfully. That is what makes his repertoire so astonishing in its range and which also enriches and enlivens the townscape. The fairly ubiquitous use of Cornish granite, often with that distinctive bluey Plymouth limestone and loud red terracotta lends many of his designs a polychromatic punch. The granite too, so hard to work and therefore impossible to make too fussy, gives many compositions an elemental quality – although nothing perhaps in Silvanus' oeuvre is quite as original as those range of buildings in giant single storeys designed by James Hicks opposite the station at Redruth. You know you are in a county like no other when you see these.

You would expect therefore such a particular set of gifts to have been recognised; but you would be mistaken. Sir Nikolaus Pevsner's 'Buildings of England' volume on Cornwall was the very first, alongside Middlesex in 1951. At that stage his Chairmanship of the Victorian Society was seven years away (as indeed was the establishment of the Society itself). Trevail was hardly mentioned and where he was, it was to bemoan, even excoriate. His monster hotel, the Headland at Newquay, had 'no redeeming features'. It is indeed fairly stolid but that remark is quite stupidly dismissive. The history of the place, not just designed by Silvanus but built for the hotel company he helped to found and the riots that greeted its proposed construction add a dimension that should be picked up by Peter Beacham in the revision of the volume that is about to start. Indeed, this whole biography should be at the right hand of all those revising the Pevsner.

Tendency towards the suicidal is often the curse, the downside of the artistic temperament. He was not alone among architects in seeking oblivion through his own hand and those that have preceded him down that doomed path – Borromini, G G Scott Jr – have, like him, strained to go beyond the conventional – a manifestation perhaps of the inability ever to be satisfied, to be content with one's own particular genius. Who knows why he did it. It hardly matters now anyway. But one can still share in the sadness that this complicated, self-destructive talent was not allowed ten, perhaps even twenty, more years to vanquish his personal demons and stamp his mark yet further on the cities, towns and villages of Cornwall.

Sources and acknowledgements

The principal primary sources of information on the architectural output of Silvanus Trevail are the many thousands of plans, elevations, drawings and sketches held in Cornwall Record Office at Truro. These have all been carefully checked, catalogued and described by Hazel Harradence, assisted by members of the Silvanus Trevail Society, including Pauline Howard, Ann and Ronald Perry, John Rapson, Helen Trist, Joy Wilson and James Whetter.

Cornwall Record Office also houses Trevail's correspondence files and letter books that contain thousands of items of information about his professional and business activities. Some years ago the letter books were summarised and the correspondence files sorted by subject matter and put into date order on a monthly basis by Ronald Perry. Also from the Record Office, a large amount of information has been gleaned from parish records, school board minutes, school log books, county and town council minutes.

Although the correspondence files and letter books offer useful indications of Trevail's political views, they tell us almost nothing about his personal life. Here we rely upon the hundreds letters, as well as ledgers, diaries, scrapbooks, photographic albums and other memorabilia in the possession of members of the Trevail family. These are listed in the endnotes as 'family papers' and for unlimited access to these we are extremely grateful to Mr Roger Trevail Brewer.

Hazel Harradence has also spent a considerable time corresponding with English Heritage and the Department for Culture, Media and Sport concerning the schedule of certain buildings on the list of Buildings of Special Architectural or Historic Interest. Several building schedules were found not to have credited Trevail as designer and some included his name in error. To the best of our knowledge these have now all been corrected.

Valuable secondary sources are local newspapers and journals, which are listed under the heading of abbreviations.

In gathering this information we wish to record our gratitude for the unstinting help and cooperation given by former and current officers of Cornwall Record Office, including Christine Edwards, Colin Edwards, Paul Brough, David Thomas and Deborah Tritton and also to the archive assistants; Cornwall Centre, including Terry Knight, Kim Cooper and Joanne Laing; and those at the Courtney Library of the Royal Institution of Cornwall, including Angela Broome and Anne Knight.

Our thanks to Diane, Lesley, Roger and Chris who proof read several times all our drafts, offering valuable comments and advice. The encouragement and advice from colleagues and friends countywide has also been invaluable.

Last but certainly not least, we wish to thank Ed Harradence for his patience and tolerance and Ann Perry for typing and retyping numerous drafts, helping to improve grammar and sustaining the authors with food and drink over a long period.

List of abbreviations

ABK	An Baner Kernewek
Boase	C T Boase, Collectionae Cornubiensia, 1890
CDP	Cornwall and Devon Post
CE	Cornish Echo
Co	Cornishman, Penzance
Corn	Cornubian, Redruth
CG	Cornish Guardian, Bodmin
CRO	Cornwall Record Office
CTel	Cornish Telegraph, Penzance
CT	Cornish Times, Liskeard
CTT	C T Trevail, Life and Reminiscences, 1927
FP	Falmouth Packet
FPT	Falmouth and Penryn Times
JCALH	Journal of the Cornwall Association of Local Historians
JRIC	Journal of the Royal Institution of Cornwall
LWN	Launceston Weekly News
RI	Redruth Independent
RCG	Royal Cornwall Gazette
SAS	St Austell Star
SIT	St Ives Times
SIWS	St Ives Weekly Summary
STSN	Silvanus Trevail Society Newsletter
WB	West Briton
WDM	Western Daily Mercury
WMN	Western Morning News

List of illustrations

Photographs by Hazel Harradence, unless otherwise stated.

Frontispiece   Silvanus Trevail, President of the Society of Architects, Fellow of the Royal Institute of British Architects, County Councillor, Justice of the Peace, Mayor of Truro

13   Birth certificate of Silvanus Trevail
14   Trevail crest as drawn by Silvanus Trevail
15   Silvanus Trevail, aged 15
18   Luxulyan Parochial School, his first professional building
21   Upton Cross Board School
22   St Ives Board School, known locally as the Stennack School
      St Mewan Board School
24   Oxford Street Board Schools, Plymouth
      Fowey Board School, for infants, boys and girls
      Port Isaac Board School
25   Mount Charles Wesleyan Chapel, 1873–1995
26   Helland Wesleyan Chapel
      Par Primitive Methodist Chapel, 1876–1988
      Mission Church of St George the Martyr, Nanpean, 1878
28   Treventon, St Columb
30   Treverbyn Board School, showing the original bell tower
31   Carclaze Board School, St Austell
33   Polperro Board School, opened for 250 children in 1878
34   Washaway Board School
      Wadebridge Board School for Boys, 1878–1991
35   St Day Board School
36   Boscastle Board School, opened in July 1879
37   Mevagissey Board School
      Brassacott (now Brazacott) Board School
39   St Teath Board School opened in 1878
43   Royal Arch in Lemon Street.

43 Welcome Arch on Boscawen Bridge
44 Peoples Arch near Truro railway station
48 Early photograph of Pentowan, Newquay
49 Trevail's drawing of Truro Post Office
50 Tregear farmhouse near Ladock
    Treator, near Trevone, built by James Julian in 1884
51 Mevagissey Congregational Church opened in 1883, now known as St Andrew's
        Church
    St Mary's Vicarage, Par, for Rev Frank Garrett
    Temple Church, rebuilt by Trevail in 1883
53 Silvanus Trevail, circa 1880
55 Memorial for the supposed death of Conybeare
56 Notepaper for County Liberal Conference with Mr Silvanus Trevail as Secretary
57 80–81 Lemon Street, Truro, Trevail's home and business quarters
58 Upper floors of Polkinhorne's warehouse in Princes Street, Truro
63 St Piran's Roman Catholic Chapel, Truro, 1884–1973
    St Mary's Wesleyan Chapel, Truro, after renovation on 1895
64 Mill house, Lanivet, 1886.
    Edgcumbe Wesleyan Chapel built by W J Winn & Sons of Helston.
65 Upton Cross Church built in 1885 next to Trevail's school
    Newquay Congregational Church burnt down in 1924
66 Helland Church where Trevail added the tower in 1888
    Tregaddick, Blisland, a holiday home for the Morshead family
67 Entrance lodge for Place, Fowey, 1882.
    Perranzabuloe Vicarage, 1888, now a private residence.
70 Great Western Hotel, Newquay, taken between 1906 and 1930
71 An early, but not original, interior of the Great Western Hotel, Newquay
72 Part of the Tolcarne estate as planned in 1883
74 Falmouth Hotel rear extension, now without the flat roof
77 Atlantic Hotel, Newquay, October 1891
    Atlantic Hotel, Newquay, after completion
80 Silvanus Trevail circa 1895
84 Part of one of the sewage schemes that Trevail studied
85 Letterhead for Chairman of the Cornwall County Council Sanitary Committee,
        Silvanus Trevail
89 Presentation silver
    Mayoral Reception for presentation of silver
91 Upper floors of the Liberal Club, St Austell
92 Tregarne Terrace, St Austell, with Tregarne House in foreground
    Trenowth farmhouse on Sir Robert Harvey's estate
93 Tredethy, Helland, new wing and facade for FJ Hext in 1892
    Princes Street, Truro, porch and steps added in 1893
94 Harrison Terrace, Truro, for railwaymen
    Wheal Agar, Illogan, cottages for miners

95   Almshouses at Tregony renovated in 1894

96   Moorland Road, St Austell, workmen's houses for Francis Leyland Barratt

97   Wesleyan Chapel, St Austell, now St John's Church, interior renovation and new facade, 1886–1892

      Trenython Chapel, Tywardreath, for Bishop Gott

98   Pendennis Hotel, Falmouth, now known as the Royal Duchy Hotel

99   Housel Bay Hotel built by Arthur Carkeek in 1894

100 Treloyhan, St Ives, built on the surface workings of Wheal Marger.

101 Draycott Terrace, St Ives, built as holiday lodgings for families

102 Carbis Bay Hotel, architect's drawing 1894

103 Polpier Mevagissey, for Dr Monro Grier in 1892

106 Trevail's copy of Truro City Council Standing Orders, drawn up by himself

108 Truro Free Library later had the Central Technical Schools added to the rear.

110 Camborne School of Mines, as seen from Trevithick Road

      Public Rooms, St Austell, opened in 1896

      Fowey Church vestry

      Trebarwith Bridge built in 1896 for Lord Wharncliffe

114 Devon & Cornwall Bank, Truro

      Cornish Bank, Helston

116 Coode & Shilson banking and solicitors offices in St Austell, popularly known as the 'Red Bank'

118 Devon & Cornwall Bank, St Ives, from a re-vamped draper's shop in 1894

      Devon & Cornwall Bank, St Agnes, built 1899

119 A shop in Fore Street, St Austell, for Henry Hodge, seedsman & nurseryman

      Burton's premises, Truro, for a china and glass showroom and warehouse

121 Vivian Brothers store, Camborne, an architect's drawing 1897

122 Public Benefit Boot & Shoe Company, King Street, Truro

      Blackford's premises, Truro

124 Hayle Institute opened by John Passmore Edwards in 1896

126 Camborne Free Library, for John Passmore Edwards, opened in 1895

128 Bodmin Free Library with Science and Art Schools, for John Passmore Edwards, opened in 1897

130 Launceston Public Library and Reading Room, opened in 1900

132 Central Technical Schools for Cornwall in Truro, showing carving of Cornish trades

134 Bowring Library, Moretonhampstead, Devon

      Moretonhampstead, Devon, Nurses Home endowed by George Wills in memory of his wife, Lucy

135 John Passmore Edwards East Ham Public Library

136 Newton Abbot Public Library designed by Trevail, together with the adjoining Technical and Art Schools.

139 King Arthur's Castle Hotel, Tintagel, opened in 1899

142 Headland Hotel, Newquay, completed in 1900 by contractor Arthur Carkeek

144 Centre portion of the Grand Hotel, Guernsey, never built

146 Ship & Castle Hotel, St Mawes, opened about 1900 by Walter Hicks of St Austell
       Brewery
     Globe Hotel, Bude, for Walter Hicks of St Austell Brewery
147 Fistral Terrace, Newquay, a personal investment for Trevail in 1896
148 On board the 'Norse King', Trevail, centre, leaning on the railings
     Trevone Bay Hotel, not enough backers were found to finance the project
150 Bon Air, Newquay, now demolished
153 1898 Election card
155 The Assistant Medical Officer's entrance at the Cornwall Lunatic Asylum
     Artisan's workshops at the Cornwall Lunatic Asylum
156 Poltair Terrace at Heamoor, a terrace of eight houses built in 189
157 Ashleigh, St Columb, a new facade and extended front rooms in 1896
     Witherdon House, Beaworthy, Devon, extension and new facade started in 1872
158 Trewince, near Gerrans, the new wing built in 1898 contained a billiard room.
     Market Place shop, St Austell, each floor only had space for one room
159 Laninval, near Bodmin, for Henry Dennis who owned the terracotta works in
       Ruabon
161 St Guron's, Bodmin, Miss Collins had at least five different sets of drawings
162 Woodside, Dublin, for iron manufacturer, John Parkes in 1901
167 Poster for Dedication of Bells Ceremony
168 The Trevail Family Memorial erected in Luxulyan churchyard after Jane Trevail's
       death
     Memorial booklet given to all Luxulyan school children
169 Devon and Exeter architects on their tour around Truro in 1902
170 Devon and Exeter Society of Architects luncheon menu, 1902
     Dining room at 80–81 Lemon Street, Truro, soon after the renovation in 1901
171 'Speed the plough' tokens minted as a memorial to John Trevail
     Service for John Trevail
173 The Society of Architects dinner menu for 1903
175 Luxulyan Church
177 Devon & Cornwall Bank, Fowey
180 Two of Trevail's letter books, each of which covers about 10 months
182 A few of the 600 plus bundles of Trevail's plans held at Cornwall Record Office
183 Luxulyan Church Memorial window erected by his sister, Laura Rundle
187 Obelisk for Joseph Trevail
188 Redruth Wesleyan Chapel
     Roche Wesleyan Chapel and Sunday school
190 Upton Cross Sunday school and church rooms
     Tretherras farmhouse, St Allen
192 Rear view of Carbis Bay terrace
195 Cowbridge, Lostwithiel
200 Door to Bodmin Post Office
201 Fiddick and Michell premises, Camborne
     Cornish Bank, St Columb

204   Nankivell & Co, River Street, Truro

210   The Passmore Edwards Hospital, East Ham. Family papers
       Fowey Workingmen's Club

213   Delabole Board School

214   High Street Board School
       St Just Board School

215   Lockengate Board School, Luxulyan parish
       St Mawes Board School
       St Merryn Board School

218   Trevarrack Board School

One
An age of adventurers

Silvanus Trevail was born in Luxulyan, a scattered moorland parish of under a thousand inhabitants some five miles north east of St Austell in 1851, the year of the Great Exhibition in London, which elevated the engineers and industrialists, who had made Britain the richest nation in the world, to the status of folk heroes.[1] In Cornwall generations of adventurers and mechanics had raised high-pressure steam technology to unparalleled levels of efficiency, supplying the UK with 80 per cent, and the world with over a third, of its copper. Trevail's locality however was mourning the recent loss of its greatest adventurer, Joseph Austen Treffry of

Birth certificate of Silvanus Trevail. Private collection.

Fowey, 'the King of Mid-Cornwall', and the biggest employer in the whole of the South West. Silvanus grew up in the shadow of Treffry's achievements; from an early age he made models of trams, inclines and Treffry's magnificent granite viaduct, an acknowledged wonder of industrial Cornwall, which spanned the Luxulyan Valley not far from his grandmother's home at Atwell.[2] His three-dimensional imagination seemed to point the way to his future career.

A childhood in 'Trevail Country'
The birthplace of Silvanus was Carne Farm, tenanted by his father John, a descendant of generations of independent yeoman farmers. According to Silvanus the family had been known locally since Norman and Plantagenet times, their armorial bearings being 'argent, a fleur-de-lys, sable', an emblem associated with medieval French royalty.[3] His mother Jane was also a Trevail, granddaughter of John Trevail of Roche, the brother of Silvanus' paternal grandfather. Luxulyan was indeed 'Trevail Country' judging by the large number of families of that name recorded in the parish. Charles Trevail, paternal grandfather to Silvanus, was farming at Higher Menadue by 1817, with acreage varying

Silvanus Trevail

Trevail crest as drawn by Silvanus Trevail (Family papers).

from 50 to 150 over a forty-year period; another John Trevail, great uncle to Silvanus, farmed at Lower Menadue by 1813 and, of his children, one son farmed at Tregarden with a hundred acres or more, another at Chetan with fifty acres and two others at Lower Menadue with twenty acres.

The first-born of four children, Silvanus was followed by Laura in 1858, who outlived him, and by John and William, born in 1860 and 1863, both of whom died in infancy.[4] He grew up in an atmosphere of self-sufficiency and independence, part of a tightly knit group. Laura did not marry until she was nearly 40, when she wed Richard Rundle, who farmed at Lanreath a dozen miles or so to the east. Silvanus never married and although he developed a wide circle of acquaintances, he never seemed to make any really intimate friendships, either male or female. Later he spent an increasing amount of time away from Cornwall, but he always kept in touch with his family, visiting them regularly and writing to them almost daily when on his travels abroad.

Silvanus appeared to be particularly close to his father, a man of strong opinions with a great contempt for smoking, horseracing and betting, and noted for his perseverance in bringing to a successful conclusion anything that he undertook. He had worked in tin streaming near Roche and had travelled to America and Canada; Silvanus later followed in his footsteps to meet his relatives there. Sworn in as a special constable during the food riots of the 1840s, his father later served for 13 years on St Austell Board of Guardians. He was also said to be greatly interested in political elections and to have 'cultivated a habit of collecting facts.[5] In all these characteristics – diversity of interests, forcefulness of opinions, desire to travel, involvement in politics and service to the local community – John Trevail clearly exercised an influence on his son.

A star pupil

Silvanus began his award-winning career at a young age, when he attended the local Sunday school at Rosemelling and two years running won books as prizes.[6] Although the Trevails were Anglicans, they probably found it more convenient for him to attend a nonconformist Sunday school because it was closer to home. There was no apparent friction between Anglicans and non-conformists in the area and indeed Silvanus later on carried out many commissions for non-conformists and got on well with prominent Methodist leaders. From the age of seven to fourteen Silvanus attended the Parochial School of Luxulyan Churchtown run by John Hobbah, who was also the Parish Clerk. Charles T Trevail, a cousin of Silvanus who was two and a half years younger, followed him into the school and gave a description of the schoolmaster: noted for his insistence on reading and writing, Hobbah was less interested in arithmetic and limited his pupils to two or three sums a day, becoming annoyed if keen scholars did any more, complaining that he could not cope with the extra work. He had a piece of wood with a round handle and a flattened end that he frequently used on boys' hands. Charles Trevail also painted a vivid picture of village life in Luxulyan. The local granite works were in full swing but when there were strikes, wet days or feast days, the public houses and skittle alleys were crowded. Luxulyan Feast was a time for wrestling, dancing and drinking and ended with a 'mayor choosing' ceremony when an inebriated reveller was taken around the village in a cart.[7]

Silvanus Trevail's next school was Ledrah House in St Austell; run by Dr H H Drake MA. This private academy offered education for the sons of clergy, solicitors, doctors and government officers and specialised in preparing pupils for the external examinations of the universities of Oxford and Cambridge, and Silvanus gave an account of it in a private letter:

> We rise at half past five and are called generally by Mr Eustace, an assistant. We are allowed half an hour for dressing and are expected in the Schoolroom at 6 o'clock. The roll is called and all that are missing have an imposition to do after school hours. After the morning lessons are past we are all called to prayer by a bell rung by one of the servants. The prayers begin generally at half past 8 o'clock and are read by one of the boys who take it in turns. We learn Scripture, Geography, Spelling, History, Grammar etc before breakfast which generally consists of nice thick bread and butter and milk and water. After breakfast we have half an hour to play when some play marbles and various other games. We are called into school again at half past nine, we either do Euclid & Algebra or Arithmetic, Grammar and Geography. We are out of school at half past 12 o'clock and at one o'clock go to dinner when we have generally a nice round of beef roasted or boiled. We are again called into school at 2 o'clock and continue until 4 o'clock. The afternoon is occupied either in Latin, French, Drawing or Writing, reading and dictation. After 4 o'clock some boys do History, others go to their homes. At 5 o'clock we have tea which consists of the same as that of breakfast. After tea we have another half an hour which is generally occupied in playing some game. At 6 o'clock we are again called into school and continue there until 8 o'clock when some boys go to bed, others do History with the Doctor after that they go to bed. I believe Latin is considered the hardest study, and Mathematics the best in our school. We are learnt to such an extent in Mathematics that it is said no other school in the West of England can equal us.

Silvanus Trevail, aged 15 (Family papers).

Silvanus was later joined at Ledrah House by his cousin, Charles Trevail, who described aspects of school life, such as land surveying, a popular subject since it allowed pupils to escape from the school confines. 'Parlour boarders' like Charles, who paid higher fees, would smoke their pipes under cover of the hedges while making the 'common boarders' carry out the measuring. In later life Charles Trevail acted as 'Architect and Licensed Valuer', although he had received no architectural training, a common practice which, as we shall see in Chapter Two, increasingly infuriated Silvanus.[8]

Although Silvanus mentioned playing 'marbles and various other games' as a schoolboy, we have no evidence that he ever took part in, or indeed showed any interest in, organised sports or athletics. Cricket was a popular activity in his youth, but rugby and soccer were not introduced into Cornwall until the 1870s. His father was said to be as contemptuous of football as he was of horseracing and Silvanus may have shared this opinion. The only physical activity that he seemed to enjoy was swimming, and one incident revealed a domineering side to his character. His cousin Charles never forgot an occasion when Silvanus took him out of his depth in the sea at Porthpean on the pretence of teaching him how to swim and then kept pushing him under. Charles feared he would drown but Silvanus called it 'fun'.[9]

According to family legend, Silvanus was known to his classmates as 'Silly Vain Ass'. Was this simply a childish play on his name, or was he already developing a touch of pomposity? Silvanus had every reason to feel pleased with himself though, for he excelled in all subjects. He passed the external examinations of the Junior Oxford and the Junior Cambridge Certificate in 1866, the Senior Oxford Certificate the next year, and the Cambridge Senior Certificate the year after. In the Cambridge Senior he gained honours in mathematics, drawing and constitutional history, a subject in which he took a lifelong interest, later giving lectures on it.[10] After passing the Associate of Arts examination of Oxford University, he called himself 'Silvanus Trevail, AA'.[11] He remained on good terms with his old headmaster after the latter retired to London and Trevail's last address book contained details of Dr Drake.[12]

Silvanus goes to London

As soon as Silvanus left Drake's Academy he joined an architectural practice, a bold decision suggesting an unusual degree of ambition on his part, since no member of his family had previously entered professional life. Moreover, by this time John Trevail's two younger sons had died, and he might perhaps have been expected to make Silvanus stay at home to continue the family farming tradition. However the Trevail family sent Silvanus to an eminent practitioner in London, Henry Garling FRIBA, of 11 Kings Road, Bedford Row.[13] It was usual to be articled to an established practitioner for a number of years on payment of a premium that covered board and lodgings, and it would have been less expensive to have been articled locally, for Cornwall possessed a number of suitable architects, such as Henry Rice, who designed many imposing buildings in the Liskeard area.[14]

On his rail journey to the capital young Silvanus must have been impressed by the architectural genius of Isambard Kingdom Brunel. Crossing the River Tamar he would have noted Brunel's name placed by admirers on every arch of the bridge completed only a decade earlier, and Brunel's castellated Bristol Temple Meads Station, built in 1839–40. On his arrival at Paddington he would surely have been overawed by the mighty glass canopies of the station, designed in 1854 by Brunel and the architect Matthew Digby Wyatt, and the magnificence of the 'Great Western Royal Hotel', commissioned by Brunel but designed by P C Hardwick. Opened in 1854 at a ceremony attended by Prince Albert himself, it was the first of London's station hotels built in the grand style with 165 rooms and twenty suites of apartments.[15] Was this the structure that sparked off his lifelong ambition to design and run Cornwall's largest and most spectacular hotels?

The battle of styles

Although born and bred in the countryside Silvanus soon developed a liking for the hustle and gaiety of great cities. Later in life, however, as he grew worldly-wise, an habitué of the magnificent boulevards and elegant squares of Paris, Berlin and Vienna, Trevail became disenchanted with the higgledy-piggledy built environment of London, and called for wholesale demolition to create a capital more worthy of its status as the hub of the British Empire.[16] Nevertheless, London in the 1860s was an exciting place for an architect. There were around 1,500 professional practitioners in the capital, nearly half of them members of the elite Royal Institute of British Architects, formed in 1834, and the 'Battle of the Styles' was in full swing. Aristocratic neo-classicists favoured the Greco-Roman model, whereas Gothicists dismissed this as the reflection of a pagan age. Silvanus would have become aware of the crucial importance of choosing the appropriate style from his mentor Henry Garling, who in 1856 carried off first prize for the design of new quarters for the War Office in Whitehall with an Italianate design, against the competition of such giants as Sir George Gilbert Scott and Sir Charles Barry. Unfortunately, after a change of government, it was decided not to go ahead with the building.[17]

By the time Silvanus arrived in London most established architects of churches had been converted to the Gothic persuasion, but the period was remarkable for the richness and stylistic diversity of its domestic and secular architecture. He must have marvelled at Joseph Paxton's Crystal Palace, the largest prefabricated building the world had yet seen. He would probably have admired the Perpendicular Gothic of Barry's Houses of Parliament and he would have witnessed the erection of Scott's gilded Albert Memorial from 1864 to 1871, with its decorative bronzes, mosaics, polished granite, marble and Portland stone, which earned him his knighthood from Queen Victoria. Silvanus would also have seen the beginnings of the flamboyant red brick and terracotta Albert Hall, designed by the engineer Francis Fowke and the artist Godfrey Sykes. Although terracotta was an ancient material it was coming into fashion as a decoration for the villas of professional men and the suburban terraces of artisans and tradesmen. In later years Silvanus was to use it on some of his most flamboyant creations, such as the 'Red Bank' at St Austell and the Headland Hotel at Newquay.

Watching such houses spring up Silvanus would have been impressed by other styles as well. A rising generation of architects favoured homes of warm red brick symmetrically pierced by tall sash windows in a style known as 'Queen Anne', another of Trevail's favourites, albeit with little resemblance to the architecture of her reign a century before. However, the nobility still tended to favour buildings reminiscent of the

Italian Renaissance, and in the City of London the houses of rich merchants were giving way to Italianate buildings, elaborately decorated with classical sculptures, as well as to the restrained classical facades of Lombard Street banks.[18] To add to the profusion a growing number of the gentry were opting for half-timbered Tudor features, while designers of churches and vicarages leaned towards Decorated Gothic, preferring it to the hard and spiky English Perpendicular.

An unpromising milieu for a budding architect?

After finishing their articles many young architects worked for a time as assistants to established practitioners before branching out on their own. But Trevail, before he was twenty-one, returned to Cornwall and embarked, single-handedly, on his career as an architect. On the face of it his homeland hardly seemed a promising place to start out. Cornish copper production had peaked in 1856 and the great Fowey Consols mine, after paying out rich dividends to shareholders for decades, was forced to ask them to put money back to keep it going. Although it continued to operate until the 1860s its workforce dwindled from eighteen hundred to three hundred and fifty and in 1867 it closed down altogether. By this time the other big local mine, Par Consols, was also in trouble and in 1870 it, too, was wound up.[19] When Silvanus set out on his architectural career nearly thirty per cent of the male work force of his parish had left to seek work elsewhere, while the cost of parish relief for the families who remained had gone up by a half.[20]

With Cornwall's mining economy crumbling into ruins, how could Trevail succeed? A happy conjuncture of events got him off to a flying start: expansion of the local

Luxulyan Parochial School, Trevail's first professional building.

china clay industry, a government edict to provide elementary education, and a little nepotism. Extraction of china clay and stone was bringing wealth to an area that had been hard hit by the mining collapse, and whereas the population of Cornwall as a whole was falling, that of nearby St Stephen, the chief clay parish, was increasing by leaps and bounds.[21] Meanwhile, concern at England's low levels of elementary education compared with its commercial rivals grew when, at the Paris Exposition of 1867, foreigners carried off most of the prizes. The government was forced to take action and in 1870 passed an Education Act decreeing that an elementary school should be placed within reach of every child.

Trevail's own parish was one of the first to respond and his uncle Joseph happened to be Chairman of the Luxulyan School Building Committee. Although not yet twenty-one years of age Silvanus grasped his opportunity and returned home to embark upon his professional career, by designing the first school in Cornwall to be built after the passing of the Act. With his own hands he proudly carved the date stone for the building – 1871.[22]

Two
'Mr Trevail's landmarks'

Silvanus Trevail's rapid rise to local fame came through designing elementary schools, so many that they were known as 'Trevail's landmarks'. At the age of 26 he told his friend Thomas Webber, Mayor of Falmouth, he had erected 'more schools than anyone west of Bristol'.[1] In accordance with the 1870 Education Act, each parish, or group of parishes, had to set up a board to conduct a census of children, make compulsory land purchase where necessary, decide how much to spend and appoint an architect to design a school. Some were slow to get off the mark, for although the government empowered boards to build schools, it left them to find the money themselves or borrow it from the Public Works Loan Commission, and repay it out of local rates. This was an unpopular move with some ratepayers, but nevertheless, within two years, twenty school boards were set up in Cornwall.[2] Some controlled existing National schools run by the Church of England, but few of these were large enough to take children of all denominations and so alterations and extensions were needed, if not complete new buildings.

Getting ahead of the field
The leaders of Trevail's home parish were not only among the first to respond, they were also unusual in choosing to appoint their own building committee rather than an official school board. A local landowner gave the site, and voluntary contributors, with great help from the vicar, raised the finance, and ran the school for three years before forming a board. Silvanus's uncle was elected Chairman of the School Building Committee, which commissioned Silvanus as architect, and by February 1871 he had drawn up the plans. In May he signed the contract (although it might not have been legal since he was under twenty-one). In June, as he wrote to his sister, 'hundreds' came, including many of the local gentry and clergymen, for the laying of the Foundation Stone by Lady Rashleigh and the tea that followed.[3] By the following March the building was completed. Luxulyan had the first village school to be opened in Cornwall since the passing of the new Act.[4]

Having got ahead of the field Silvanus made sure that he stayed in front by a relentless pursuit of commissions. Never one to hide his light under a bushel he is said to have written to every parish in Cornwall informing them of his prowess in school building.[5] In December 1871 the St Austell School Board advertised for designs for a new school at Mount Charles, to the east of the town, offering a prize of £5 for the best set submitted. Six architects competed and Trevail was chosen; the board also chose him for two more schools, one at the port of Pentewan and a large Central School within the town at West Hill, the latter a particularly large and challenging project for an architect not yet twenty-one years of age. Mount Charles opened in December 1872 and was at first hailed as Cornwall's first official Board School, until the Illogan Board, near Redruth, claimed that distinction for a school that had begun construction in March and was finished in September.[6]

During 1873 he took on four more school commissions around St Austell, at St Mewan to the west, St Blazey Boys School to the south east and St Columb Major and Padstow to the north. In 1874 he added another three at St Wenn, Mevagissey and Brazacott. In the following year he won no fewer than a dozen school commissions, from Port Isaac on the north coast to Fowey on the south, Upton Cross on Bodmin Moor and Lanner and St Day near Redruth.[7] Work on a further six schools followed in 1876 from Polperro on the south coast to St Mawgan-in-Pydar on the north and Delabole in the north east.[8]

In the later 1870s the construction of branch railways, and the conversion to passenger traffic of the Newquay, St Ives and Fowey lines made it easier for Trevail to spread his activities further afield. In 1877 he won a further ten commissions, ranging from Crantock Road at Newquay and St Ives to Fowey Grammar and Gorran.[9] From 1878 to 1880 he added another seven new schools, including his first venture across the Tamar, Oxford Street School in Plymouth.[10]

Upton Cross Board School, includes a playground shelter.

Top: *St Ives Board School, known locally as the Stennack School.*
Bottom: *St Mewan Board School, opened in 1874 and still in use.*

The high quality of a Trevail school

What was a Trevail school like? They varied greatly in size, from Sharplands (a small building for eighty pupils in a remote area between the rivers Lynher and Inny) to his most expensive school project, Stennack school for 800 children at St Ives, which cost £5,000, including an unusually large master's house. Trevail later claimed it was 'the best school in Cornwall', and Sir Charles Reed, MP for St Ives and chairman of the London School Board, said of it 'not a more convenient nor better designed Board School existed in all London'.[11] Anne Treneer, in her best-selling autobiography *Schoolhouse in the Wind*, described Gorran school, near Mevagissey, where her father was master, as 'strong and symmetrical, without beauty, but not mean'.[12] It soon lived up to its name when a gust of wind smashed two large panes of glass in the classroom door.[13] The local historian R S Best went to another Trevail school at St Mewan, near St Austell, where 'the rooms were very high, giving the children more than enough air-space but too little floor space or elbow room. The doors were very heavy and cumbersome and the windows were highly placed to prevent us from out of door distractions ... the worst disgrace were the toilets, if that is not too grand a word for them. They were not even of the bucket type, but merely a deep pit with a seat over it'.[14]

These were hardly flattering descriptions, but it must be remembered that Trevail was following increasingly severe guide lines laid down by the Department of Education in London, and working within tight budgets imposed by local school boards who were not noted for extravagance. The size of a school was calculated according to the number of pupils, allowing eight or nine square feet each, with class sizes ranging from 30 up to as many as 80 children. Although the ceiling height was not specified by the Board of Education, the fashion was for high ceilings in public buildings, banks and shops, which meant that schoolrooms were light and airy in summer but freezing in winter. Junior school galleries had to be instantly removable and larger classrooms had to be divisible into four; lighting had to come from the back of the rooms so that it shone onto the blackboards.

Within these strict parameters Trevail always chose the best available local materials and insisted upon high standards of craftsmanship. Wherever the budget allowed, he used granite quoins and surrounds to give solidity and durability, and roofs of Delabole slate, but transport along roads that were sometimes little more than rough, muddy cart tracks was costly. Local sandstone was both cheaper and easier to work, and in the china clay area he used cheaper bricks made from clay waste on the less prominent parts of the building; sometimes, as at St Blazey Boys School, he alternated bands of white and red bricks to add a touch of colour to arches.

Although Trevail's natural inclination was for the decorative and the flamboyant, local boards demanded buildings that were 'attractive without being expensive'[15] and while he managed to slip in a picturesque feature like a bell turret or a clock tower wherever he could, these were crossed off the plans when funds ran low. At Padstow they allowed the clock tower, but never provided the clock.[16] Self-appointed watchdogs, determined to minimise expenditure on an elementary education that they deemed a waste of time, kept an eagle eye on progress. Sanitary facilities were often the first to feel the pinch, as at Treverbyn in the clay district. Yet, as Trevail repeatedly pointed out, London schools cost £8 to £12 per pupil, those in rural England cost £8 to £16, but his only came to £4 to £6 a head.[17]

Professional recognition

Despite the financial and design constraints imposed upon him, Trevail won prizes and swift recognition from his peers for his professional skills on a widening scale. Already by 1874, within three years of starting up his professional practice, he had qualified for, and been elected to, membership of the Architectural Association.[18] His plans and drawings appeared regularly in British architectural magazines, St Blazey School being the first to be mentioned in the prestigious journal *The Architect* on 6 September 1873.

Top: *Oxford Street Board Schools, Plymouth.(CRO: AD396/643)*
Bottom left: *Fowey Board School, for infants, boys and girls.*
Bottom right: *Port Isaac Board School, on the edge of the cliff also had a board room.*

In the following year a design for one of his earliest works, the Central Schools at St Columb Major, together with those for Padstow Board School, and a 'well executed drawing of Buckingham Palace' won the Silver medal of the Royal Cornwall Polytechnic Society at their annual exhibition, as well as being featured in the *British Architect*.[19]

Another feather in his cap was a commission, gained against the stiff competition of 33 entrants from all over England, for the erection of the Oxford Street School in Plymouth. It was a large project, with separate accommodation for Seniors, Juniors and Infants as well as Babies' Rooms, his 'greatest success', he wrote to his sister. 'Has any young man in Cornwall,' he asked her, 'done such a thing during the past ten years?' He also requested that she sent him any references to the building that she might have read. The Plymouth Selection Board could hardly believe that anyone west of the Tamar could produce designs of such quality and complexity. 'No Cornishman could draw plans like that,' one of them commented.[20]

Trevail's designs won him international recognition in 1878 when the Royal

Institute of British Architects selected his school plans for Fowey, St Ives and Plymouth to represent the best of British practice at an exhibition in Paris, and subsequently sent some of them to International Exhibitions in Sydney and Melbourne.[21] He was particularly proud of his Certificate For Architectural Design, classified as 'Commended', from the prestigious Sydney Exhibition of 1879, for which a magnificent wooden 'Garden Palace' was built.[22] He had the certificate framed and hung in his office for the rest of his life. Drawings for Wadebridge School appeared in *The Architect* of 1880.[23]

When renovating or extending existing schools, Silvanus always respected the work of earlier architects. For instance at Chacewater the old National School had been extended in 1861 by William White, in 1878 by James Hicks and then in 1894 tactfully treated by Trevail himself.[24] Nanpean, Downend at Lostwithiel, St Wenn, Biscovey and St Mawgan in Pydar were other extensions of older schools. His additions were always sympathetic and blended in well, enabling some of the schools, such as Downend and St Mawgan in Pydar, to be listed as Buildings of Special Architectural or Historic Interest. Other Trevail schools are listed in their own right: Indian Queens, St Merryn, Padstow, Port Isaac and St Teath among them. His rebuilding in 1883 of the ancient church at Temple, standing on the site of a house of the Knights Templar, won rare praise from Pevsner. In his architectural survey of Cornwall, Pevsner singled out for attention Trevail's fidelity to the 'language of the Middle Ages', calling him 'one of the more original later Victorian architects'.[25]

It is greatly to the credit of Trevail and the builders he employed that a century or more later, when his schools were adapted to other uses, their internal structures were found to be in excellent condition, despite years of neglect in some cases; which is more than can be said for the work of certain of his competitors. As we shall see, some of the buildings of H Syd Hancock, Clerk to St Austell School Board, seem to have been adapted from Trevail plans, but built in a most unsatisfactory fashion.

Churches and chapels

Despite his increasing involvement in school design it did not take Trevail long to branch out into other architectural fields. Whenever he designed a school in a village or town there was a good chance that he would find a client for something else, often a church. His commissions for religious buildings, like those for his schools, varied greatly in size and complexity, from the simple addition of a porch at St Paul's Penzance[26] to the renovation of St Austell Wesleyan Chapel costing £3,000. In March 1872,

Mount Charles Wesleyan Chapel, 1873–1995.

Top left: *Helland Wesleyan Chapel had space for the Minister's pony and trap.*
Top right: *Par Primitive Methodist Chapel, 1876–1988. Family papers.*
Bottom: *Mission Church of St George the Martyr, Nanpean, 1878.*

while completing his first school in Luxulyan, he renovated Rosemelling Wesleyan Chapel, also in his home base of Luxulyan parish, furnishing him with his first ecclesiastical as well as his first educational commission. By November of that year, before finishing Mount Charles School, his Mount Charles Wesleyan Chapel

was under way, and Thomas Crowle of London, who had given the site, laid its foundation stone in April 1873.[27]

From 1875 to 1880 he took on the renovation of St Columb Congregational Church and the building of the Congregational Church at Lostwithiel.[28] This was followed by the design of new buildings for Par Primitive Methodist, Sweetshouse and Helland Wesleyan and Lank Free Methodist chapels, and the new Church of St George the Martyr at Nanpean. He also made additions or alterations to Roche and Feock Wesleyan and Bodmin Bible Christian Chapels and to St Austell Congregational Church.[29] Several of his chapel alterations adopted the Anglican pattern of pew arrangement, porches, accommodation for organs, and communion tables; he also added larger and better-supported galleries. At Roche Wesleyan, an organ chamber was added at first floor level with a room for the minister below, and new roof, ceiling timbers and upper windows were installed, the original 1835 building being virtually gutted before Trevail began his work.

The chequered career of some of the chapels reflected changes in the size of communities and alterations in the relative strength of different religious persuasions. The Primitive Methodist Chapel at Par is a case in point; Sir Colman Rashleigh laid its foundation stone in 1875 and it opened in 1876.[30] A decade later however, its purchase was announced by the Reverend George Graham for use by Catholics,[31] and a decade after that it was described as a Bible Christian Chapel.[32] The Mission Church of St George the Martyr at Nanpean had the distinction of being the first new Anglican church to be commenced in Cornwall after the restoration of the ancient Bishopric in 1877.[33]

Not all of Trevail's attempts to gain commissions were successful and unfulfilled projects included schools at Dobwalls, Lanivet and Shortlanesend and Public Rooms at Bodmin. The fate of some of his plans to build cemetery chapels illustrates the variety of problems that he faced. St Austell Burial Board received designs from twelve architects in April 1877, after advertising in *The Builder* as well as two local papers. A London architect, Lewcock, was favoured if the chapel could be built for £1,200; if not then a design by Lovegrove and two by Trevail were also to be considered. However, when Lewcock's design was rejected as too expensive, Trevail was ignored and Lovegrove was invited to alter his plans by substituting granite for Bath stone dressings to the chapel, and white brick for Bath stone at the lodge.[34]

A different kind of disappointment occurred at Padstow after the Burial Board interviewed Trevail about a new site in December 1879. He drew up plans, only to be asked by the Board six months later to delay until the details of the new Burials Act were available. When it was found that the Bishop of Truro would consecrate the new ground without the need for a chapel the project was abandoned, but Trevail later received fifteen guineas for his trouble.[35]

Domestic and commercial projects
During this time Trevail was casting his net wider. He added a large billiard room, kitchen and servant's quarters to Treventon at St Columb, the home of Henry Whitford, partner in a long established local firm of solicitors.[36] He took on workers

cottages at Menna, and for William Coode at Witherdon, across the Devon border. For Charles Prideaux-Brune, the landowner of Prideaux Place in Padstow, he designed farmhouses at Killivose, and Tretherras in St Allen as well as farm buildings at Gwarnick.[37] Silvanus later became a friend of Charles Prideaux-Brune. On the east face of the memorial cross to his mother, Silvanus copied a design from a cross in the grounds of Prideaux Place at Padstow.

Other commissions included a workingmen's club at Fowey in 1877 that contained a library, reading and bagatelle rooms and a meeting hall. At Camborne a house in Chapel Street was designed for a local auctioneer and valuer, A J Tangye. Trevail's first foray into the sphere of adult education came in 1880 when he designed the Art School in Morrab Road, Penzance, which was doubled in size a decade later by a local architect, Henry White, through the addition of a Public Library. White duplicated Trevail's facade, joining the two buildings together with balustrades and twin gables, decorated with red terracotta motifs.[38]

As for Newquay, Trevail site plans exist, dated 1876, for fourteen numbered housing plots on the main Newquay to St Columb road.

Treventon, St Columb, had a new billiard room and servants wing in 1879.

No dwellings were erected, but this is possibly the place where the first hotel that he designed, the Great Western, was erected in 1878.[39] In 1880 Trevail designed a handsome granite villa, Pentowan, illustrated in *The Architect*, overlooking Newquay harbour, for George Hicks.[40] Born in the area, Hicks had returned after a colourful 30-year career in Spain and South America, including failure in a cotton plantation in Peru and success in running large railways in Bolivia and Chile, and was later to play a significant part in Trevail's enterprises.

Trevail also designed a small Masonic Hall in Newquay[41] and a substantial villa above Porth, to the north for William Stephens, a landowner with extensive properties in Devon and Cornwall. He also began to plan a large seaside estate on Stephens' land, which led to problems that will be discussed in Chapter Five. An unusual project was Tywardreath Reservoir, built in 1873 to supply Par Green and Par, but which fell into disrepair and was demolished in the mid-1900s.

On the south coast, facing Fowey, Trevail surveyed a shipyard at Polruan, run by the redoubtable Jane Slade; during this project he displayed his impetuosity, and his penchant for blaming other people for his own mistakes. Always a man in a hurry, he fell in the water while trying to get off the Fowey to Polruan Ferry. In a letter to the *Western Morning News* he complained about the dangerous state of the landing place, alleging that earlier someone had drowned there. The ferry owners retorted that despite their warning, he had tried to disembark before the ferry had properly docked and rumours spread that his real motive in complaining was to get a commission to design a better landing place.[42]

Three
Competition, income and travel

As he moved further afield in his quest for commissions, Trevail met increasingly strong professional competition. Formidable rivals to the east included the Plymouth architects James Hine FRIBA and Henry John Snell. With various partners, Hine extended Bodmin Asylum in 1871 and 1880, as well as erecting schools in Lewannick and St Pinnock, chapels and churches at South Petherwin, Davidstow, Delabole and Bude and a post office at Launceston. Snell designed schools at Calstock and Blisland. At Looe, schools and the town hall were the work of J F Gould of Barnstaple, and A E Skentlebury of Looe was responsible for schools and chapels in the Liskeard and Looe area, while Edward H Harbottle ARIBA of Exeter was the architect of Bude UM Church. C P Wise of Launceston designed schools in Lelant and Liskeard, and Otho Bathurst Peter ARIBA designed schools in his home town of Launceston.

Henry Rice, creator of so many fine buildings around Liskeard, was still active in the early 1870s, designing a chapel there, a school at Callington and a bank in Truro, later extended by Trevail. One of Rice's pupils, the Liskeard-born architect Richard Coad, designed churches at Tywardreath and Liskeard in Cornwall and others in Lincolnshire and North Wales, as well as a London bank. Coad also took over from Sir George Gilbert Scott, for whom he had worked, the continuing improvements to the great mansion of Lanhydrock in the 1880s.[1] Scott, who had earlier designed Redruth workhouse, made additions to the mansion of Polwhele near Truro around 1870.

Perhaps the strength of competition from the east explains why Silvanus tended to look increasingly to the west. Not that he failed to come up against some worthy opponents in West Cornwall. James Hicks of Redruth, his near contemporary, and Trevail were two of a kind; men in a hurry, with interests in local politics and other commercial ventures, who swept aside anything or anybody who got in their way. Until his early death in 1896, Hicks ruled the roost in Redruth, indeed contemporaries dubbed the town 'Hicksville', and for Trevail it seemed almost a closed shop.[2] Trevail kept a sharp eye on Hicks' activities and Trevail's private papers included a cutting from a newspaper which described how Hicks had been ordered to leave a meeting of Redruth Local Board of Health after he had 'made an unwarrantable attack on the Chairman' when the Board opposed his plans for a new building,[3] an episode that was to be echoed many times in Trevail's own career.

Penzance was another place endowed with gifted architects and Trevail designed little here. J P St Aubyn FRIBA, of a distinguished West Cornwall family, restored or designed many churches throughout Cornwall over a long period. Penzance-based architects included Henry White FRIBA, who doubled the size of Trevail's Art School in that town, John W Trounson FRIBA and Sons (to whose church Trevail added a small porch) and, active from the 1890s onwards, Oliver Caldwell FRIBA.

Surveyors, charlatans and plagiarists

Qualified professional architects, however, were far from the only practitioners against whom Trevail had to compete. Adding to the field were a host of local builders, among them John Ennor senior and junior of Newquay and Thomas Smith of St Austell. Local builders doubled as furniture makers, undertakers or general handymen and they were also capable of solid and well-crafted vernacular architecture, especially when they were able to use or adapt plans drawn up by professional architects for whom they had worked as contractors. Plagiarism was not unknown, and Trevailian architectural features appeared in other school buildings of the time.

For instance H Syd Hancock, Clerk to the St Austell School Board, may have taken possession of Trevail's plans for Board schools in the district, for although there is no record of any dissatisfaction with Trevail's work, the board began to use Hancock instead of Trevail. Over a number of years Hancock took on contracts for additions to Trevail's Central School at St Austell, Carclaze School, the master's house at Treverbyn and new schools at Boscoppa and Charlestown. Hancock's designs may have been

Treverbyn Board School, showing the original bell tower.

cheaper at the time, but the buildings later developed severe cracks due to inadequate foundations or ground settlement. One of the roofs had to be re-slated well before an earlier Trevail building needed attention, and a schoolmaster's house had to be rendered to keep out damp.

As his career progressed, Trevail became more and more infuriated by the activities of what he called charlatans and plagiarists. Local councils, acting upon the recommendation of their surveyors, got into the habit of requiring duplicates of complete sets of drawings made by architects whose projects they had approved.[4] Their surveyors then visited persons known to be interested in building a property and offered to carry out the

duties of an architect at cut rates, with a guarantee that their plans would be passed. The surveyors then simply made tracings of existing plans in their possession and used them with slight modifications. This was a perennial concern for Trevail and probably coloured his relationships with Borough and County Surveyors, which were often far from amicable. This problem was by no means confined to Cornwall. The Architects Association of Ireland later tried to prevent surveyors, who were already paid handsome salaries from 'scooping up the best part of the private practice that was available'.[4]

Carclaze Board School, St Austell, where Hancock's extension on the left was added in 1893.

Time and again Trevail attacked this practice, he was very upset by cases where 'board schoolmasters, builders' clerks, auctioneers, land agents, general contractors, clerks of works, boys from the nearest art school, photographers, highway surveyors and in one instance a marine store dealer' made 'absurdly impractical drawings' leading to disasters which gave the whole architectural profession a bad name.[5] This, however, was one campaign that Trevail did not win. It was not until an Act of Parliament of 1931, when an Architects' Registration Council was set up, that use of the title 'architect' was restricted by law. Before then, only membership of one of the professional bodies gave architects any sort of recognised status.[6]

Excellence plus advertising
In the face of this competition, Silvanus followed the example of successful tycoons of his era. His recipe for success was a combination of restless energy, superior skills as a designer and a flair for self-publicity. Items in his letter books show that some of the most flattering tributes in local newspapers and professional journals were penned by his own hand. A typical account would emphasise the superior quality of the materials selected by the architect, with flattering references to local notables involved in the ceremonies of laying the foundation stone and opening the building. Congratulations on the way in which the 'skilful designer' had enhanced the architecture of the locality were followed by the name of the builder and, of course, the name of the architect himself. Since a building often took years to complete, reports appeared in the press every

few months, which, in the manner of modern 'spin doctors' announced the same item of news as something fresh, usually however adding a few new features. Trevail also succeeded in incorporating descriptions of his buildings in local business directories, an unusual achievement for the time.

Nor was he backward in bringing his successes to the notice of prospective clients, or in knocking the reputation of rivals. Replying to a newspaper invitation for designs from Gwennap School Board, he first congratulated the Chairman for 'one of the most sensible advertisements I have yet seen advertised by a School Board'. He then informed the board that he was busy with designs for similar-sized schools at St Endellion and Linkinhorne and that his designs for the last of these had been preferred to nine entries from Liskeard, Launceston, Plymouth, Exeter, Bristol and London, as well as one from St Agnes 'which was a complete laughing stock for the Board'.[7]

Architectural overload

How did Silvanus cope with such an enormous workload? Of course his energy was phenomenal and his letter books record him dealing with correspondence in the early hours of the morning after a busy day of professional and political activities, and taking care to point this out to builders or suppliers who were slow in responding to his orders. It is not that clear how much assistance he had. The first record we have found of clerical or professional assistance is a rather frosty letter of 1875 from his office and signed by E M Houston. This informed the recipient that his application for a job could not be entertained since he had not 'quoted even approximate terms, whilst all others sent definite terms with ten specimens of their work'.[8] Possibly Houston was an architectural assistant, although he may have simply been a clerk and Trevail was seeking an assistant.

Even with assistants, in trying to control so many projects spread over such a wide area, Trevail was almost bound to run into trouble. Already, by the end of 1874 he had ten on-going projects, at varying stages from initial sketches to final preparations for the opening. During the following year the number he was controlling increased to twenty-one, and in the year after that to twenty-nine, peaking at thirty-eight in 1877. Output then declined slightly to thirty-five in the next year, to twenty-two in 1879 and nineteen in 1880. By this time he was responsible for work from Plymouth and west Devon down to Penzance, and from Newquay on the north coast to Fowey on the south. Before school plans could be passed by the Department of Education, he had to survey the site and discuss matters with the School Board at least twice, sometimes three or four times as at St Mewan and St Austell, and on occasions as many as eight or nine visits were needed as at Lanner, St Day, Polperro and St Stephen in Brannel.

He could travel to some of these sites by rail, but others, tucked away in remote rural areas, took hours to reach along roads no better than cart tracks. To add to the complexity of his workload he was, as we saw in the previous chapter, taking on a greater variety of commissions, ranging from mansions, villas and cottages to public halls and a hotel. To cut down his work he occasionally used some of his school drawings more than once, with minor alterations to meet the demands of local boards and the site, and paid for old drawings by builders of existing structures in the case of additions.[9] But meet-

Polperro Board School, opened for 250 children in 1878.

ings with boards, estimating costs and supervising the construction all took time, even when things went smoothly.

Problems of organisation and control

Of course things quite often did not go according to plan. For example, extra foundations were found to be necessary at St Blazey because of the difficulties of building on the sands of Par Bay, while at Biscovey a juggling act was required to enlarge an existing mixed school and build a new infants section in such a way that they could later be separated into boys' and girls' classrooms. The Port Isaac School site was bounded on one side by a fifty foot drop into the sea and the frontage was about eight feet below the road and, because of its exposed position, special attention had to be paid to copings, flashings and slating.[10] Despite all this the school was completed within in a year of the foundation stone being laid in April 1876.[11]

To add to his difficulties, local school boards were apt to demand special features and change their minds about details at frequent intervals. It was standard practice to provide preliminary sketches and draft specifications of materials for the boards then alter them as needed to provide more precise drawings and specifications for the contract. In addition plans had to be amended to conform to modifications made by the Education Department or the Public Works Loan Commissioners in London, and an estimate was needed to assist selection from the tenders presented by builders.

Professional fees and expenses

For this work Trevail charged the normal professional fee of five per cent, and he later described the duties that were covered by this commission. These were preliminary sketches in pencil, revised until the wishes of the client were exactly ascertained; approximate estimates of cost; preparation of a full set of one-eighth scale drawings (with one traced copy for the builder); detailed specifications of materials (with a builder's copy); one quarter inch or one half inch scale drawings for the craftsmen and

34

SILVANUS TREVAIL

full instructions for the execution of his work; and personal supervision on a monthly or six weekly basis. All other work including surveys, liaison with adjoining owners, travelling and out of pocket expenses and extra copies of plans were to be charged separately.[12]

For school buildings the architect had also to certify to the Education Department and to the Public Works Loan Commissioners, at regular intervals, how much the builders would receive in payment at various stages of the building programme. As we shall see, there were many occasions when Trevail failed to practise what he preached. At the beginning of his career he took on the job of Clerk of Works as well, being paid £40 to supervise schools at West Hill St Austell, and Pentewan.[13] At Mevagissey he agreed to visit the site fortnightly or more often if required to save the expense of a Clerk of Works [14] and in his early years he made no charge for travelling or other expenses, only adding them later when his projects became more far-flung.

Unsurprisingly, as his practice grew, the simultaneous supervision of a multitude of projects stretching over a wide area posed more and more problems, as Trevail's experience with the St Breock and Egloshayle United School Board illustrated. In 1875 the board wanted to treble the size of the girls' school at Wadebridge, design a new school

Top: *Washaway Board School was only for infants who lived a long way from Wadebridge.*
Bottom: *Wadebridge Board School for Boys, 1878-1991.*

for boys on the Wadebridge to Padstow road and an infant school at Washaway on the Bodmin Road. He swiftly completed the designs and they were approved within a month, but two months later the Board asked for alternative estimates and specifications for the boys' school using either granite or brick surrounds for doors and windows. They also required detailed and alternative specifications and prices for desks to be made of wood or iron. Trevail originally designed school desks himself although later these were standardised by the Department of Education.

Next the Board cancelled a proposed bell-turret and water closet for the master's house. Building proceeded but six months later disaster struck when an arch gave way and the Board reprimanded Trevail for a lack of supervision. They then reinstated the bell tower and the water closet, altered plans for the walling and decided to install gas. Understandably the building was not completed on time (there was a fine of £5 per week for delay) and the Board wrote a stiff letter of complaint to Trevail, but also made further demands, including railings and more boundary walls, and the removal of a telegraph pole.[15]

A lack of supervision

As his projects became more far-flung and his personal supervision less thorough, school boards complained of his failure to attend site meetings, or to supervise the builder, or quarrelled with details in his accounts. In May 1875 Talland and Lansallos United Board objected to some expenses on his bill, the chairman consulted a solicitor, an extraordinary meeting was called and the Clerk was ordered to write to Trevail asking for the dates on which he had inspected the Polperro building. The matter went to Liskeard County Court, where Trevail won his case with costs, but only on a technicality.[16] Again, after plans had been approved for the St Day and Lanner Schools, he postponed meetings to present specifications, so the board appointed its own Clerk of Works, although supervision was included in Trevail's fees. He then failed to turn up at

St Day Board School had 27 boys on the first day, out of a possible 400.

Boscastle Board School for 70 children opened in July 1879.

three consecutive monthly meetings and, when he finally appeared, did not bring the contracts and specifications required, promising to produce them at the next meeting, which he then failed to attend. It took nearly five years to reach a settlement of his final accounts, which meant that the builder also had to wait for that period for his own final payment.[17]

Trevail also seems to have been negligent in his dealings with Boscastle Board. He eagerly contacted them in 1875 within a month of the board's formation and their decision to purchase building land. Having secured the commission, he quickly sent plans for a mixed school with a divided playground instead of a girls' school as requested. Three months went by before he sent amended plans, which still did not conform to instructions and the board minutes record their resentment. To save time they sent the plans to the Education Department expressing their regrets that the stupidity of the architect had caused such a delay, with a copy to Trevail himself. His estimates were also very vague, based as he admitted on an average cost for that size of building of £470 to £500. The only tender received, however, came to £615 and this was eventually accepted, but the agreed completion date came and went, and it was another four months before the school was ready.[18]

Delays accumulate

Building delays, then as now, were commonplace and the completion of a project could take five years, through a combination of alterations in Department of Education regulations, changes of minds by school boards, dilatoriness of the builders and inadequate supervision by Trevail himself. At Mevagissey the Board asked Trevail to enlarge their Church School for Boys and build a new girls' and infants' school on another site. He was prompt in furnishing site plans on Tregony Hill, but the site was turned down by the Department of Education. He then had to redraw them for a new location chosen by the Board on St Austell Road (now School Hill). After these were accepted, John

Top: *Mevagissey Board School, took over three years to build, but was finished in 1877.*
Bottom: *Brassacott (now Brazacott) Board School had mixed junior classes and an infants class.*

Hoskins was appointed builder and Trevail became Clerk of Works, promising to inspect every fortnight. But after months of slow progress and absence of supervision, the board appointed their own Clerk of Works. When the builder used inferior stone and a few months later the roof fell in, the Board became incensed and insisted that Trevail himself bear the extra cost of supervision.[19]

Another occasion on which Trevail was badly let down by his builder occurred in 1874, when the North Petherwin Board commissioned him to build a school at Brassacott. He arranged for one of his preferred contractors, John Oliver of Bodmin, to tender, but Oliver was already busy with three other Trevail schools and, perhaps deliberately, sent in a tender that was much too high. Trevail then advertised for a contractor in a Plymouth paper, but received only one response, from Trenouth and Powers of

Week St Mary in north east Cornwall. By now the Board had also had second thoughts about the cost of using Yeolmbridge stone and asked Trevail to substitute cheaper materials. Not until December 1875 did the Board amend the contract and construction began with a delayed completion date of midsummer 1877. After some months the Board complained of the slowness of the operation and asked Trevail to inspect it, which he did. By November the Board, still concerned about slow progress, asked him to visit again. Five years after the original decision to build, the school was still not finished and the Board themselves took the work out of the hands of the contractor.[20]

On the other hand, Trevail had cause to be disgruntled by members of the Liskeard Board after he had submitted plans for Dobwalls School. They preferred the plans of the Lostwithiel architect, Skentlebury, in February 1879, but the following December they changed their minds and chose other plans by Webb and Pearce.[21] Silvanus wrote to the Board demanding that his own plans, and those of the new designers, should be sent to the Education Department in London for them to decide. But, after considering his letter, the Board 'decided to pass on to the next business', and there was no further discussion on the matter.[22] Fowey Board also kept him waiting for a decision on his plans, dated 1875, which were considered good enough to be published in *The Architect*. Not until March 1877 did John Julian of Truro sign the building contract, but the school that eventually appeared bore little resemblance to the first set of drawings.[23]

How much did Trevail earn?

In the absence of Trevail's accounts for the period we can only make tentative estimates of his gross income. School building and alterations perhaps amounted to around £60,000,[24] while chapel restoration and building possibly added another £6,000.[25] Calculating the cost of his other work is even more problematic, because it varied greatly in size and refinement, including surveys of seaside estates, a dock, and a number of projects which never came to fruition, but for which he may have received a fee.[26] On occasions he received an income as Clerk of Works to his projects, but it is unlikely that he could have carried on with this kind of work when he was juggling with thirty or so undertakings at the same time. In addition he received various small sums as prizes for his more ambitious designs.[27]

The total cost of the projects he designed during the first decade of his professional life possibly came to £70,000. His income probably rose from a hundred pounds or so per annum in his early days to over four hundred a year by the early 1880s, although arguments over claims sometimes went on for years. Out of this money he had of course to pay many expenses. He always expected, or hoped, that travelling expenses would be paid, but he was not always fortunate. The contracts for schools at Lanner, St Day, St Stephen in Brannel and Wadebridge stipulated that he paid his own expenses, although Wadebridge Board later relented and allowed him £5 a year. Some School Boards, as at Port Isaac, St Teath and Delabole, made a fixed allowance of six shillings (30p) per visit, while Padstow made a single payment of £15 to cover all visits on a fortnightly basis. St Austell Board paid him £40 to cover the cost of supervising both St Austell Central and Pentewan Schools. St Ives board struck off his claim for over £18 travelling expenses from the bill he presented, but nonetheless he gave them, and the contractors, a celebratory dinner on completion of the project.

He also had to pay for any professional assistance he received in producing plans, elevations and blueprints or special 'artists' impressions' of his more elaborate buildings. In his earlier days he possibly managed without help and he remained with his parents at Carne Farm.[28] In this case, his working accommodation might have cost him little or nothing.

How did his income compare with that of other professional men? Over eighty per cent of the British workforce averaged only £38 a year and even the middle classes, who made up an eighth of those receiving income, only averaged £70 per annum. An enormous income gap existed between the middle classes and the top 4.2 per cent of wealthy landowners and rich industrialists who averaged £855 a year,[29] Silvanus was obviously not in their class but nevertheless with no dependants, and with perhaps no household and few office expenses, he probably had more disposable income than most Cornishmen except the great landowners, 'mining lords' or 'clay lords'.

What did Silvanus spend his income on? Like his father John, he did not waste time or money on frivolous pursuits. Already, in his early twenties, the photographs in his albums (he had studio portraits of himself taken at frequent intervals) gave the impression of a much older person, solidly built with a bushy black beard, who took his social responsibilities, and himself, very seriously. Throughout his life however, he was capable of acts of generosity and consideration for others. At the age of twenty-one he collected subscriptions for the relief of families who had suffered through a dynamite explosion in the house of a Luxulyan quarryman who had taken explosives home to dry on his stove. A year later he gathered money to present the Vicar of Luxulyan, prime

St Teath Board School opened in 1878.

mover in raising funds for the school that launched Trevail's career, with a silver teapot.[30]

Unlike some other prosperous professional men, he always lived in rented properties and never acquired a horse or carriage. In the summer of 1876 he left home and rented a house in Tywardreath, south of St Austell, giving long and precise instructions to his sister about packing his belongings, including architectural drawings and plans. At first he seemed to live in some disarray. He was much behind with his work, he told his sister, and warned both her and his mother not to visit him until he had 'sorted things out'. He asked her to send him three nightshirts, since his shirts were 'spoilt by being slept in'. Later he acquired a housekeeper.[31]

Trevail's travels

His major extravagance was foreign travel. From 1874 through to 1902 he toured the continent and made frequent trips to many other parts of the world. This was the era of the grand hotels, palatial structures that sprang up as the railways and steamships opened new vistas in Europe and America. Silvanus stayed in the best of them, dined in the finest restaurants and developed a taste for high living. In the summer of 1874 he visited Western Europe, including Brussels and Antwerp[32] and in the autumn of 1877 he went further afield, describing his visits in a series of articles in the *West Briton* newspaper.[33] At Le Havre the wide central boulevard, in contrast with the cramped and twisting thoroughfares of Cornish towns, immediately impressed him. In Rouen he admired the harmony and symmetry of the Church of St Ouen but criticised the 'disorder' and 'jumble' of the Cathedral. Arriving in Paris in the midst of its grandiose modernisation by Baron Haussman, he marvelled at the 'new buildings in every stage of progress in every direction', a transformation impossible in 'smoky, muddy Oxford Street or the Strand'.

Flattered to be given a personal tour of the site of the 1878 International Exhibition, he praised its layout and noted it would cover an area five times that of the Great Exhibition in London of 1851. He then travelled to Italy, visiting Turin, but returned to Paris because he was 'getting tired of the extreme heat'.[34] These experiences created, or reinforced, his belief in the urgent necessity of town planning, a subject he returned to in later years when President of the British Society of Architects. Once home he lost no time in giving lectures in aid of local causes at the Town Halls of St Blazey, Fowey and elsewhere,[35] where he showed postcards and photographs he had collected of the sites he had visited.

By 1878 he was a member of Cornwall's leading literary and cultural society, the Royal Institution of Cornwall at Truro and also a prominent Mason. In 1880, at the Quarterly Conclave of the Unity Chapter of Tywardreath, 'Companion S. Trevail the Treasurer' was requested to forward a cheque to the Truro Cathedral Fund for a memorial to Masons.[36] To achieve the rank of Master Mason and then be exalted to membership of the Chapter and probably to the status of an Excellent Companion before being elected Treasurer in a secret ballot normally took several years.[37] Not yet thirty years of age, Silvanus had established a reputation that extended outside his home territory. He was now ready to take his place upon a wider social, political and professional stage.

Four
Triumphal arches, harbours of refuge and politics

At the beginning of the 1880s Silvanus could look back with pride upon his first decade as an architect. Still only 30 years old, he had designed about a hundred buildings of various kinds and now the time had come for him to look to new horizons. The question was, where should he go? Although he was an ambitious man with a passion for foreign travel, he did not join the army of 'Cousin Jacks', the popular name given to Cornishmen who were emigrating to all parts of the globe. As he explained later in life, 'being the only son, my father did not want me banished from the Old Country. Therefore I remained to carry out his wish, although I have had offers from other parts of England as well as India.[1] (He was later to visit India).

Inside Cornwall he had a number of options, for it was not a 'city-region' with an obvious single centre, but rather a configuration of small towns, a dozen or so miles apart, each with its own characteristics,[2] and his professional activities took him to most of them. The Cornwall-wide range of his interests is shown by the notice he inserted in the *West Briton*: 'Building Sites of Freehold and Long Leases Commanding the most picturesque and charming scenery in the county may be had in the following locations: Truro, Falmouth, St Mawes, Pentewan, St Austell, Par, Fowey, Wadebridge, Penzance, St Ives, Newquay, St Columb Minor, Porth, Padstow, Tintagel, Boscastle. For particulars apply to Mr Silvanus Trevail'.[3]

We do not have any records of how Silvanus came to make his decision to move away from the St Austell area, but it seems reasonable to suppose that he was looking for a place that was not over-full of talented architects but offered scope for his widening social and cultural interests. For while St Austell was the commercial centre of the rapidly growing china clay industry, it lacked an infrastructure of scientific or intellectual institutions. Penzance was well equipped with these, but was perhaps too far to the west and was already well endowed with gifted architects, while Falmouth was handicapped by an unsatisfactory branch railway service. Camborne and Redruth, twin flagships of the once-great mining economy, formed Cornwall's largest urban agglomeration, and James Hicks had a tight grip on architectural work in Redruth.

On the face of it Bodmin seemed a promising location. It was the county town and housed Cornwall's Lunatic Asylum, Her Majesty's prison, the Duke of Cornwall's Light Infantry, the East Cornwall Hospital and Dispensary, the Royal Cornwall Rangers Militia, and the headquarters of the police and the judiciary. But its population was small, only 5,000 including 600 mental patients and 250 prisoners; the main railway line was four miles away and it offered little potential for tourism.[4] Nothing much seemed to have changed since Carew's description of the town in Elizabethan times: a single street leading east and west with the church as the only building of note.

Truro, on the other hand, offered a promising professional, social and cultural milieu. Its population of 11,000 was smaller than that of Falmouth-Penryn, Penzance-Newlyn or Camborne-Redruth, but it occupied a more central position and boasted the County Library, founded in 1792, the Royal Institution of Cornwall, with its lecture room and laboratory, dating from 1818, and an ancient Grammar School. As we shall see Silvanus was to play a role in all of these.

Probably the deciding factor in Truro's favour, though, was that it had beaten off the challenge of St Columb Major and Bodmin to become the seat of the new Anglican Diocese and in 1877 Queen Victoria had declared that it should henceforth be styled 'The City of Truro'.[5] Bishop Benson had set his sights on a new cathedral that would rival in magnificence the grand medieval cathedrals of England and France. Trevail would, no doubt, have liked to submit plans for this but the Cathedral Executive Committee chose John Loughborough Pearson, a leading Gothicist, from their own short list of six.[6] Throughout the rest of his career Trevail lived almost literally within the shadow of its construction, and as a Cornishman he was proud that it was 'the last cathedral completed, and in all human probability the only one commenced and finished within the period of one generation'.[7] Sadly he never lived to see its completion, but towards the end of his life he took part in the celebrations that marked the construction of the central tower in 1903.

In anticipation of an influx of clergy and professional people, builders were erecting houses and commercial premises at a rate that had not been witnessed since the heyday of mining, and local tradesmen quickly cashed in on Truro's new status by calling their firms 'City Boot-Makers' or the 'Cathedral Luncheon Rooms'.[8] Trevail was aware of these developments, and his files contain plans signed by Nicholas Whiteley for an estate of fifty villas, detached residences and terraced houses on the estate of F G Enys, near Truro railway station. He also knew that the Redruth-based James Hicks, his main rival in school and church building, had designed elaborate Dutch-gabled residences in Farley Terrace and supplied Truro Council, free of charge, with plans for a Corn Exchange that would cost £1,300 to £1,400.[9] James Henderson, a well-established, locally based mining and civil engineer, was also turning to architectural design.

The Triumphal Arches of Truro

The time seemed ripe for Trevail to step in. He moved to premises at 31 Boscawen Street in the middle of the City, and quickly brought himself to the notice of the general public and the Cornish establishment in the most flamboyant way. In 1880 the foundation stone of the new Cathedral was to be laid by Edward, Prince of Wales and Duke of Cornwall, and for this historic occasion, the construction of the first entirely

Top: *Royal Arch in Lemon Street (Family papers).*
Bottom: *Welcome Arch on Boscawen Bridge (Family papers).*

44

SILVANUS TREVAIL

new cathedral in England since the middle ages, a Cornwall-wide holiday was declared. The ceremony, with full masonic and ecclesiastical rites, was expected to attract a vast concourse, and to mark the occasion Trevail suggested that 'Rather than dig out the rather tired bunting used in other towns' Truro should erect a set of Triumphal Arches at every entrance to the city. The council agreed and Trevail designed five structures of wood and plaster, the height of a two-storey building, each differing in style and richly decorated with flags, flowers, coats-of-arms and loyal greetings.[10]

This project marked a major stepping-stone in Trevail's career. Although he had taken every opportunity to bring himself to the public eye, the arches gave him free rein, for the first time and before a wide audience, to display an artistic imagination that had been held in check by the strict constraints of school boards, parish budgets and bureaucratic regulations. He rose to the occasion by exhibiting a mastery of architectural styles, from Greco-Roman, Gothic and Tudor to Moorish. He also displayed a talent for the organisation of a large-scale project on a number of sites, carrying out the design and erection of these arches entirely on his own in just two weeks, acting as his own Clerk of Works, visiting each site ten or twelve times a day and supervising the local craftsmen who made them.[11]

A single arch with the words 'Welcome' and 'God Bless Our Duke and Duchess' in gold at Boscawen Bridge greeted the Royal Couple on their arrival from the east. A Royal Arch near the Lander Monument at the top of Lemon Street in Gothic style proclaimed the message 'Welcome to England's Hope and Pride' looking down the street, with 'Commerce, Peace and Plenty' looking up. At River Street a Cornish Arch with four battlemented towers on its corners was adorned with thirteen medallions of the Borough Seals of Cornwall and the arms of distinguished Cornish families – Boscawen, Carew, Lemon and Trelawney. Outside the railway station another arch, decorated to simulate blocks of Sienna marble, and of intricate Moorish design, spelt out 'Welcome, One and All' and 'Welcome to England's Prince'. At Lemon Bridge the inscription 'Hail Grand Master' on the Masonic Arch was a greeting to the Duke of Cornwall as head of the Masonic movement, of which the Provincial Grand Master was the Earl of Mount Edgcumbe.[12]

As he wrote to his sister, Trevail enjoyed the freedom of 'having my own way in everything',[13] and he was so proud of his designs that he kept large drawings and photographs of them in his study and he mounted the medallions from the River Street arch in a frieze around his office.[14] For his 'unswerving exertions' he received a special commendation from the Truro Cathedral Committee[15] and also found

Peoples Arch near Truro railway station.

favour with local notables who played a part in his professional life as clients or colleagues. Lemon Street was lined by mounted men commanded by the architect James Henderson, Captain of the Rifle Volunteers, who later worked closely with Trevail on the Harbours of Refuge Committee. One of the members of the organising committee was Charles Prideaux-Brune of Padstow, the High Sheriff of Cornwall, for whom Trevail designed farmhouses and a large estate. For another member of the committee, Lord Robartes of Lanhydrock, Trevail carried out various commissions.

Climbing the social ladder
Trevail's triumphal arches were intended to flatter royalty, but they also covered their architect in a blaze of glory. The talk of the town, they gave him entry to the social elite. In 1881 he was elected to a committee to raise funds for a going-away present to J H Collins, a leading geologist and mining expert, who was joining the mighty Rio Tinto Mine in Spain, and this brought him into contact with prominent members of the Cornish establishment. They included W M Grylls, Redruth banker and nationally known dairy farmer, who was later a useful ally when Trevail was involved with designing Truro Technical School, and Howard Fox, influential merchant from the important Falmouth Quaker family, for whom Trevail designed an extension to Falmouth Hotel.[16]

While still at Luxulyan Trevail had joined the Royal Institution of Cornwall in Truro, one of the most prestigious of Cornwall's learned societies, and at one of its meetings he read a paper on 'Cornwall and its Prospects'. Later he informed members of a letter he had received from Richard (later Sir Richard) Tangye, son of an Illogan farmer who had made an engineering fortune in Birmingham, proposing the formation of an art gallery. This 'well known and public spirited gent' as Trevail called him, offered £100 as soon as £900 was contributed by others and Trevail suggested that the existing museum in Pydar Street could be used to house a collection which would grow through bequests. Trevail also offered to keep the accounts for the project, and to draw up a list of contributors which would 'encourage rising artists in a county that has all the characteristics to form a School of Painting'. The editor of the *West Briton* pressed for the suggestion to be taken up by 'our county gentlemen and Cornish gentlemen in London'.[17] Ironically, at a time when painters in Newlyn were founding one of Britain's most famous art colonies, the scheme came to nothing.

A lengthy visit to North America
Somehow, in the midst of his frenetic schedule, Trevail found time in the autumn of 1881 to travel across the United States and Canada on a trip that lasted from the middle of August 1881 to the end of January 1882. We have a detailed account of his journey in his letters to his sister. He prepared for his long absence with his habitual thoroughness, leaving envelopes and cards to cover his itinerary with his sister so that she could keep him in touch with family affairs. On other trips we know that he instructed his assistant to send him copies of every drawing on a daily basis and he probably did the same on this occasion. He told his sister that he was pleased with the way that 'Mr Cook was dealing with matters'.[18]

Before embarking from Liverpool, he stopped off in London for a few days and then travelled to Birmingham, where he visited the Tangye family, as well as Kenilworth, Warwick Castle and 'Shakespeare's place'. At Liverpool he stayed with acquaintances, the Rutters and the Watts. The latter lived at Elm Hall 'about the size of Prideaux Place' and 'kept 14 horses and carriages'. On board the 'Cynthia' he made friends with the Captain, 'a great swell', and got to know Samuel Hoxley, MP for Bristol. In New York another acquaintance, Mr Drew, met him and took him to Staten Island. Following in his father's footsteps, he went to Niagara Falls, where he looked through visitors' books for his father's name, but found the volume for 1848 had been destroyed by fire. In Canada he visited friends and relations and informed his father of their news. After a month of these visits, however, he wrote that he 'was getting very tired of Canada and glad to be back in the States'. The Canadians were 'not go-ahead enough for me' and he found the country 'generally flat with bunches of trees in every direction and hundreds of miles of wooden fences'. Back in New York, he headed west to Chicago, Cincinnati and Washington, and attended a reception where he shook hands with the President and was interviewed by the *Washington Post*.

On his return, as was his wont, he lectured about his travels, and sent a copy of his lecture to the President of the United States; receiving a friendly reply from the Private Secretary, he had it published.[19] An amusing account of his visit, 'Trevail in the Rockies', was later displayed in one of his hotels. As always Trevail made good use of his contacts abroad, and illustrations of his more ornate buildings began to appear in American architectural journals. He added descriptions of his North American trip to his repertoire of talks about his visits to English cathedrals and the Lake District, and these proved 'so instructive and enjoyable' that he 'was induced to present the remaining photographs of his collection'.[20] An inveterate post-card collector, his albums included sets of the Kings and Queens of England, views of Edinburgh, Glasgow and the Scottish Lowlands, Italian art and the Italian lakes. These he lent to clients such as the Prideaux-Brune family.

Trevail and politics

Trevail had moved into Truro at a time of mounting public involvement in imperial, national and local politics. Successive reforms widened the Cornish electorate from 10,000 to 50,000, which meant that all middle class men and a proportion of male artisans and skilled workers, including skilled miners, now had the vote.[21] Even the most parochial of newspapers devoted pages to international and parliamentary affairs and as the influence of the aristocracy and gentry waned, radical views came to the fore. To discuss such matters, Trevail was the prime mover in the foundation of a debating society. After writing to the *West Briton* to give notice of a meeting, Trevail took a prominent part in its affairs and was soon elected Secretary. The first debate, 'The Sanitary Condition of Truro', was followed by 'Future Policy in Egypt', and 'The Trade Prospects and Improvement of the City of Truro'. Significantly, a later paper argued for the adoption of the Public Libraries Act that was to lead to some of his most prestigious commissions.[22] Trevail was constructing a platform for the launch of future professional work.

His entries in the suggestions book of the Cornwall Library Reading Room (a private subscription library) showed his progressive opinions. He recommended that members should donate or loan copies of foreign or colonial newspapers, and protested when political tracts were banned from the Room. Members, he argued, should be aware of all shades of political opinion, even controversial ones on such burning topics of the day as the Irish Home Rule question, and he won the day on this issue.

Again, during an international crisis of 1882, when Egyptian forces rose against the Franco-British condominium, he urged that telegrams with the latest news should be posted in the Reading Room every evening. This would have cost each of the members five shillings (£0.25), and he paid for copies of 'Central News' for a month, at a cost of thirty shillings (£1.50), asking members to contribute towards the expense. To encourage female participation and noting that 'no ladies' novels or works of fiction' were held, he suggested that a notice should be displayed asking ladies to propose 'light reading, as they are more competent judges' of this genre. He did not, however, assume that females lacked interest in wider issues, for he also asked for copies of 'The Lady' to be kept so that all members could benefit from 'views of Imperial Politics from the ladies' standpoint'.[23]

Imperial politics

The growth of the British Empire was a subject that touched Trevail deeply. His life was spent in an era when the Empire was reaching its highest point as soldiers, politicians and adventurers coloured large expanses of the map of the world pink. He was elected a member of the General Committee of the Imperial Federation League[24] founded in 1884, later the British Empire League. He lectured on the politics of colonial growth throughout Cornwall and further afield, and was later invited to join a Select Committee of the League but declined because of pressure of work.[25] He read papers on subjects such as 'The Expansion of the English Races' and 'The Expansion of Great Britain into a Greater Britain' to Institutes in Redruth, Bodmin and Plymouth. He also dealt severely with the 'Radical School who preached disintegration', especially the Liskeard MP, Leonard Courtney.[26] The *West Briton* approved; 'Good missionary work in a good cause, Mr Trevail'.[27]

A Harbour of Refuge

Trevail was by now occupying positions of prominence on a Cornwall-wide front, notably in the development of Harbours of Refuge for ships caught in the violent storms that sometimes struck the coasts of Britain.[28] The issue came to the fore from time to time, usually after a particularly tragic maritime disaster – one-sixth of the loss of lives around the seas of Britain were said to occur between the Severn Estuary and Land's End – and then floundered when funds were not forthcoming. The year 1884 was one such occasion and Trevail, after witnessing ships in a storm from the Great Western Hotel that he had designed at Newquay, called for urgent action.[29] Having made an impressive contribution at a meeting of the Central Committee for Harbours of Refuge for Cornwall, he was elected to a small executive committee. The Chairman was Edward Carus-Wilson, a banker and county and Truro city magistrate of Penmount, north of Truro and Trevail was elected joint Honorary Secretary with James

Henderson, the Truro civil engineer and architect.

Again this activity brought him in touch with Cornishmen with whom he remained closely and usefully associated throughout the rest of his life. They included George Hicks, for whom Trevail had already designed the mansion of Pentowan above the port of Newquay. Hicks shared an interest in promoting the expansion of the town and was strongly in favour of Newquay as a site for the proposed Harbour of Refuge. Chairman of the newly established Newquay Waterworks Company, Hicks invited Trevail to its

Early photograph of Pentowan, Newquay (Family papers).

inaugural luncheon held in the Great Western Hotel.[30] George (later Sir George) Smith, one of Cornwall's leading industrialists, was another member of the harbour committee who was later to give valuable support to Trevail when the latter was facing criticism as Chairman of the Central Technical Schools for Truro.[31]

Trevail and Henderson sent a circular to all districts requesting information on their views, and organised local commit-

tees.[32] Almost immediately, however, trouble arose when Josiah Harris, Honorary Secretary of the main committee, complained of the treatment he received from Trevail. 'For Carus-Wilson', he said, 'I have always desired to cherish a true respect, but it is utterly impossible for me to work with him while he takes Mr Silvanus Trevail under his wing'. The upshot was that Harris resigned,[33] but Trevail continued. He wrote a thirty-two page report[34] and was one of the members of the committee who gave evidence before the Select Committee of the House of Commons, who took a deplorably long time to deal with it.

Local disagreement, central indifference

A memorial, in the drafting of which Trevail played an important part, was presented to the President of the Board of Trade in May 1885 and the committee sent a circular to all the candidates in the Devon and Cornwall parliamentary election and to many of the seaports in Britain, soliciting their support. All this was harder work, Trevail recalled later, than his railway campaigns, but their efforts met with no more success than all the other attempts to finance a Harbour, for much the same reasons. The government was not interested and Cornishmen could not agree on a site. Trevail was a member of the deputation to Joseph Chamberlain, then President of the Board of Trade, who received them in what Trevail described as a 'most nonchalant manner'.

As the Earl of Mount Edgcumbe, who headed the movement, explained a decade later, 'there were no places in Cornwall that could make up their minds as to where the Harbour should be ... some said Padstow, others said ridiculous, it should be at St Ives, and vice versa'.[35] The Harbour of Refuge project was clearly going nowhere. Trevail was not the man to waste time on such ill-fated ventures and he took no further active part in it.

The saga of Truro Post Office

All these social and political activities were superimposed on a crushing schedule of architectural work, such as the construction of a new post office for Truro. During the course of 1880, reports appeared about a building to be shared by the Post Office and the Corn Exchange, for which James Hicks of Redruth, as mentioned earlier, had submitted a free set of plans, and in 1881 Trevail prepared drawings for a site next to City Hall, with the Post Office facing Boscawen Street and the Exchange at the rear. But in 1883 the Post Office authorities abandoned this scheme as too costly and also declined Lord Robartes' offer of a site at High Cross, near the Cathedral. They called for new plans but, as one of Trevail's well-wishers declared, he had received no payment for his previous plans and could not be expected to provide alternative designs for nothing. A year later Trevail declared in the *West Briton* that the Post Office would be erected as planned, but this turned out to be a mere branch office at Alderman Heard's shop in what is now Cathedral Lane; and so Trevail embarked on designs for a new office at High Cross, for which tenders were invited.[36]

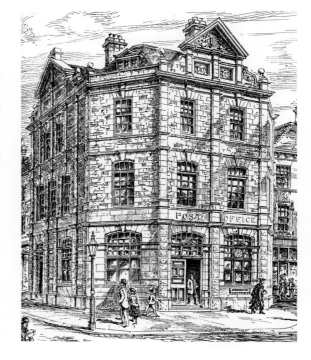

Trevail's drawing of Truro Post Office (CRO: AD396/613).

A further eighteen months went by before the *West Briton* reported that 'chiefly through the indefatigable efforts of Mr Trevail', a new post office was to be erected near the site of the Cathedral. However, further disputes arose because his plans required a space larger than the land available from Lord Robartes and the estimated cost of the building would have entailed payment of a higher rent than the postal authorities were willing to pay. Truro Council owned adjoining property which would enable the structure to be built, but were reluctant to sell it. Eventually, after a series of heated exchanges between Trevail and local officials, construction began in the summer of 1886 and a building arose which, according to the *West Briton* 'elicited universal admiration', indeed 'the handsomest and also the largest Post Office in Cornwall'.[37]

The Post Office project was marked by a growing number of conflicts between Trevail and Truro Council. The surveyor objected to a clause in Trevail's letter stipulating that as the plan had been approved by H M Office of Works, he would permit no further alteration by the surveyor. On this occasion the surveyor accepted the plans, but the Mayor and Council resented Trevail's attitude. As a correspondent wrote to the *West Briton*: 'Mr Trevail may be able to hit very hard blows, but if people choose to retort, possibly heavier blows may be given'. This controversy, however, did not prevent Trevail from designing an Exchange in Boscawen Street, with similar balustrading to that he used later for Burton's shop in Pydar Street and the Devon and Cornwall Bank on the corner of Lemon Street.[38]

When the Post Office finally opened, the West Briton fancied that 'our readers will regret, with us, that monetary difficulties prevented the first ideas of Mr Trevail from being carried into practical effect'. His original four storey design, with granite facings, oriel windows and Dutch gables would have been more impressive than the actual building, in the classical Queen Anne style.[39]

Some country dwellings

One of the architectural fields into which Trevail diversified was the construction of country cottages, farms and mansions. Some of these projects were small, such as alterations to farmhouses and outbuildings at Terras and at Penhale, near St Stephens, for Edmund Beauchamp Beauchamp, descendent of a distinguished family who had taken a very active interest in the early mining industry. Trevail was firmly instructed that old materials should be reused as far as possible, limiting the cost to £35 or £40 per project. However, Beauchamp also commissioned a substantial farmhouse at Tregear, Ladock.[40] Another small commission was the erection of a mill house at Lanivet Churchtown, for although it had five bedrooms, the tiniest was only six feet square. William Martyn Richards, a Justice of the Peace, had Woodlands, also a five bedroom house but larger, built outside Padstow,[41] and another Trevail project of the time was the construction of a terrace of four shops and a post office in a large empty frontage in Honey Street, Bodmin, which was marked by a minor mishap when the chimney collapsed, happily with no casualties.[42]

One of his finest ecclesiastical works was constructed during this period. In

Left: *Tregear farmhouse near Ladock for the Beauchamp family.*
Right: *Treator, near Trevone, built by James Julian in 1884.*

February 1881 the Congregational Church Building Group of Mevagissey appointed him architect, by August the memorial stones were laid, and the opening ceremony took place in January 1883. All these occasions were marked by luncheons, teas or public meetings, reported in great detail in the press, with references to the structure as 'an ornament to Mevagissey' and, of course, the name of the architect. But certainly the Chapel with its granite buttresses and dressings and its grand, three-light, Gothic arch west entrance, was worthy of praise.[43]

A St Austell project of the time was the renovation by Trevail of St Austell Congregational Church, with an arched organ chamber and rostrum replacing the narrow pulpit with new pews for the congregation. The building was later awarded a Grade II listing but was demolished in the 1970s. Nearby, St Mary's Vicarage, Par, was designed by Trevail between 1880 and 1882, using a pink stone, probably from a quarry on the Carlyon estate, Major Carlyon of Tregrehan having given the site. Red brick was used for the window and door reveals and the chimneys.[44]

Alterations to Wesleyan chapels at Redruth and St Agnes, porches added to Bodmin Bible Christian Chapel and Penzance St Paul's Church, a vestry for Fowey and a new tower to Helland Church were other Trevail renovations, probably the best known of which was at Temple, one of the most ancient of Cornish churches. There was so little of the old structure remaining that it could almost be classed as a new building, and the driving force behind the restoration was the newly installed Rector of Helland, the Reverend J R Brown who raised £450 to enable the work to go ahead. Trevail generously provided the plans without charge.[45]

Top: *Mevagissey Congregational Church opened in 1883. Now known as St Andrew's Church.*
Bottom left: *St Mary's Vicarage, Par, for Rev Frank Garrett.*
Bottom right: *Temple Church rebuilt by Trevail in 1883.*

Although only in his early thirties, he was also making a name for himself outside Cornwall. In 1885 he was elected to membership of the Society of Architects, formed a year earlier to 'look after the business side of the profession', as Trevail later put it.[46] He was soon made a member of its Council and embarked upon yet another of his crusades: to ensure that persons calling themselves 'architects' should be properly qualified and registered, as were doctors or lawyers, before being allowed to practice their profession. He continued to pursue this mission when fifteen years later he became President of the Society.

Five
Trevail 'gets his knife' into some powerful men

A recurring feature of Silvanus Trevail's life was the way in which he became embroiled in feuds and vendettas with influential men who stood in his path. One of them was Arthur (later Sir Arthur) Pendarves Vivian MP and another, discussed later in this chapter, was Truro's Chief Clerk, F Hearle Cock. Vivian was a rich and powerful man with a wide circle of political friends. He had become MP in 1868 at the invitation of an elite of wealthy landowners including J M Williams, Lord Robarts and Lord Falmouth,

Silvanus Trevail, circa 1880 (Family papers).

whose tenants were naturally expected to vote for him. But the Reform Act of 1884 had widened the suffrage and Cornish constituencies had also been reshaped. Camborne and Redruth, up to then in separate constituencies, had been combined in a 'Mining Division' creating a radical grouping of working class and lower middle class voters.

Instead of being chosen behind closed doors, as in the past, Vivian now had to present himself to a meeting of over five hundred Liberals for re-selection as a candidate. He was opposed by a rich barrister from Essex, Charles Augustus Vansittart Conybeare, and although Vivian was selected Conybeare declared the whole procedure a sham and presented himself as a rival Liberal with a political platform that was far bolder than Vivian's. Calling himself the 'miners' champion' Conybeare advocated the abolition of the House of Lords, the disestablishment of the Church of England, female suffrage and the repeal of the game laws which prevented tenants from killing game. He even supported devolution of central government powers to Cornwall. His opponents called him a 'Red-hot

Radical Agitator' and in a bitter political campaign furniture was broken and windows smashed during public meetings.[1]

While Trevail was, as we saw in Chapter Four, an imperialist, he held progressive views on many matters and entered the fray strongly on Conybeare's side. He had fallen out with Vivian over the seaside estate he designed for William Stephens, mentioned in Chapter Two, at Porth Veor to the east of Newquay. His plans comprised 148 numbered plots for villas, semi-detached and detached houses of varying sizes, tennis courts, recreation grounds and a church, with space for further development.[2] Unfortunately for Vivian, this scheme surrounded Glendorgal, which he had bought as a secluded holiday retreat overlooking the sea, and he showed his annoyance by impeding Stephens in the diversion of a road by a few feet through the proposed estate to his home.

According to Trevail when, as a matter of courtesy, he approached Vivian's agent to inform him of the deviation, the agent warned him that Vivian was a rich man who would not hesitate to take Stephens to court to get his own way and, if necessary, build a wall 40 feet high around Glendorgal which would ruin the sea view of any prospective development. As a result Trevail claimed he would lose commission on a possible £20,000 of architectural work.[3] Vivian then left Glendorgal, selling it to Richard Tangye, the Cornish-born manufacturer mentioned in Chapter Four, as a seaside family residence.[4] Tangye proved more amenable, not only agreeing to the deviation but defraying half the expenses of improving the road. Since Tangye's arrival, Trevail asserted, the blight on the development of the estate had been removed and a substantial area had been sold.

However, Trevail was not one to let bygones be bygones, and in 1885 when Vivian stood for election as a Liberal, Trevail published two pamphlets with Northey, a well-known Liberal activist. These contrasted Vivian's 'conservatism' with Tangye's 'liberality', a paradox in terms because Vivian was standing as a Liberal. Vivian was furious with these attacks by Trevail, and Stephens, returning to Cornwall, was incensed that a purely private dispute had been brought into the political arena by Trevail and quickly dissociated himself from Trevail's remarks. Tangye too was greatly displeased and wrote to Vivian regretting that he had unwittingly been 'dragged into a personal and violent attack'.

Tangye's version of events contradicted Trevail's. According to Tangye, Trevail had 'vehemently denounced' Vivian for costing him commission, and said that he had 'got his knife into him', and would see to it that Vivian would never again be elected MP for a Cornish constituency.[5] Yet, Tangye claimed, there was no demand for housing plots and the only purchase was by Tangye himself who had paid £300, five or six times the market rate, simply to ensure that no development took place.[6]

Perhaps though Tangye was ingenuous in blaming the need to purchase surrounding land upon Trevail. He had written a letter to the press complaining about the 'rough ladies and gentlemen of Newquay' who strolled in his gardens and stared at his guests, which he felt was a poor compensation for all the improvements he had made to the walks, cliffs and paths of Newquay.[7] His purchase of the additional land could be seen as a means of enhancing the resale value of Glendorgal.[8]

Conybeare's campaign was enlivened by the publication of rival pamphlets. A number of copies of them have been found in Trevail's papers, including several sheets of doggerel, 'composed by Mr Conybeare's supporters'. One of them, to be sung to the melody of 'John Brown's Body', referred to a burning issue of the day, Irish Home Rule:

> Serf and sailor they shall both be free,
> And the green land of Erin over the wide sea,
> The liberty for us shall be liberty for thee,
> And we'll go marching on.

Another, set to the tune of 'And shall Trelawney die?' dealt with another matter on which Trevail had strong views, the reform of the leasehold system on land:

> We'll all have our Rights, our house, our land,
> The stewards shall not prey,
> With 'One and All' and hand in hand,
> And who shall bid us nay.

Whether Silvanus had a hand in composing these verses we shall never know, although it might be thought that he would have shown more literary skill. However, he was accused of what would now be called 'political dirty tricks', by publishing scurrilous attacks on Conybeare that were claimed to be the work of Vivian's supporters. One document took the form of a funeral notice, edged in black, lamenting the death of Conybeare on election day. Another was a cartoon of an elephant, presumed to be Conybeare, also meeting its death on the same day. Trevail was forced to write to the press denying all knowledge of them,[9] but the fact that a number of them were found in his papers leads us to wonder whether he had had something to do with the matter.

Memorial for the supposed death of Conybeare (Family papers).

Trevail as a Liberal campaigner

In the end Conybeare did not meet his political death at Camborne; on the contrary he pulled off a famous victory, albeit by a narrow margin. He remained a life-long friend of Silvanus, a companion on trips to Paris and an investor in some of his projects. Now that the parliamentary vote had been given to working men, political meetings drew large audiences and Trevail's involvement in the turbulent election campaign of Conybeare in Camborne had brought him fame, or notoriety, in local political circles. Already, when a National Liberal Club in London had been proposed in 1882, he had become a country member. He initiated a series of debates upon issues, including Home Rule for Ireland, on behalf of the Liberal Club of Truro, and he was delegated by the Liberal Association of Truro to go to London to see a candidate who would support Home Rule.

While in America in 1881, Trevail had attended a 'wild Irish political meeting', com-

✦ CORNWALL ✦
COUNTY LIBERAL CONFERENCE, AT TRURO,
◦ Friday, 15th April, 1887, ◦
Under the auspices of the National Liberal Federation,
The RIGHT HON. The EARL SPENCER, K.G.,
(LATE LORD LIEUTENANT OF IRELAND, AND OTHERS.)
County Committee:—
SIR ARTHUR D. HAYTER, BART., Chairman.
MESSRS. T. H. LAKE, and Hᵗ LOWRY, Treasurers.
MR. SILVANUS TREVAIL, Secretary.

Truro,   188

Notepaper for County Liberal Conference with Mr Silvanus Trevail as Secretary (Family papers).

menting that 'the Paddies are pretty savage with Gladstone ... America applauds our government'.[10] Gladstone's attempts to establish Home Rule for Ireland split the Liberal party and had a particular resonance in Cornwall because of anti-Catholic feeling among nonconformists, as well as suspicions that if Irishmen got Home Rule they would raid Cornish fishing grounds. Trevail also lectured on similar issues in other towns, including Redruth and acted as Secretary-Organiser for a Cornwall-wide Liberal Conference.[11] He remained a Liberal all his life, and was one of the principal mourners chosen by the Truro Liberal Club to attend the lying-in-state of Gladstone in 1898. The 1885–6 period, however, marked the peak of his involvement in Parliamentary politics for, as we shall see, he soon became preoccupied with local government.

The problems of Truro Baths

Away from the excitement of his political life, Trevail was increasingly frustrated with what he saw as stick-in-the-mud municipal councillors and officials, in other words anyone who opposed his schemes. In addition to problems of Truro Post Office, described in previous chapter, another example concerned the construction of Truro Public Baths. Truro Council had enthusiastically approved the project in the early 1880s, but it was not until 1885 that a site meeting was held at which 'Mr Trevail expressed himself a thorough believer in public baths and thought every town should be provided with them'. As with the Post Office, an alternative site, owned by Lord Falmouth, was available in St George's Road. He appeared ready to invest in the scheme although the cost would be high, and Trevail prepared a scheme for Lord Falmouth, keeping it below £2,000. Eventually it was decided to transform some rooms in a smaller YMCA site in St Mary's Street at a cost of around £1,500, including the freehold.[12]

After a further two years of inaction, the Mayor of Truro appointed a committee of local leaders including Aldermen and Councillors, as well as the heads of Truro School and the Wesleyan Middle Class School and Trevail himself, to expedite the matter. In less than three weeks they compiled a list of potential shareholders and a company was formed, with Trevail as director and shareholder, with a capital of £1,500. Trevail who had 'recently visited some of the most efficient metropolitan baths' was appointed architect. The building finally opened in 1890, and Trevail was complimented upon 'making a good job out of a comparatively unpromising site'. But the project did not pay because not enough people displayed a desire to bathe in the winter months, and so the floor was covered over and the premises used for entertainment.[13]

Silvanus Trevail, JP and Truro councillor

The year 1886 was a significant one for Silvanus Trevail. He was elected Justice of the Peace at the comparatively early age of thirty-five, and moving to a large house at the

bottom of Lemon Street, he successfully presented himself as a candidate for election to the city council. His experience of road widening in Newquay, to be discussed in Chapter Seven, had given him ideas on the way that Truro's street network could be enhanced and he attended a meeting in May 1886, the result of a public enquiry into the state of Truro, at which the council present-

80–81 Lemon Street, Truro, Trevail's home and business quarters.

ed its planning proposals. First to take the floor he expounded, at what a reporter considered inordinate length, prefaced with 'a lot of irrelevant history of the town', his criticisms of their scheme. He was supported in this by Edward Roberts, local superintendent of the Prudential Assurance Company, but they were warned by Councillor Jacob, an influential local retailer, not to press their attacks too strongly or Truro could end up with nothing achieved. They were invited to join them in a deputation to the Government Inspector of Public Works to finalise the project, but they were disappointed to find that little heed was taken of their ideas.[14]

Meanwhile Trevail was crossing swords again with the Council, and its authoritative City Clerk, F Hearle Cock. Trevail had fallen out with him on minor matters before, but the main disagreements arose during the long drawn out case of the Polkinhorne warehouse that had begun early in 1885. Samuel Polkinhorne, a prominent cattle breeder and corn merchant from Malpas near Truro, had acquired some dilapidated buildings at Boscawen Bridge, including the Bridge Inn, on the river at Truro and wanted to knock them down to build a new store and office.[15] Since Truro was then a port, the prosperity of which had been affected by the collapse of mining, it was vital to maintain its status as an agricultural centre. A new warehouse would promote Truro's mercantile life, offer employment to local people and bring in several hundred pounds a year of rates to the Council.

Instead of welcoming the project with open arms, the Council, guided by the Town Clerk, Hearle Cock, seemed to place obstacles in its way. Admittedly Trevail had first upset him when, as on a previous occasion, he reserved to himself the right to change the materials he used before or during construction. The council resented this but, in view of the importance of the building, did not stand in his way. But the Town Clerk had also noticed that the proposed foundations projected about a foot into the river bed, which belonged to the Duchy of Cornwall and, instead of resolving the matter amicably with the Duchy agent, the clerk ordered Trevail to redraw his plans.

Trevail refused and the dispute then dragged on for over three years. Trevail demolished the old buildings leaving rubble, which caused annoyance to the citizens of Truro and which he refused to clear away. Polkinhorne threatened to abandon the scheme and move his base to Falmouth, and Trevail wrote angry letters to the press, attacking what he called the unwarranted interference of the Council and its Clerk. When the Surveyor issued a circular, reminding developers that no new buildings could be erected unless he had approved both the front line and the floor level, Trevail took this as a personal affront, 'a usurpation of power that the inhabitants of the city will do well to be on their guard against'.[16]

Polkinhorne finally opened a warehouse in 1888, designed by Trevail, but on another site in Prince's Street. A highly ornamented and massive red brick structure, it overshadowed the older, elegant and restrained classical buildings on either side, the Mansion House and Prince's House. For the first time Trevail had adopted Dutch gables, which he later used on Bosvigo School in 1895.[17] Trevail was perfectly capable of building in a classical manner that would have been consistent with the neighbouring buildings; had he, or Polkinhorne, deliberately introduced this incongruent construction to get his own back on the authorities?

Upper floors of Polkinhorne's warehouse in Princes Street, Truro.

Councillor Trevail makes a quick impression

Meanwhile, in November 1886, Trevail had been elected to the Town Council for the Eastern Ward of Truro.[18] He took great pride in the manner of his achievement, making a great play of rising above the rough and tumble of local politics, although as we have seen his conduct in the Conybeare parliamentary election was open to question. He had, he claimed, not asked any person for his vote, nor stooped to 'vote catching, promise-squeezing or boycotting'. This was hardly true, since he had made one of his customary forceful speeches at a ratepayers' meeting which led to his being asked to stand for election; another meeting was held at the Corn Exchange at which he also expounded his views. He issued a series of pamphlets in the months before the election, entitled 'Half a Dozen Reasons why Mr Trevail Does Not Canvass', 'The City of Truro Municipal Election' and 'The Reverend Canon Mason and the Truro Municipal Election'. In these he argued that a candidate should not actively campaign, but simply let his record of public achievement speak for itself. On this occasion his high principles proved successful but, as will be seen, he had to pay a high price for them later on.[19]

At his first Council meeting, Trevail followed his customary practice of making his presence felt by a number of swift interventions. He claimed the privilege, as junior member of the Council, to support Edward Heard, Senior Alderman, in proposing the new Mayor, Robert Macleane Paul. In doing so he heaped praise not only upon the Mayor and upon Heard, proprietor of the *West Briton* and one of the most influential men in Cornwall, but also on Paul's father and uncle, both former Mayors. These pleasant formalities performed, Trevail reverted to his customary, more combative manner, demanding to know why he had not been appointed to three prestigious sub-committees, notably that on Finance, occupied by his predecessor. His elders quickly reminded him of his position as junior member, also pointing out that he had failed to attend a preliminary gathering at which committee places were allocated. Unabashed, Trevail then made what seemed a presumptuous request for information on the Town Clerk's duties that would justify his salary.[20]

A vendetta with the Chief Clerk

It was customary in the English legal system for the Town Clerk to be a local solicitor in private practice. However, the Clerk occupied a position of great authority. He advised councillors on all legal matters, staff appointments and dismissals, attended every meeting and coordinated the activities of the subcommittees. As a result this post was the most coveted in local government, 'practically for life, with rich perquisites'.[21] Truro's clerk was a respected solicitor who had served the council for over 20 years and whose knowledge of municipal affairs was such that he was deferred to on all adminis-trative decisions.

Hearle Cock was outraged by Trevail's impudence. He regarded himself as the equal, if not the superior, of the councillors, yet Trevail was treating him as a mere employee, as he later made this quite clear to the Clerk. 'I suppose you think you are a great man. Let me tell you, Sir, that you are merely a servant and before I have done with you I will show you your place,' Trevail asserted, inviting the Clerk to come out-side into the street where he would 'give him satisfaction'. The longer-serving council-lors were shocked by such behaviour, especially when Trevail pursued the vendetta with the Clerk in meeting after meeting. Alderman E G Heard, doyen of the Council and proprietor of the *West Briton* newspaper, declared that in all his years on the Council he had 'never heard anything so disagreeable'.[22]

However, Trevail had done his homework. After making enquiries in towns of a similar size, he had calculated that clerks in such places earned on average £114 a year. Since Hearle Cock received £120 this did not seem out of place. It was, though, only the tip of the iceberg as Trevail revealed in subsequent meetings. The Clerk also acted as Secretary to the Local Sanitary Committee, composed of exactly the same persons as the town council, which doubled his salary. This, again, was by no means unheard of. What really was irregular, as Trevail had found, was that Hearle Cock charged the coun-cil separately for every item of legal work he carried out for them, although this should have been part of his Clerk's duty.

What was worse, he made the public pay for all their dealings with the Council, and instead of letting them use standard printed forms which cost a few pence, he drew up expensive legal documents. In these ways he was earning an income of several hundred pounds a year.[23] Moreover, Hearle Cock, as Trevail discovered, was receiving this income for work that only occupied him one day a week, allowing him to act as clerk to other bodies and carry out private practice as a solicitor. If these activities paid as well as his local government post, he must have been one of the highest earners in Cornwall.[24]

Bringing these matters to the attention of the councillors was one thing. Getting them to do anything about it was quite another, as Trevail was soon to learn. The longer-serving members were embarrassed by his discoveries and no doubt would have preferred to sweep them under the carpet, but Trevail's revelations were being reported in the local press and also gained the support of some of the newer councillors. One of them was Henry Buck, who had come to Truro as a railway clerk and then set up as a grocer, before becoming a prominent wine and spirit merchant. Another was John James, a bank manager who was associated with the influential Quaker bankers, Tweedy's. Buck had been elected on a promise to cut down Council expenditure while James, as a Quaker, was disturbed by hints of corrupt dealings. Together they helped Trevail produce a report that recommended cutting out the Clerk's legal charges.

Hearle Cock's disdainful reply to all requests to reduce his professional charges was quite simply: 'very well, then, increase the Town Clerk's salary!' And as a rejoinder he produced a bill for over £1,000 in unpaid charges. The older councillors, anxious to hush things up, offered £800 which Trevail and his supporters opposed and which the Clerk, in any case, refused. So the quarrel dragged on. Every time the older councillors seemed to be reaching a rapprochement by paying the Clerk more money, his opponents would create a fresh impasse by making new allegations of malpractice. When the appointment of a School Attendance Officer was discussed, Trevail asserted that this was one of the duties of the Clerk that he had failed to carry out. Trevail and Buck also accused the Clerk of 'gross negligence' in selling a Council property at well below market value as well as holding on to Council funds and earning interest on them. For such irregularities they proposed to fine him £20.[25]

Under this relentless pressure the Clerk resigned. But if the councillors thought that their troubles were over they were greatly mistaken. For Trevail then played his trump card. By burrowing through the Council's records he had unearthed an old agreement between the Clerk and the Council which clearly stated that all the extra work for which the Clerk had been charging, and for which the Council had paid without question, was covered within the Clerk's duties. To make matters worse, they had twice increased his salary while condoning these improper payments. Trevail, Buck and their supporters were all for taking the clerk to court. The councillors who were party to the agreement took no action, perhaps because they were unwilling to risk being arraigned for wasting the ratepayers' money.

Hearle Cock, it must be said, did not lack audacity. Despite clear evidence of his dubious activities, he refused to hand over Council funds in his possession until he was paid another £400 for his illegal charges. This time it was Trevail who, as newly appointed Chairman of Finance, offered him £200 to close the matter, and Buck's turn to accuse Trevail of 'sacrificing principle to expediency'. Nor was this the end of the Council's questionable practices. When they advertised the dual post of Town Clerk and Sanitary Committee Secretary at the reduced salary of £200, to include all the items for which the Clerk had been charging extra, they received 48 applications from well qualified and experienced solicitors from all parts of England, including four solicitors who were members of Truro Council, one of them being the Mayor himself. Obviously the Clerk's post was highly prized, even on the new terms. The Council then excluded all the non-Council applicants from the short list and the Mayor got the job. Trevail, surprisingly, not only accepted this blatant favouritism but openly backed the Mayor's candidature, although another Councillor condemned the proceedings as a 'pure farce'.

Trevail had not finished rooting out irregularities. He accused the Assistant Surveyor, Albert Clemens, of purchasing bricks at a price £100 above the going rate in order to receive an 'illicit commission'. Then, defeated on a vote to reprimand Clemens, he threatened to press charges against him privately under the Public Health Act. Some councillors, like Theophilus Lutey Dorrington, a watchmaker in Cathedral Lane, defended Clemens, arguing that Trevail had greatly exaggerated the difference between the price that Clemens paid and the normal price. A report by the Improvement Committee of the Council found no proof of any secret commission, but Trevail threatened to challenge it 'paragraph by paragraph' in an effort to overturn its findings. He was again defeated and no charges were made against Clemens; yet a few months later he suddenly departed without giving the customary notice. Whether this was an admission of guilt, or a reaction to Trevail's treatment is not known.[26]

Yet another of Trevail's multifarious tasks was to inspect new housing projects and supervise housing accounts for Kenwyn, a district of Truro. In 1890 this led him into disputes reminiscent of his earlier vendettas with the Truro Town Clerk, discussed earlier. In a meeting attended by ratepayers, he conducted a heated quarrel with J H Sampson, assessor-surveyor for St Clement near Truro, accusing him and other officials of claiming extra expenses for work that formed part of their paid duties. He also attacked the 'most despotic and ill-advised backstairs' influence on magistrates, by what the *West Briton* called a 'handful of Tory squires', who overrode the decisions of Kenwyn citizens.[27] Financial deficits in the Kenwyn accounts continued to trouble him for a number of years.[28]

Finally, it is interesting to note that, according to Trevail's own calculations, the Council had paid Hearle Cock no less than £2,912 during the period when Trevail was trying to cut his salary. In later years, Trevail often referred to the way that he had re-organised Truro's finances, saving the ratepayers much money. Perhaps it would have been better if he had left things alone.

Six
The 'Chancellor of the Exchequer' meets a setback

The personal vendettas that Silvanus Trevail conducted never seemed to interfere with his architectural activities and his progress was, as always, aided by his flair for publicity, although this sometimes met with disapproval. For instance when he stamped the periodicals he had contributed to the Truro Library Reading Room with 'Silvanus Trevail, Architect', a writer in the suggestions book criticised this as tantamount to self-promotion. Trevail replied with typical self-assurance that he might 'safely assume that every subscriber knows what my occupation is'.[1]

He took a prominent part in the annual conference of the Society of Architects of the UK held at Plymouth in the autumn of 1885, serving on the panels that awarded prizes for architectural drawings and presented a paper arguing that architectural competitions were becoming more and more numerous, imposing an 'intolerable burden' upon professionals, especially since the winning designs in so many instances appeared to satisfy nobody.[2] Was there a pressing reason for his concern since, as we shall see, he was now beginning to lose commissions to other architects? Shortly after, the *West Briton* reported that he had been elected a member of the Society, proposed by no less a person than its President, Hugh Romien Gough FRIBA.[3]

Some commissions in Truro
Trevail's contacts in Truro also gave him plenty of opportunity for obtaining work. A small commission of 1885 was the design of stables for J H Martin, later converted to other uses and finally demolished at the end of the twentieth century to make way for the relocation of Marks and Spencer's when they opened a store facing a new piazza in Truro. A more important work that has since disappeared was the addition of two mock-Tudor storeys to the Red Lion, to be discussed in Chapter Ten.

St Piran's Roman Catholic Chapel, designed by him in Dereham Terrace in Truro was almost dwarfed by the six-bedroom, three storey presbytery which he designed next door. Built by James Julian of Truro, the two buildings cost about £2,000 and were illustrated in *The Architect*[4] in 1885. In the same year he altered St Mary's Wesleyan Church in Union Place the interior of which, one observer remarked, contrasted with

Top: *St Piran's Roman Catholic Chapel, Truro, 1884–1973.* Bottom: *St Mary's Wesleyan Chapel, Truro, after renovation in 1895 (Family papers).*

the factory-like appearance of the exterior. Even here Trevail could not avoid contro-versy, being accused of favouritism in the selection of Battershill, a well-known local craftsman, an allegation that Trevail refuted in his customary robust fashion. His alter-ations cost around £2,000, the same as the new St Piran's buildings.[5]

At the re-opening ceremony for St Mary's it was announced that a large new school-room would be built behind the chapel and a new chapel erected in William Street, requiring a total outlay of over £6,000. Trevail designed both, and the school with its elegant assembly hall, high moulded plaster ceilings and elaborate wrought iron balustrade for the gallery, contained not only twelve classrooms but facilities for ladies' working groups, institute meetings and prayer gatherings, with a kitchen to cater for large social events.[6] The William Street Chapel replaced an old Wesleyan Chapel, built in 1833 and generally referred to as Lemon Chapel, in what was then called John Street. Two cottages were demolished to make a new site. Since the specifications were the same as those for the Wesleyan School Trevail tried to persuade William Clemens, the City Surveyor, that a repetition was unnecessary, but without success. The Chapel, built at a cost of about £1,000, opened in October 1887.[7]

Other Cornish commissions

Bottom left:
Mill house,
Lanivet, 1886.
Bottom right:
Edgcumbe
Wesleyan Chapel
built by WJ Winn
& Sons of
Helston.

One of the best surviving examples of his renovation skills is his work on the large Wesleyan Chapel in Station Road, Redruth, in 1888. Internally, the ground floor at the sides was taken down to the level of the centre, the old pulpit replaced with a handsome rostrum and slender pillars were installed instead of the heavy wooden gallery supports. The old pews were replaced as were the front panels of the gallery and the few remain-ing older features were embellished with red felt or paint.[8] Unfortunately for those seated nearby, the swing doors leading to the gallery pews moved in the wind, causing considerable discomfort.[9] St Agnes Chapel received similar treatment and the 1880 renovation of Roche Wesleyan Chapel may well have been on the same lines as that of

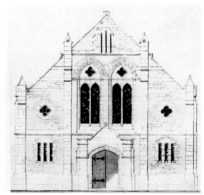

St Austell Congregational mentioned in Chapter Four, with an arched organ chamber and rostrum replacing the narrow pulpit.

Commissions of 1886 included a miller's house at Lanivet Churchtown (now a private residence), and the small Lank Free Methodist Chapel (since demolished) and St Austell Wesleyan Chapel, not completed until 1892. The original building dated from 1827 and the work proceeded in two stages. Trevail planned for a rostrum, seating and the introduction of electric light and central heating. New windows were then installed with leaded lights. One stained glass window bears the inscription, 'Presented by Silvanus Trevail, Architect, for the renovation of this Chapel, 1892'.[10]

Further to the west, Trevail's Edgcumbe Wesleyan Chapel at Wendron was close to being destroyed in October 1886, only six months after being opened, possibly due to overheating of the warming apparatus. Fortunately the fire was discovered in time and only some internal woodwork and a new harmonium burnt. It is not clear what form of heating was in use at this time because in 1888 it was decided to change the system and to heat the chapel by means of hot air. The very open site, exposed to the weather, meant the trustees incurred considerable expenditure over the first few years to keep the place warm and free of damp – moving a doorway, installing curtains to protect pews, boarding in a stair well, re-pointing the front wall and plastering a side wall.[11]

A year before this Trevail had designed the largest of his three Anglican churches at Upton Cross, Linkinhorne, an apsidal building as at Nanpean, accompanied by a Sunday school.[12] Meanwhile at Newquay the momentum of the Congregationalists in this expanding town was enhanced by the arrival of a new Minister, the Reverend W H Fuller, and a new building was erected in Bank Street to replace an old decaying structure. Trevail drew up the plans, James Julian of Truro was the contractor and the Liberal MP, W A McArthur, laid the foundation stone in May 1888, at a ceremony attended by Richard Tangye, with whom Trevail had earlier crossed swords.

Within six months the money was raised to finish the Chapel, and Pastor Fuller entertained the building workers at a dinner held in the Commercial Hotel, at which he congratulated both Trevail and Julian for the excellence of their work. Unusually for this time, the Chapel contained a small pulpit, although this was later replaced with the more fashionable rostrum.[13] Elsewhere another energetic cleric, the Reverend J R

Left: Upton Cross Church built in 1885 next to Trevail's school. Right: Newquay Congregational Church burnt down in 1924 (CRO: AD396/133).

Left: *Helland Church, where Trevail added the tower in 1888.*
Right: *Tregaddick, Blisland, a holiday home for the Morshead family.*

Brown, prime mover in Trevail's rebuilding of the historic Temple Church, was active in raising funds to add a tower to his parish church at Helland. In 1888 Trevail produced a sturdy design with battlements and pinnacles to house a peal of eight Harrington bells.[14]

An ambitious undertaking was the design of Tregaddick Lodge, Blisland, for Sir Warwick Charles Morshead. Although Cornwall was not his main residence, Sir Warwick had family connections as well as land in Cornwall.[15] The lodge was built as a summerhouse for him and his second wife, Sarah Elizabeth Wilmot, and their initials and the date 1886 are displayed above the front door. But the couple soon found the accommodation too cramped and Trevail added two large ground floor rooms with additional bedrooms above, together with stabling and possibly the gatehouse. Their residence in Cornwall was warmly welcomed by the *West Briton*, for a number of Cornish landowners were spending much more time up country following the improvement in railway transport,[16] with a consequent loss of local trade. Here again Trevail made use of his American connections to have the plans published in *The Scientific American* in New York in July 1886 as the model of an English Country House.[17]

Some professional disappointments

Like other architects, Trevail was not always successful in his pursuit of commissions. One that he failed to win in 1882, rather surprisingly in view of his close collaboration with Treffry on other matters, was the Masonic Hall on Treffry land in Fowey, where the design of A S Clunes was used. However, he did design an entrance lodge for Treffry's home in Fowey that still stands, an attractive small building along Passage Lane, its main elevation almost untouched.[18] A later frustration was the failure in 1884 to obtain the commission for Trewirgie School near Redruth, one of the largest new schools in Cornwall, although when the chosen drawings were displayed Trevail challenged them, asserting that while his own and one other set of discarded plans conformed to official guidelines, the winning plan did not. He requested that all sets of drawings should be sent to the Education Department in London for their decision,

Top: Entrance lodge for Place, Fowey, 1882. Bottom: Perranzabuloe Vicarage, 1888, now a private residence.

but it seems that the Redruth Board did not carry out his suggestion.[19] Not content with his heavy professional and political programme in 1887 he applied for, but did not get, a post as surveyor of bridges and main roads in West Cornwall.[20]

A further project that did not come up to expectations was the erection of a new vicarage for St John's Church, Truro, in 1887. Along with James Julian, A C Clemens and W Swift of Lemon Street he was invited to send in plans, but it was Swift who received the commission.[21] Another parish in need of a vicarage was Perranzabuloe. Since the 1870s both its incumbents had served the area without

fulfilling their hopes of a building, although Trevail's plans of 1884 had been counter-signed by the Reverend W Parkhouse, the vicar at that time. Delays were possibly due to alterations to the plans by the Ecclesiastical Commissioners or by the incumbents themselves, and it was not until 1887 that work started on a large and handsome house in buff coloured brick and stone for the Reverend C R Meeres.[22]

Trevail had earlier failed to persuade the public of Truro to finance alterations to the Royal Institution of Cornwall (RIC) to accommodate an art collection, but he returned to the attack as the Golden Jubilee of Queen Victoria approached. Anxious to celebrate the event in a manner acceptable to Truro and Cornwall as a whole, he took out a full-page supplement in the West Briton to make the case for a cultural centre. He suggested that the RIC, at that time located in Union Place, should be extended as far as Pydar Street to house a library on the ground floor with an art gallery and painting room above. A public meeting was held to promote the scheme and a committee appointed to raise funds to supplement those promised by the RIC for the project. But it never got off the ground, although the mayor expressed the indebtedness of Truro's citizens to Trevail for the time and money he spent on it.

Bodmin was also the source of some major disappointments. In 1879 the Town Council had asked him to prepare plans for a new guildhall and he was consulted again on this matter in 1888 and 1889. A year after this the newly formed Bodmin Public Hall Company advertised for plans for a building and twelve architects competed, but not Trevail, who decided that after more than a decade of 'shilly-shallying' he would not take any further part. The building was designed by an Exeter firm and finally completed in 1892.

An unforeseen defeat

Although Silvanus Trevail took these architectural disappointments in his stride, a more serious blow to his self-esteem occurred in 1889. In November his term of office as Truro Councillor was up and he confidently presented himself for re-election. He could look back on his three year's work with satisfaction, especially his time as what the West Briton called Truro's 'Minister of Finance' or 'Chancellor of the Exchequer', when 'he had done what no man before has done', according to E G Heard, doyen of Truro Council. 'He has worked night and day and for the first time enabled us to understand the financial position,' claimed Heard, and other councillors complimented him on his 'elaborate and exhaustive' summaries of Truro's affairs. As a result of his reorganisation of Truro's tangled finances, he claimed that he had secured the eventual extinction of a burden of municipal debt that had been accruing for decades.[23]

His diligent research into Truro's official records, apart from uncovering the town clerk's mispractices, had also illuminated many interesting details in its history and Heard again congratulated him upon investing a large amount of time and labour in the work: 'No man in the last fifty years has done so much.' Trevail produced an abstract of his historical research and the Council allocated £10 for preserving documents.[24] They also thanked him for the 'able and efficient manner' in which he improved the municipal building in readiness for its use by Cornwall County Council for its first full meeting.[25]

But then Trevail made a serious mistake. True to his belief that a candidate should let his record of public service speak for itself, he took himself off to the International Exhibition in Paris during the Truro Council election period in November 1889, thinking that his re-election was a mere formality. He had not realised that while his reforming zeal had won the respect, indeed admiration of some, his conduct had irritated and offended others. The press had noted his habit of making what they called 'long historical digressions' on Truro Council and his fondness for giving detailed particulars about relatively minor matters, such as the length of notice required to present documents in other local government areas,[26] and 'exercises in hair-splitting' over whether an 'iron pipe' should be referred to as a 'metal pipe'. Perhaps wary of boring their readers, reporters used such phrases as 'Mr Trevail spoke at some length' in their accounts of Council proceedings[27] and his speeches elsewhere.[28] Again, when Trevail complained about delays in planning matters Councillor Chirgwin, Truro's leading accountant, retorted that Trevail himself was largely responsible.

And so, with Trevail away, a group put up a rival candidate. Trevail claimed to have gone to Paris for the worthiest of reasons, to attend an industrial and commercial exposition, but it was not difficult for councillors like Henry Buck to imply more frivolous motives for his visit and to infer that he thought so little of his responsibilities as to neglect them at a crucial moment.[29] To Trevail's utter astonishment he was defeated.[30] The shock must have been all the greater since, only a few months earlier, he had been returned unopposed as one of Truro's two representatives on the newly formed Cornwall County Council. This was a great honour for such a comparative newcomer to municipal politics. Alderman Heard had passed a resolution in Truro Council complimenting Trevail on his election,[31] 'briefly acknowledged' by the mayor, according to the *West Briton*. Trevail's reply, it noted, was 'not so terse'.

Trevail had met with the first major setback in his life. Until that moment his professional and social career had been marred by minor vexations, aggravations and occasional disappointments, but to suffer a political defeat was a new and painful experience. Of course, as a man of great ambition, his habit of sweeping aside anything or anybody who got in his way upset many people; but he had always prevailed in the end. Yet, while he was doubtless deeply hurt by the apparent lack of appreciation of his work by his fellow citizens, he compensated for this affront to his dignity by directing the full force of his administrative energies into his new role as County Councillor. In the 1890s he was to make himself known, if not loved, by local authority officials throughout the length and breadth of Cornwall. Truro's loss was Cornwall's gain.

Seven
Grand plans for tourism

Later in life Silvanus Trevail claimed that his ambitions as a tourist developer began in 1872 at the early age of twenty-one when, in association with 'gentlemen from East Cornwall', he had planned a hotel, together with gas and water works, at Newquay.[1] Just what the project was is not clear, but in any case it was abandoned because of difficulties in obtaining Parliamentary approval for the public utilities. Nevertheless, his choice of locations was prophetic for Newquay, rising star of the holiday trade, was to become Cornwall's first purpose-built tourist resort and the scene of some of his greatest triumphs and disappointments. In 1876 a branch line of the Cornwall Minerals Railway from Par to Newquay opened for passenger traffic. Although it ran at a loss for

Great Western Hotel, Newquay, taken between 1906 and 1930. Major alterations took place after this date (John Fitter collection).

An early, but not original, interior of the Great Western Hotel, Newquay (John Fitter collection).

several years[2] by 1878 the Newquay board were boasting that they were lighting the streets by gas, had revived the Newquay Regatta and had persuaded the Great Western Railway, which had acquired the line, to add a new platform with toilets to the station.

It was at this time that Trevail designed the Great Western Hotel as well as George Hicks' villa, Pentowan, and other structures in Newquay, described in Chapter Two. The Great Western Hotel still stands on the cliff top almost opposite the railway station, although the original modest two-storeyed gabled building was later altered beyond recognition to its vaguely art-deco state in 1931. But now things were not going so well for the new resort. Visitors were complaining of uncleared streets and the much vaunted gas lighting had been seized in payment of debt, so that residents had to use candles placed in turnips. According to Hicks, a native of the town, the problem lay in the 'many religious cliques' that absorbed all the town's wealth but distributed nothing for the benefit of its citizens. Nevertheless Hicks, Chairman of Newquay Waterworks, was a generous benefactor to many local causes and, along with another resident, financed a tunnel through the cliffs to improve access to the harbour.[3] Richard Tangye, along with Hicks, contributed to the construction of the waterworks, and also bought £1,000 of shares; the Great Western Railway also subscribed £2,000.[4]

Meanwhile, Trevail was drawing up grandiose plans for seaside estates in the Newquay area. A large coloured plan dated 1881 shows a development of part of the manor of Towan Blistra, which belonged to C E Treffry. A 'Bird's Eye View' of this project includes over 50 sites for villas, detached, semi-detached and terraced housing overlooking the cliffs to the east near the harbour, with extensions for a further 60

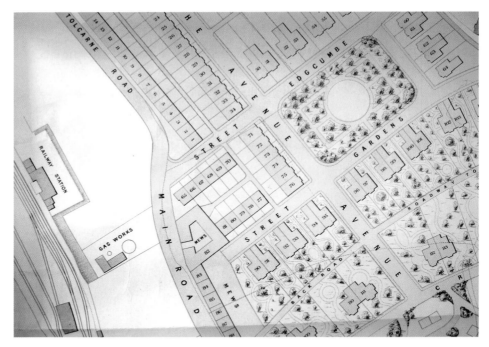

*Part of the
Tolcarne estate as
planned in 1883
(CRO:
AD396/240).*

numbered and over 100 unnumbered plots to the southwest in the area later occupied by the golf course above Fistral Bay. As we shall see in later chapters these ventures were thwarted. In the same year he prepared plans for Stephens' Porth Veor estate north east of Newquay,[5] discussed in Chapter Five, but again little development took place.

Two years later he designed a layout for the Tolcarne Estate on the property of Edward Pearce, son of a mayor of Bodmin and grandson of a Camelford banker. Trevail's plan included 125 numbered plots with three villas, 40 large semi-detached residences, a public garden, tennis courts and 'Edgcumbe Square', which was to be surrounded by housing. Pearce's death in 1885 held up progress but development was continued by his son Edward (later Sir Edward) Pearce-Edgcumbe, who had acquired the Edgcumbe name by marriage. But Trevail reaped little benefit from this scheme although his successor Alfred Cornelius was commissioned to design at least nine houses on the estate after Trevail's death. The gardens, the square and the tennis courts, however, were never developed.[6]

Railways fail to fill the bill

Although Hicks blamed Newquay's difficulties in attracting visitors on squabbles between its religious cliques, they were part of a general problem of Cornish tourism: poor rail links to the big cities of England. For all but the shortest of journeys, railway access was the key to success for the Victorian holiday promoter, and after Brunel bridged the Tamar from Plymouth in 1859, Penzance and Falmouth, those two Grand Old Ladies of the Cornish holiday trade, had quickly responded, erecting the first hotels specifically designed for middle-class railway passengers; the Queen's Hotel on the promenade at Penzance and the Falmouth Hotel opposite the railway station. However, the Falmouth Hotel Company, which had originally announced plans to double its size, never paid a penny of dividend until 1882 when it was reconstituted with a capital of £19,200, on which a modest dividend of 5 per cent was paid.[7]

The problem was that the railway route to Cornwall skirted the south Devon coast before passing through Plymouth and a chain of intervening resorts offered the traveller to the West Country superior amenities such as the Grand Hotel at Weston-Super-Mare and the Imperial Hotel, Torquay. To make matters worse, in order to maximise their passenger traffic, Great Western Railway trains tended to stop at every town and minor halt on the way and before they introduced corridor trains in the 1890s, long comfort stops were needed for the convenience of passengers. Only the hardiest and most determined of holidaymakers, it seemed, would spend the extra time and money to travel to Cornwall via the south coast line.

An obvious way to circumvent competition from Devon resorts en route, and also to shorten the trip to some parts of Cornwall, was to build a track directly from Exeter to the North Cornwall coast, and Trevail devoted much time and energy in promoting this idea as we shall see in later chapters. In the early 1880s merchants and landowners revived an old dream to build a railway from Exeter to Padstow with a branch to Wadebridge and Bodmin. Padstovians aimed to make their port a centre for the building of iron-clad steamships, using iron from mines in the area, as well as becoming the premier resort of North Cornwall, with regular passenger steamship services from Bristol and Weston-Super-Mare.[8] However, not for the first time nor the last, dreams of a north coast railway faded away as local enthusiasm was not matched by hard cash. While the *West Briton* asserted that 'Londoners will be blind to their own interests if they do not come forward', the City men in fact proved farsighted enough not to back a project which, when it was finally built, never proved to be profitable.

Trevail surveys Newquay

After Padstow's failure to secure a railway link, Newquay's leaders redoubled their efforts to make their town the premier north coast resort and Trevail added to his heavy professional load by acting as the town's Assistant Surveyor. In 1884 he was asked to devise a new road layout, with a limit of £1,000 expenditure and within a couple of weeks presented plans which typically upped the cost to £1,320. Nevertheless, the Board sent him to London to negotiate with the Great Western Railway for land adjoining the station that he needed to implement his plans, by then costing £1,600, which he presented two months later to a Local Government Board of Enquiry.

These plans widened the narrow road through the town from the Great Western Hotel to the Commercial Hotel from 13 to 30 feet and continued it up to Mount Wise by removing some dilapidated cottages. Trevail then negotiated the acquisition of more land from Edward Pearce, who gave it free of charge on the understanding that his property was properly fenced.[9] Trevail carried out further work for the Newquay Board until, as so often happened, his relationship with them shifted from cordiality to acrimony. The Board rejected his expense claims as excessive, Trevail did not deign to resubmit them and the dispute dragged on for years.[10]

Falmouth Hotel
rear extension,
now without the
flat roof.

Hotels encircle Cornwall

Although he had focused his attention upon Newquay as a holiday centre, Trevail's architectural activities in other parts of Cornwall made him aware that rival architects were winning commissions to design hotels. In the late 1870s the Great Western Railway opened a branch line to St Ives and leased, and later purchased, a large private mansion well above the harbour, converting it into the castellated Tregenna Castle Hotel. Fowey also benefited from a branch line and in 1882 a twenty-one bedroom hotel was designed by A S Clunes of Fowey for £14,000 on the esplanade, which was soon enlarged, and then further extended in 1891 by the Plymouth architect H J Snell.

At Falmouth handsome villas and terraces were springing up on the heights overlooking the town to the south, and in 1889 the Falmouth Hotel Company commissioned Trevail to add a large extension.[11] Nearby, the Lizard peninsula attracted invalids and others in search of solitude, fresh air and unique botanical specimens, and after many difficulties in fund-raising, a line opened from Helston to the main Great Western route at Gwinear Road in 1887. Boarding houses were built or developed from existing properties and a large hotel, Polurrian House, was built on the coast half a mile from Mullion and later extended by James Hicks. So successful was it that the owners were rumoured to be erecting an even larger hotel nearby, probably the Poldhu, although this idea did not materialise until the end of the 1890s.[12] In smaller places like Perranporth, superior accommodation was being built for 'very distinguished and aristocratic families who came year after year for lodgings',[13] whose numbers were expected to grow as hordes of day trippers invaded holiday resorts near the big cities, forcing the better off to move further afield.

Trevail plans a chain of hotels

After the Great Western Railway took over the Cornwall Railway, it announced plans to convert its unique broad gauge lines to the standard British gauge, allowing easier access from other railway companies. The time was ripe for Trevail to launch the most ambitious tourist project ever seen in Cornwall, nothing less than a ring of hotels of uniform size and standards around the coast. In 1890 he formed the Cornish Hotels Company, with himself as Company Secretary and Chairman, with an initial capital of £60,000 of which, he claimed, £10,000 had already been promised.[14] As Chairman he secured a colleague on the County Council, Alderman William Trethewey JP, who had taken over from his father as steward of the vast Hawkins estate around Truro, and was a widely known and respected cattle breeder and agricultural businessman in his own right. The Vice Chairman was John Jose JP, another County Councillor who had left Lanner near Redruth and made a fortune in South America, returning to become Director of banks, mines and other commercial ventures. One Director was Major John Mead JP, Falmouth Councillor, son of a Penryn miller and partner in ferries, a newspaper and a hotel. Two other Falmouth-based directors were William Rowe, Chairman of St Mawes Steamship and Ferry Company and other ventures and Charles Gatley, who had many local business interests.

The company prospectus, written by Trevail, exuded confidence. The hotel business, it proclaimed, was the 'best paying in the west' and, as a first stage, arrangements were already in hand to acquire prime sites in Newquay, St Ives, the Lizard and Falmouth. A chain of hotels of similar size and tariffs would be built so that guests might transfer from one to another as the mood took them. Building plans and elevations in Trevail's records show that they were to be of relatively modest dimensions, not the 'Grand Hotels' that he so much admired on his travels. He aimed at the rapidly rising class of merchants and industrialists with middling incomes for, as the editor of the *Redruth Independent* argued 'wealthy people to whom cost was not the consideration did not patronise Cornish resorts'.[15] Standardisation, Trevail asserted, would create economies of scale in design, construction, purchasing and marketing. A familiar concept today, it seemed revolutionary to Victorian Cornwall.

Too imaginative in fact, for even with the backing of his wealthy and influential directors, Trevail could not raise enough capital locally, and had to launch the venture on the London money market. There, however, he suffered a cruel stroke of ill fortune, for his share flotation coincided with one of the greatest financial crises of Victorian times. The great merchant banking firm of Barings was near to collapse because of failed investments in Argentina, and although they were bailed out by other banks on the advice of the Bank of England, the confidence of the investing public was low and few were willing to speculate on Trevail's project.

The initial reaction of the directors of the Cornish Hotels Company was to drop the project, but Trevail had other ideas. If he could not develop a chain of medium sized hotels, then he would design one big building, the largest that Cornwall had ever seen, indeed 'the finest west of Ilfracombe'.[16] He went to London, secured a promise from the Great Western Railway for £2,000 in debentures and persuaded Cornwall's leading bankers, merchants and industrialists to invest in his scheme. There were 86 shareholders in all, and it is of interest to record the names of some of them because they illustrate the way in which he used his contacts in the County Council and Truro Council to back his ventures.

The great landowner Lord Robartes headed the list, with shares to the value of £800, and Thomas Lang, who built the hotel, contributed a like sum.[17] John James, Truro bank manager, fellow Truro Councillor and member of the consortium that made extensions, designed by Trevail, to the Red Lion Hotel in that town, invested £600. Purchasers of £400 in shares included Michael Williams, County Councillor and member of one of Cornwall's richest mining dynasties; J C Daubuz, County Councillor, smelter and landowner; Thomas Bedford Bolitho, Chairman of Cornwall's largest locally-owned bank; and Trevail's confidante, George Hicks. Subscriptions of £200 each were made by his Truro Council colleagues Joseph Rogers, E G Heard and Thomas Chirgwin.

Other substantial investors among his fellow county councillors were Alfred Lanyon, prominent Redruth merchant; Francis Barratt, who provided him with many St Austell commissions; Richard Stephens, related to the Porth Veor Estate owner; Charles Treffry, Lord of the Manor at Newquay; and John Branwell, prominent Penzance trader. More modest subscribers were Arthur Carkeek, contractor for several Trevail projects, John Ennor, the Newquay builder and developer, and the Earl of Mount Edgcumbe, Chairman of the County Council. (Robert Tweedy, the wealthy Quaker banker, risked £8!) Of the Board of Directors, the Chairman Trethewey contributed £240, Jose the Vice Chairman £400, Mead £240, Rowe £244 and Gatley £460. Trevail himself took up £200 in shares.[18]

Early rumours suggested Falmouth as the site,[19] but instead he chose Newquay, partly because the other places on his list already had a first class hotel, partly because the town was expanding at full pace. New villas and terraces were being developed by John Ennor and Son, the leading local builders, and the Great Western Hotel was awaiting enlargement, but not by Trevail.[20]

The Atlantic Hotel, Newquay

For his new hotel, Trevail chose one of the most commanding positions on the north coast, a place that was destined to become the scene of violent clashes in later years. However, initially, in March 1891, the local population was pleased to learn that the Lord of the Manor, Charles Treffry, had given them five acres of the headland to the west of the harbour,[21] and Trevail plans exist for the laying out of the site with shelters, tennis courts and shrubberies. Fishermen had always regarded the headland as theirs to use for drying nets and protested when in 1885 William Hoyte, lessee of the land, had installed gates on the harbour side, erected hedges on the Fistral Bay side and ploughed up grass around the coast guard lookout. After a meeting was arranged by the town crier, Newquay Board paid Hoyte £4 a year to allow fishermen access to the headland and Hoyte restored the ground to its former condition.[22] Treffry's gift formalised public use for part of the headland but some were dismayed when a month later, in April 1891, Trevail announced, at a meeting of the Cornish Hotels Company, that another three acres of the headland overlooking the harbour had been leased from Treffry for

Top: *Atlantic Hotel, Newquay, October 1891 (Family papers).* Bottom: *Atlantic Hotel, Newquay, after completion (Family papers).*

the site of what was to be called the Atlantic Hotel.[23]

Treffry had a legal right to dispose of his land in this way, however, and there was nothing that objectors could do about it. Some residents were also annoyed because they believed the town had been overdeveloped already. In the summer of 1889, hoteliers and lodging house proprietors had been forced to reduce their tariffs by a half to fill their rooms, 'Not a moment too soon,' commented the editor of the *Redruth Independent*, claiming they had become 'intoxicated by dreams of fabulous wealth'.[24]

Nevertheless, as building progressed, flattering reports appeared in the London and Cornish press about Trevail, the Atlantic Hotel and Newquay, 'the healthiest place in the country' and 'rendezvous of students and bathers, natural historians, tennis players, golfers and women with sketch books'. Newquay Mercantile Association welcomed the hotel as a boost to the town's claim to be a 'winter Riviera as well as a summer holiday ground' and R C Collins of Newquay Local Board, who had been spending more money on public health than most Cornish places to foster the town's claim as a health resort, praised Trevail as 'a man that Cornwall could not be without'.[25]

Four storeys high under a mansard roof, with 61 bedrooms, the hotel dominated the landscape for miles around. Now, unfortunately, its classic symmetrical appearance has been disguised by later alterations. Inside, elaborate gasoliers illuminated luxurious walnut furniture, marbled mosaic floors and ornamental iron balustrading. Although its opening in July 1892 was marred by a local outbreak of scarlet fever and a water shortage, about which Trevail complained bitterly to Newquay Board, nonetheless it proved to be an astonishing success. Far from being a white elephant, as some had predicted, in the first few months of trading it made a profit of 12 per cent on paid up capital of £15,000 at a time when 10 per cent for a full year was considered more than satisfactory, and annual profits later rose from 15 per cent to 20 per cent.

At the 1893 Annual General Meeting Major Mead, one of the directors who had argued against building on such a scale, had to admit that profits were 'much larger than the most sanguine expectations' and praised Trevail as 'a man of large ideas and a lot of go'. James Pearce of Newquay Board awarded Trevail the entire credit for bringing the project to a triumphant conclusion in the face of opposition and even derision from all sides. John Jose, who succeeded to the chair of the Hotel Company after the death of Trethewey, paid tribute to the skill of Trevail and the constructor Lang on erecting such a massive structure on so difficult a site 'perhaps the most trying in the county', according to Trevail.[26]

'One and all' or 'One that's all'?

After such a resounding success, Trevail could hardly be blamed for assuming that the directors would want to press on with his original scheme of building a chain of hotels. To his astonishment, they would have none of it. As he afterwards confided to George Hicks, 'the gallant Major Mead and his Atlantic crew' were very fond of quoting the old Cornish pledge of solidarity 'One and All', but when he asked them to finance another hotel their reply was always 'One that's All'.[27] In later chapters we will see how Trevail went it alone to fulfil his grand plan, although not in the way he had originally intended, and not, unfortunately, with the same financial success.

Eight
County Councillor, educational and health crusader

The Local Government Act of 1888 marked a watershed in Cornish administration. For over 500 years the main authority had been the Court of Quarter Sessions, comprising of JPs who set the county rates and supervised a multitude of different committees and boards responsible for highways, public health, sanitation and relief of the poor. The new County Council, elected by the voting public, took over most of these functions. Prominent landowners, farmers, industrialists and merchants vied with one another for election to this new and authoritative body,[1] and Silvanus Trevail was one of them.

At the first meeting of the County Council in the municipal buildings of Truro in April 1889, Silvanus Trevail as usual lost no time in making his presence felt among the 66 councillors and 22 aldermen.[2] He seconded a proposal by John Tremayne of Heligan to elect the Earl of Mount Edgcumbe as Chairman of the Council in terms that flattered both gentlemen. In this and subsequent meetings he spoke with increasing length and frequency on a wide range of topics including finance, highways, river pollution, public health, mental health and theatrical performances. Together with two prominent councillors, Colonel Tremayne and Richard Gundry Rows, he successfully resisted attempts to rob the Council of its powers to regulate weights and measures.[3]

Despite being one of the youngest members, he displayed a mastery of administrative law that few of his fellow councillors could match, achieved by a painstaking study of the parliamentary bill which set up County Councils. Indeed so great an authority was he on the subject that the Earl of Mount Edgcumbe invited him to join a deputation to the President of the Board of Trade to suggest alterations in the Bill that affected Cornwall. According to Trevail, all the proposals that he made were adopted.[4] He did not wear his learning lightly, however, and his habit of expounding at ever-increasing length on the minutia of the law was not always welcomed.

On one occasion he alarmed his audience by brandishing 300 pages of notes he had amassed on the Local Government Act, reassuring them that he would make a brief speech on the subject. As they feared, it proved to be a very lengthy one and it was not long before he was demanding more frequent meetings of the County Council to get through the business. This suggestion was countered by his colleagues who argued that if he was less loquacious the problem would be solved. During one debate Colonel Tremayne, who had obviously been counting Trevail's interjections, congratulated him on scoring 48 not out! Nevertheless, Trevail carried out much useful work for the County Council, particularly in the fields of agricultural education, technical instruction and public health. And, with his usual flair for combining public service and private profit, these interests led to lucrative architectural commissions.

Establishing Truro as the centre of technical excellence

First, however, Truro had to be selected as the seat of the County Council, rather than Bodmin or St Austell, both of which had their supporters. While still a member of Truro Council, Trevail had recommended to his fellow councillors that they placed their meeting chamber at the disposal of the County Council. And in a number of lengthy speeches he had tried the patience of Truro councillors in detailing the results of his research into Truro archives that showed Truro, rather than Launceston, was historically the premier borough of Cornwall. With Alderman Heard, Trevail drew up an impressive document that set out Truro's case as the best location for the new County Council. They were successful, and the full Council held four meetings a year in Truro's municipal buildings. At the first ceremonial dinner of Truro's Mercantile Association, the Secretary Hugh Rice toasted Trevail, along with Thomas Webber of Falmouth, as two men who had done most to advance Truro's case.[5]

Silvanus Trevail circa 1895 (Family papers).

Soon after the County Council was formed, Trevail spotted his chance to further a scheme for a college in Truro with an agricultural bias. His opportunity came with the passing of the Technical Instruction Act of 1889, perhaps the most significant piece of fresh legislation with which the new council had to deal.[6] Britain's leaders, alarmed that the nation was falling behind its rivals in scientific education, passed an Act of Parliament that gave County Councils the powers to provide technical instruction, but did not provide them with the money to pay for it. Since many councillors were also principal ratepayers, they were unwilling to foot the bill. Cornwall was by no means alone in its lack of response and it took a windfall from the Chancellor of the Exchequer to get things moving. In the hope of reducing public drunkenness, he had raised taxes on liquor so as to be able to subsidise publicans who gave up their liquor licences, but a public outcry at his use of public funds blocked this project. Instead he allocated some of the 'Whiskey Money', as it was called, to another of his pet schemes, the provision of technical education.[7]

Trevail versus Buck on technical education

Michael Williams, a member of one of Cornwall's richest mining and smelting families, was Chairman of the committee charged with allocating Cornwall's share, which amounted to £6,282 for the first year. He invited comments from individuals or bodies throughout Cornwall and was amazed to find he had opened a pandora's box of conflicting opinions. Farmers, fishermen and miners disagreed about the size of their allocation, independent-minded towns displayed what the *West Briton* called a 'terrible and unreasonable jealousy' about their share, and those who favoured a single centre of advanced scientific knowledge clashed with others who wanted local provision at a more elementary level.[8]

These issues were debated in meetings throughout the length and breadth of Cornwall and Trevail put his case at a 'largely attended and influential' gathering in Truro.[9] His principal opponent was the Truro Councillor Henry Buck. As we saw in Chapter Five, in the early days of their association on Truro Council, Buck and Trevail supported each other. By now, if one thing was certain it was that any proposals by Trevail would be opposed by Buck, and vice versa. Buck asserted that the 'labouring classes', because of their low level of basic education, were not capable of understanding the advanced scientific theories that a centre of excellence would offer. What was needed, he argued, were scholarships for the brighter students to attend 'continuation classes', and for the village schoolmaster, with appropriate training, to impart the rudimentary skills that were all that were needed for workers to carry out their tasks efficiently.

Trevail immediately attacked Buck's proposals. 'Surely no one would be such a fool,' he demanded, 'as to fritter money away in penny packets of pseudo-scientific knowledge presented by parochial schoolmasters.' Truro, he insisted, should build a centre of advanced learning, particularly in agricultural education, and appoint highly qualified staff who would spread their knowledge to all parts of Cornwall. It should not, he warned, rely upon the moribund Royal Institution of Cornwall (RIC) in Truro to carry out the task, for this body 'refused to come out of its shell' and 'dilly dallied' in promoting technical education. Major Parkyn of the RIC, who was present at the meeting, objected that it was already providing four classes averaging 25 students apiece in geology, minerology, botany and hygiene; Buck insisted that the RIC was doing 'grand work'. Whereupon the Truro Councillor Blenkinsop, wine merchant and Trevail's ally, retorted that the Egyptian mummy in the RIC's entrance epitomised the mental stupor of its members.

Cornwall divided about centres of excellence

Trevail's appeal to the civic pride of Truronians easily won the day, and the meeting unanimously passed a resolution calling upon him to present the County Council with a scheme for a Central Technical School for Cornwall, with particular reference to agriculture, to be built in the City. In many other parts of Cornwall though, where distrust of book learning was only equalled by suspicion of outside experts, the idea of a centre of excellence was not even considered. In the china clay district, for instance, the debate focused exclusively upon the kind of classes that should be provided in each parish. At a farmers' dinner in Lostwithiel, the local County Councillor James Thomas argued against a central college for agriculture on the grounds that young farm hands could not make the long journey to attend evening classes, and favoured grants to existing parish schools. All the other speakers at the meeting agreed with him. Digby Collins, powerful Tory landowner, contended that too much book learning would give farm hands ideas above their station. Representatives from Hayle, St Ives and Penzance emphasised their towns' successes as centres of technical education and pressed for the direct allocation of funds.[10]

The County Council was inundated with proposals from towns and parishes and had to appoint a special committee to advise on the allocation of funds. Its Chairman was Richard Gundry Rows, former Helston farmer and powerful local religious and political leader, and his committee, which included Silvanus Trevail, contained merchants and industrialists who were strongly in favour of centres of excellence. This aim ran directly counter to the desire of many councillors however. 'What a man can't learn on his own farm is not worth knowing,' one of them asserted, while another saw no point in visits from 'peripatetic quacks'. An ounce of practical experience, they argued, was worth a ton of theory.

A curious compromise

After hours of wrangling in the County Council a compromise was reached. A Public Health Act of 1872 had divided Cornwall into over twenty urban and rural sanitary districts and, rather than creating a separate set of bodies to administer technical education, the County Council decided to use them to devise schemes.[11] Supporters of central provision, including Trevail and Rows, were appalled at this decision, but the County Council set up a new Technical Instruction Committee to allocate funds and Rows was persuaded to chair it. Meanwhile, district meetings were held to elect Local Technical Instruction Committees, usually headed by a County Councillor. It did not take long for tensions to arise between the central committee and the local bodies, especially when Rows tried to cut their allocation from £90 to £25 each. After further lengthy and acrimonious debates, Edward Hain, member of the central committee and Chairman of the Fisheries Training Sub-committee, of which Trevail was a member, proposed a compromise of £50. Rows, after threatening to resign, accepted this solution.[12]

The central committee appointed an organising secretary and Trevail tried unsuccessfully to insist that this official reside in Truro. Further disagreements arose between districts and the central committee on how much they should contribute to peripatetic lecturers sent from Truro, and Trevail assisted Rows in keeping a tight grip on the activities and expenditure of the districts. In the end, despite its unwieldy structure, the technical education system worked reasonably well and at the end of the first year nearly 6,400 students had enrolled for day and continuation classes and over 2,000 had taken vocational examinations in such useful subjects as building, surveying, mining and china clay techniques, arable and dairy farming methods, book-keeping and foreign languages.[13]

A striking example of how, in the midst of his other activities, Trevail was always willing to honour those who served Cornwall well, was his recognition of the work of H S Stokes, distinguished Cornish writer, poet and public servant. Trevail suggested that the County Council should commission a portrait of Stokes in acknowledgement of his work as Clerk to the Council. Trevail acted as Honorary Secretary to a committee to achieve this aim, chaired by the Earl of Mount Edgcumbe with Lord Robartes, Lord Kinsale, Alfred Lanyon, E G Heard and Chirgwin among the members. At the presentation to Stokes, Lord Mount Edgcumbe praised Trevail's 'devotion, energy and ability'.

'Mr Trevail's Health Crusade'

In 1892 a new County Council was voted in. During its three years of existence, a sense of comradeship had developed among its members, and whereas originally some seats had been bitterly contested, in every case where a sitting member stood for re-election he was returned unopposed.[14] Silvanus Trevail was therefore re-elected, but although Rows continued to head the Technical Instruction Committee, Trevail was no longer on it. In the earliest days of the council, he had been invited to join a sub-committee appointed to examine reports from the medical officers of Cornish districts, run by Michael Williams. By 1891 his capacity for work and reforming zeal had been recognised and led him to a higher status as Chairman of the Sanitary Committee, responsible for overseeing public health administration in Cornwall.[15] Nonetheless, he retained a strong interest in scientific training since it was one of the issues where what was good for Cornwall was undoubtedly good for Trevail and, as we shall see in later chapters, he picked up some of his most lucrative commissions designing technical schools in Cornwall and Devon.

Public health was another area where Cornwall's and Trevail's interests fruitfully coincided. It was an issue of national importance as rapid population growth created overcrowded and unsanitary towns. Until the 1860s Cornwall experienced the same high rate of population increase as other industrial regions with outbreaks of typhoid, diphtheria, tuberculosis and cholera, and Truro was one of the most notorious centres for these diseases. In 1840 Dr Charles Barham, physician to the Royal Cornwall Infirmary at Truro, reported that the 'ill constructed houses, many of them old, with decomposing refuse close upon their doors and windows, open drains bring the oozing of pigsties and other filth to stagnate at the foot of a wall ... a row of small dwellings where there is only a very narrow passage'.[16] Despite the appalling state of Truro's drainage system, with rivers doubling as open sewers, little was done until 1888 when the City Surveyor was asked to design a sewerage scheme. By this time Truro's condition was notorious. In the words of the editor of the *Redruth Independent*: 'elegant streets, fine market, disgusting rivers'.[17]

Apart from his humanitarian concern for the suffering caused by typhoid, cholera, diphtheria and tuberculosis, Trevail was also well aware, as a tourist developer, that a bad health record held back progress in the holiday trade. Time and again, in his speeches to Truro and county councillors and to outside bodies, he warned tourist promoters that, while it was all very well advertising Cornwall as a gigantic sanatorium, this message was negated by regular reports in the press of outbreaks of diseases and by guide writers who advised readers to avoid, literally like the plague, picturesque fishing resorts that were hotbeds of infection.

Trevail's preoccupation with public health in fact dated back much earlier. From 1874, he had noted in his diary all the deaths in Cornwall that were attributed to sewage pollution, so as to build up a case for public health reform. These matters became almost an obsession after his arrival in Truro, a city with a notoriously bad drainage system. Ever since a fatal outbreak of disease in 1875, Truro councillors had employed the time-honoured delaying tactics of setting up committees of enquiry into the sanitary problem, engaging consultants to prepare reports and then debating them without reaching a conclusion. Trevail suffered the full effect of their procrastination when he moved in 1886 to a house at the bottom of Lemon Street overlooking a stream that was liable to flood in wet weather and served as an open sewer when it was dry. After one warm spell in 1887 he supported a scheme to build a stone sewer at a modest cost of under £100, and a much more ambitious plan to construct a new drainage system estimated at £6,900. His fellow councillors accepted neither scheme; most of them lived at a comfortable distance away from the city centre, had their own unpolluted water supply and, as principal ratepayers, were reluctant to dip into their own pockets to solve the problems of others.[18]

During Trevail's first few years on Truro Council he, in his customary manner, mastered the details of the two studies by the City Surveyor and another four by London sanitary engineers, for schemes costing from £8,600 to £15,000. He denounced them all at great length, whereupon one of the consultants retaliated by describing him as

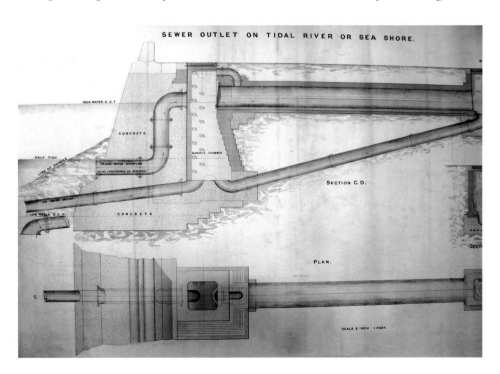

Part of one of the sewage schemes that Trevail studied (CRO: AD396/89).

'partial, prejudiced and bigoted' while another 'passed over' his comments 'in contempt'. These quarrels only played into the hands of the opponents of reform who, like his enemy Henry Buck, made light of the whole issue, arguing that 'a bottle of carbolic would do the trick'. To bring matters to a head, Trevail proposed in 1892 to adopt the Public Health Amendment Act, which would force the council to take action, but the Chairman of Truro Sanitary Committee, the accountant Chirgwin, postponed any decision because he had not looked at the Act.[19]

Meanwhile, Trevail had joined enthusiastically in a county-wide struggle to bring into line those district sanitary authorities and medical officers of health who winked at abuses of the reporting requirements for infectious diseases. Soon he had publicly identified eight 'foul spots' where cheese-paring committees were guilty of 'gross neglect' and noted 'appalling conditions' in Redruth and Helston. The editor of the *West Briton*, whose office in Truro was near to a sanitary black spot, asserted that Trevail deserved 'hearty thanks' for his effort: 'For a young man, I don't know of anyone who has done such an enormous amount of public service'.[20]

The Sanitary Committee

When Trevail took on the chairmanship of the Sanitary Committee in November 1891, it was the smallest in number, with nine members, compared with the 26 in the Contagious Diseases (Animals) Act Committee, which perhaps says something about the public attitudes to animals as opposed to humans. However, he made it into probably the most active and certainly the most controversial of the council's bodies. He quickly asserted his authority by sending detailed instructions to every Sanitary Authority and Medical Officer of Health, demanding full monthly returns instead of the perfunctory annual statements that some of them got away with.[21]

Trevail's actions stirred up a hornet's nest among health administrators from one end of Cornwall to the other and he was attacked as overbearing, high-handed and headstrong. Penzance and Launceston were among the sanitary authorities who refused point-blank to do his bidding. St Austell's Medical Officer of Health demanded extra payment for the form filling involved. Falmouth rejected his requests as 'impertinent and impudent'. Bodmin protested after he reported a smallpox outbreak, when a woman leaving a train was said to be covered in spots. At Hayle he was denounced as a 'self-seeking Pope of Cornwall', the pontiff of course being a figure of hate in some quarters. But rumours of an outbreak of cholera at Falmouth and steps taken to prevent the spread of typhoid at Bodmin and Port Isaac showed that he was not always far off the mark. 'By a singular coincidence', he reported to the County Council, it was in the districts that complained the most 'that the greatest sanitary defects occur'. After 'shrieking' a bit, he claimed, most of them fell into line.[22]

Although never slow to criticise other Cornish

Letterhead for Chairman of the Cornwall County Council Sanitary Committee, Silvanus Trevail (Family papers).

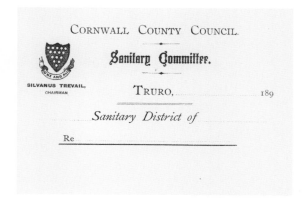

districts, Trevail still reserved his greatest displeasure for Truro, where he repeatedly antagonised his fellow councillors by condemning their 'appalling ignorance' of health matters and warned them that 'should cholera once get a hold, people will die like flies'. No fewer than 54 sanitary engineers from all parts of Britain competed for prizes to design a drainage system for the city. Trevail read them all and criticised them at great length. In one debate, a fellow councillor objected to Trevail's numerous interjections and comments: 'he has been up 20 or 30 times already'. Trevail lost his temper on more than one occasion, as when Henry Buck, who dismissed all sanitary schemes as 'fads and fancies', tried to delete clauses from regulations that stopped people from throwing rubbish in rivers. But Trevail had his admirers as well as his critics. Edward Goodridge Heard, editor of the *West Briton* and Truro and County Alderman, applauded Trevail, 'the very embodiment' of the Cornish health reform movement, for his battles to purge 'the foul stain that soils the fair name of the city'.[23] Nevertheless, so strong was the resistance to change that the struggle continued with even greater ferocity into Trevail's mayoral year of 1894–5, as we shall see in Chapter Fifteen.

Nine
Railway hero, fisheries, housing the rich and poor

While Trevail was leading a crusade for public health reform he was also conducting vigorous campaigns for improved rail access. Here, again, his own interests coincided with the wider needs of Cornwall since improved rail links meant more visitors, more tourist accommodation and more architectural commissions. He had to tread warily though, because what he called his 'great railway battles' attacked the Great Western Railway Company (GWR), which had gained a stranglehold on Cornish rail transport by buying existing lines and adding new ones. He needed the GWR to help finance his hotel developments: without them, as we saw in Chapter Seven, he might not have been able to build the biggest hotel in Cornwall, the Atlantic at Newquay. On the other hand he felt obliged to stir the Great Western into action, since it was dubbed by some 'The Sleepy Giant' because of its slowness in enhancing its facilities. Having said this, it was always swift to thwart any attempt by its rival, the London and South Western Railway (LSWR), to drive a line through Cornwall.

Cornish discontent with the GWR reached boiling point early in 1893 when rumours spread that it was about to raise its charges by an average of 30 per cent. The editor of the *Redruth Independent* called for the railways to be nationalised, and a hastily summoned Railway Rates Conference at Truro was attended by representatives from most towns in Cornwall as well as from Plymouth. The delegates heard of a proposed increase of 100 per cent in the tariffs on market garden produce and a rate per mile on the carriage of beef that was twice that charged from Aberdeen. Timber charges per mile were reported to be rising to double those paid by importers of wood. R G Rows, Chairman of Cornwall's principal bacon factory at Redruth, contended that a rumoured increase of more than 100 per cent on the transport of bacon would 'strangle and throttle our infant industry'.

Trevail proposed a resolution, unanimously passed, that 'an object of first importance is to promote the extension of a second railway from Launceston to Truro' and to expedite this a powerful committee was formed, with T B Bolitho the banker as chairman, together with Edward Hain the shipping magnate, R G Rows and Trevail. Another unanimous resolution set up a deputation, which was led by Bolitho and included Rows, Hain, Rickard and Hugh Rice, Honorary Secretary of Truro Mercantile Association and organiser of a Fisheries Exhibition, (but not Trevail) which went to London to confront the director of the GWR.[1] The deputation returned to announce that most of the proposed railway tariffs had been reduced to their former levels, some even below them, such as the charge on bacon. The GWR announced the doubling of the railway line from Bodmin to Launceston and from St Austell to Par, with other sections to be doubled later, together with an acceleration of the express train to Cornwall and the introduction of corridor trains to Penzance and Falmouth. The *West Briton* reported 'general satisfaction' with the outcome.[2]

Further good news for rail users came in November 1893 when the North Cornwall Railway (NCR), which had been advancing slowly towards Wadebridge and Padstow master-minded by the LSWR, gave notice that it was putting a Bill before Parliament to continue the line past Padstow to Newquay and then south to Truro, with the right to use GWR lines to Falmouth and Penzance. Sixteen miles shorter from London to Truro than the GWR line, the NCR route involved easier gradients meaning faster trains, and Trevail, who had attended the opening of the NCR station at Camelford, was full of praise for the enterprise of Tremayne the Cornish landowner and Chairman of the NCR. Tremayne however was more cautious, warning that although Lord Robartes had given land free of charge to construct the line, other landowners, after promising to do the same, had allowed their agents to charge exorbitant rates.[3] Nevertheless Trevail remained optimistic and, with his usual panache, walked the entire proposed route of the line and predicted it would be 'one of the best ever made' in Cornwall. Typically, he claimed credit for the introduction of the route, asserting he had proposed it himself to the GWR years earlier.

Then, out of the blue, a Newquay Junction Bill appeared before parliament to build a line from Newquay to Truro. The proposers were Henry Buck and Joseph Rogers, secretary to the Falmouth Hotel, with whom Trevail had worked on the Pendennis Hotel and the Red Lion Hotel projects. Why had they done it? The *Royal Cornwall Gazette* suggested that it was because 'Buck automatically opposes everything Silvanus Trevail supports'. But Trevail had drawn other conclusions. He told a Parliamentary Select Committee, set up to consider both the plans, that for five years he had pressed the GWR to build a Newquay to Truro line but without success, and the only reason they were now proposing one was to block the NCR scheme. If the GWR won, he predicted that their scheme would never see the light of day.

The GWR denied this, but offered to back the Buck-Rogers project if others financed it.[4] A vast body of support for the NCR plan was then presented to the Parliamentary Committee from organisations including the Fish Trade Association, the Duchy of Cornwall, Falmouth docks and Falmouth Chamber of Commerce. The editor of the *West Briton*, on behalf of Truro Council, claimed that 'Not one Cornishman supports the bogus Newquay Junction scheme'. Hugh Rice, Honorary Secretary of the County Corn Exchange and of Truro Mercantile Association, asserted that the NCR line would greatly benefit fishermen, fish processing and ports on the north coast. T H Lake, Truro corn merchant, contended that it would be of great service to tradesmen in Truro as well as Padstow.[5]

Amazingly, in the face of such overwhelming support for the NCR scheme, the Select Committee rejected it in favour of the rival proposal. Protest rallies were held and when Buck tried to speak for his Bill he was booed and hissed until he sat down. Yet all opposition appeared fruitless as his Bill moved, in apparently irresistible fashion, towards its final reading in the House of Commons. Then Trevail made an impassioned speech to the County Council. 'Railways exist for Cornwall,' he said to great applause, 'Cornwall does not exist for the railway system'. He had, he explained, a 'few shots left in my locker', and a special Committee of the County Council was formed to lobby MPs, chaired by Colonel Tremayne and including J C Williams MP, Thomas Chirgwin the Mayor of Truro and Trevail. Trevail set off for London, armed with over 100 petitions supporting the NCR scheme, canvassed every Member of Parliament and persuaded most of the Cornish MPs to sign a letter rejecting the Bill. It was defeated at the third reading: Trevail had achieved, according to the *Royal Cornwall Gazette*, 'a feat unprecedented in Parliamentary history'.[6]

Trevail receives a public testimonial

He returned to Cornwall the hero of the hour, a Cornish David who had defeated the Goliath of the Great Western Railway. So great was public appreciation of his success that a committee was formed to collect subscriptions for a testimonial. It was supported by the powerful Robert (later Sir Robert) Harvey, who had left Truro as a young apprentice to make a vast fortune in South American nitrates. Harvey was a particular admirer of Trevail, perhaps recognising in him some of his own buccaneering spirit, and Trevail designed buildings for him that will be discussed later.

The list of subscribers to the testimonial read like a roll call of the Cornish political, commercial and industrial establishment: great landowners like the Earl of Mount Edgcumbe, Lord Falmouth, Lord Robartes and Prideaux-Brune; the MPs W A McArthur and Edwin Lawrence; Truro and County Councillors including Colonel

Left: *Presentation silver (Family papers).*
Right: *Mayoral Reception for presentation of silver (Family papers).*

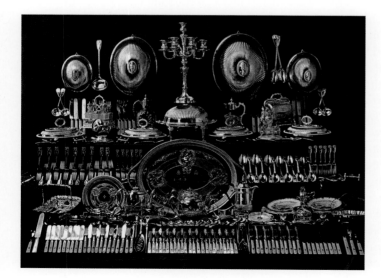

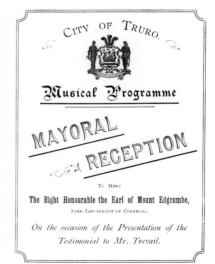

CITY OF TRURO.

Musical Programme

MAYORAL RECEPTION

To Meet

The Right Honourable the Earl of Mount Edgcumbe,

LORD LIEUTENANT OF CORNWALL.

On the occasion of the Presentation of the Testimonial to Mr. Trevail.

Tremayne, J C Williams, G J Smith, Edward Hain, Digby Collins, Thomas Webber, E G Heard, John Lanyon, J C Daubuz, Francis Barratt, W Cole Pendarves and John Jose; business associates like the Bolithos, Shilsons, Holman Brothers, Howard Fox and Trevail's contractor Arthur Carkeek.[7]

In February 1895, at a special meeting, Lord Edgcumbe presented Trevail with a handsome silver service and a substantial cheque.[8] Speaker after speaker rose to praise Trevail's energy, courage and public spirit. 'He worked night and day for several weeks' on the project, commented the St Austell attorney D H Shilson. In his reply Silvanus took care to keep on the right side of the GWR. 'No one has a stronger appreciation of the Great Western than I,' he asserted, and he called their managers his 'strong personal friends'.[9]

The Truro Fisheries Exhibition

Meanwhile, in another project reminiscent of the Triumphal Arches that had first brought him fame in Truro, Trevail designed temporary conference halls and accommodation for an exhibition held in Truro in 1893. While serving on the Technical Instruction Committee of Cornwall County Council he had been a member of a small group, chaired by Edward Hain the shipping magnate, concerned with the training of fishermen. Trevail had no obvious links with the industry, but in his usual way he launched himself enthusiastically into his new role and made a series of speeches bringing to the public's attention the plight of Cornish fishermen, whose fishing grounds were being invaded by giant steam-driven trawlers from other regions. Inevitably, Trevail was surrounded by controversy when he advocated sending a local man to America to study fishing methods. Most Cornish fishermen, like many Cornish farmers, were convinced that they had nothing to learn from outsiders.[10]

To demonstrate the importance of fishing to the Cornish economy, the County Fisheries Committee, impressed by the success of a Fisheries Exhibition in London in 1883, set about holding a similar event in Cornwall. Trevail offered to design the buildings and Evelyn Rashleigh, a County Councillor, acted as Secretary and asked 'every lady and gentleman in Cornwall' to guarantee £5 to cover the estimated costs of £200 to £300. Delays, caused by national mourning for the unexpected death of the Duke of Clarence, postponed the proposed opening in the autumn of 1892, perhaps to the relief of the organisers, since exhibits from all over the world were late in arriving. A further setback was a disastrous fire at James Julian's, the contractor, destroying all the workmen's tools, which were their own property and were not insured. With typical generosity towards the working man, Trevail drew up a list of all the losses and organised a collection to reimburse them.[11]

The Exhibition opened in July 1893 on the Green at Truro (site of the present bus station). The buildings were of wood with corrugated iron roofs and the main hall, 200 feet long and 40 feet wide, was probably the largest temporary structure ever erected in Truro. Four smaller arcades ran off at right angles and the whole structure covered some 16,000 square feet. The walls were decorated with paintings of the fishing industry, arranged by Stanhope Forbes, doyen of the Newlyn school. South Kensington Science Museum sent appropriate exhibits and local collectors contributed marine artefacts. At the inaugural luncheon Travail made flattering references to distinguished guests and lectures were given on technical matters and also more popular subjects such as ways of cooking fish. At one well-attended meeting the audience loudly condemned non-Cornish trawlermen who were scooping up the bulk of the local catch, and ruining the trade by catching immature fish. So successful was the exhibition that it was extended until the 20 August.[12]

Architectural commissions in the early 1890s

At forty years of age, Trevail's high profile involvement in education, public health, railway access, fisheries and political life had brought him to the attention of every Cornish family of note. It was therefore no coincidence that many of them commissioned him to design private and public buildings of all kinds in a great variety of styles. Although the great Gothicists had died or retired from practice, the style continued to dominate ecclesiastical architecture,[13] but mixed or 'free' styles had developed for other buildings and Trevail was master of them all: picturesque 'Old English'; romantic arts and crafts; up-dated classical, symmetrical 'Queen Anne'; Tudor; Flemish or Dutch. His qualities as an architect had been further recognised by his unanimous election to Fellowship of the most prestigious professional body, the Royal Institute of British Architects. Nominated by J Piers St Aubyn, FRIBA, he was seconded by the President of the Institute. 'A well-deserved honour', commented the editor of the *St Austell Star*, 'a distinguished recognition of his high ability'.[14]

One of his most important clients, both in terms of his political influence and the commissions he gave to Trevail, was Francis Barratt, County Councillor for the St Austell district and later, as Sir Francis Layland-Barratt, MP for that town. Son of a mining captain who had played a leading role in developing the immensely profitable Hodbarrow iron mine in Cumberland,[15] Barratt was a generous benefactor in Cornwall, and also in Devon when he was MP for Torquay. For him Trevail designed, in 1890, the Liberal Club in St Austell, of which Barratt was president. In what Trevail called the 'Queen Anne Renaissance' style, it still stands relatively untouched on the outside. Two shops

Upper floors of the Liberal Club, St Austell.

on the ground floor, with a central entrance and stairway, led to the Club, which occupied the two storeys above, including a reading room, smoking room, library, billiard room, secretary's room and kitchen. The wall of Hawke's premises and the facade of his shop had to be rebuilt and Trevail also added a second storey.[16] An archway to a yard that gave access to the premises of the ironmonger, George Hawke, next door has since been filled in with retail premises.

The Liberal Club opened in a blaze of glory, for which Trevail claimed his fair share. The *St Austell Star*, the local voice of Gladstonian Liberalism, published a special edition, followed by a supplement with plans, drawings and full descriptions of the building, and an illustration of it later appeared in the London *Daily Graphic*. Applauded at the opening ceremony, Trevail seconded a flattering vote of thanks to Francis Barratt and was equally extravagant in his praises of the two local Liberal MPs, McArthur and Conybeare, as well as Sir George Trevelyan, a member of Gladstone's cabinet, who officially opened the building. Sir George reciprocated by comparing Trevail with the classical architects of Italy in his skill in 'raising a very fine building indeed on a confined town site'.[17]

Trevail did not fail to mention that on the very next day Sir George would be laying the foundation stone of yet another of Trevail's buildings, the Public Rooms at Camborne. This building replaced a Temperance Hall and Rosewarne Dairy on the opposite side of the road from the site where Trevail was later to erect his Free Library. It comprised a large meeting hall with gallery and stage, together with dressing, billiards and reading rooms and a kitchen. The County Surveyor Hickes put forward a number of objections when the directors applied for a licence to perform stage plays, but Trevail took great pleasure in demonstrating his superior knowledge of building regulations and demolishing the surveyor's arguments.[18]

Housing the rich and the poor
Barratt provided Trevail with commissions for many workers' cottages, discussed later in this chapter, as well as for the elegant granite-dressed Tregarne Terrace near St Austell railway station. An attractive mixture of larger double-fronted and smaller semi-detached dwellings rather than a straight run of identical houses, the terrace was intended for middle class occupants. Barratt retained one dwelling, Tregarne House, extended by Trevail in 1900, for his own use when he came to Cornwall from his bases in Devon and London.[19]

Robert Harvey, mentioned earlier, was another tycoon who furthered Trevail's career. He had purchased an estate at Trenowth near Grampound Road from James Hendy in 1890 and Trevail quickly drew up plans for a new two-storey farmhouse and outbuildings, including stables and a barn at an estimated cost of nearly £2,000. Harvey,

Left: *Tregarne Terrace, St Austell, with Tregarne House in foreground.*
Right: *Trenowth farmhouse on Sir Robert Harvey's estate.*

Left: *Tredethy, Helland, new wing and facade for FJ Hext in 1892.*
Right: *Princes Street, Truro, porch and steps added in 1893.*

like Barratt, expected swift action. The advertisement for tenders produced a very large response and within hours James Julian, later the constructor of the Fisheries Exhibition, had been chosen. Fewer than six weeks later, men were working on the farmhouse as well as on cattle houses and other buildings for the home farm.[20] The double fronted house in white brick and random stone, with granite quoins and keystones, has the initials R H carved in stone above the entrance; the date stone of 1900 on one building suggests that work continued for the decade.[21]

Other work carried out for country gentlemen included Tredethy at Helland, a seventeenth century country house added to by Francis John Hext in 1868 and further extended by Trevail in 1892/3 with a new wing, porch and facade, with fresh panelling on existing ceilings.[22] At Cowbridge, Lostwithiel, Trevail designed two wings at the side and the rear of a house for George Hext in 1894. The new build included drawing and dining rooms, study, butler's pantry, kitchen and scullery, with eight bedrooms and two dressing rooms on the first floor. Coloured plans and blueprints exist in Trevail's files, dated 1893–4, for 'proposed alterations and additions' to Witherdon House, Beaworthy, Devon, originally a farmhouse but developed from 1872 into a manor house by Luxmore, who became the local squire. He designed extensive additions for William Coode, and altered these designs slightly for the later occupant T Hugh Carlyon. They included a new facade, a new rear wing for kitchen facilities with bedrooms over them, stables and coach houses. Nothing was built immediately, but the work was carried out in 1897 and 1898.

In Trevail's correspondence file for March 1893 are site plans, undated, for seven large plots adjoining the south side of the St Austell to Charlestown Road, entitled 'Edward Coode Esq. Building Estate, Watering, St Austell'. In August of that year, Trevail added the imposing porch and steps to an eighteenth century house in Prince's Street, Truro, for the agricultural dealer Samuel Polkinhorne, next to the warehouse that Trevail had designed for him in 1885. Another important client was the Right

Reverend, the Bishop of Cornwall, John Gott, who bought Trenython near Tywardreath as his residence in 1891 because he was not able to house his large and valuable family library in Lis Escop, the official residence.[23] For Gott, Trevail designed a gatehouse with an open front porch and a lobby, living room, dining room and kitchen with pantry, and three bedrooms upstairs. The exterior had Tudor style woodwork on the upper floor and plain barge boards.[24] Trevail also added a chapel to the property, to be discussed later.

Working men's cottages
Another example where Trevail's radical views coincided with architectural commissions was his campaign to provide better accommodation for working people, including railwaymen, than the squalid hovels in which some of them existed. A regular guest at the annual supper of the Truro branch of the General Railway Workers' Union, he

Left: *Harrison Terrace, Truro, for railwaymen.*
Right: *Wheal Agar, Illogan, cottages for miners.*

was elected chairman of a union meeting to discuss demands for reduced hours of work, part of a Europe-wide movement to improve working conditions. He recommended moderation, arguing that the Great Western Railway had a good record on worker relations. But this was disputed by R Bell of the Amalgamated Society of Railway Servants, who asserted that Trevail's information was unreliable and that he, Bell, had been 'hounded and spied upon' in Cornwall.[25]

At the next annual supper, which Trevail was too ill to attend, he sent a letter congratulating them on achieving their demands for 'Sunday Pay', and for following his advice to act moderately. 'Whenever I have the opportunity of putting in a good word for railway men, I never fail to do so,' he wrote, adding, 'The next matter is to get better housing.'[26] Truro suffered from a particular shortage of working class housing because of an influx of railwaymen and their families from the Midlands, Wales and the north of England. According to Trevail, Truro needed a hundred dwellings of this kind, and a few years earlier he had appealed for benefactors to finance them but only one man, James Ball, came forward offering to fund the construction of a single house.[27]

As a Truro Councillor, Trevail made himself unpopular by accusing his council colleagues of failing in their duty because of their ignorance of the requirements of the 1890 Housing of the Working Classes Act, quoting in support the criticisms of a Sanitary Inspector about acute overcrowding. One difficulty was the high price of building land, another was the perennial problem of constructing houses of an acceptable standard at a rent that working men could afford.[28] Trevail practised what he preached. A previous mayor of Truro, Councillor E Roberts, had praised Trevail's efforts to find cheaper building land and negotiate a rent from Lord Robartes, at 50 per cent below the market price for a plot in Harrison Terrace, near the railway station, between Clifton Villas and Adelaide Place. There, in 1892, Trevail planned an experimental group of four houses, which still stand, each with six rooms, a restrained contrast to the later housing which surrounds them.[29]

The following year though, a violent scene erupted in Truro Council when the new mayor complained that the houses were not complete and Henry Buck asserted of Trevail: 'He poses as the working men's friend, but he is their enemy'. A furious Trevail demanded Buck to retract his words, arguing that he had negotiated exceptionally favourable terms for the land and had 'not asked a farthing' towards the cost of the plans or the legal expenses. But, he said, he was 'only the messenger for Lord Robartes', and the delay was caused by the slowness of Pearse Jenkin, Robartes' agent, to build a road and a wall on the adjoining land.[30] A year later the houses were still not finished.[31]

Trevail's interest in working class housing as a Truro Councillor continued when, as Chairman of the County Council Sanitary Committee, he had to deal with dozens of reports on housing conditions from all over Cornwall. In his new role he once again

Almshouses at Tregony, renovated in 1894.

Moorland Road, St Austell, workmen's houses for Francis Leyland Barratt.

annoyed Truro councillors, as well as those of such places as Polperro and Falmouth, by publicly criticising their lack of action. He designed 25 pleasant stuccoed houses for workers on Lord Robartes' estate at Illogan, near Redruth at a low cost of £140 each, with a new road near Wheal Agar mine from the main highway between Redruth and Camborne on a site selected by Pearse Jenkin, Robartes' steward, commanding views of the sea.[32]

A social housing project of a different kind was Trevail's restoration of Tregony Almshouses, originally built from a bequest of 1696 for accommodating 'decayed housekeepers' from the Boscawen family. From a ruinous state, a long-standing eye-sore, he transformed them in 1894 into a picturesque half-timbered addition to the village and they are still occupied today.[33]

Trevail later designed seven blocks of simple but attractive workingmen's houses, six to eight in each block, along Moorland Road in St Austell for Francis Barratt, a project that continued for a number of years.[34] The plans for each block were similar but not identical, some having a more decorative gable, and the block at the end of Moorland Road running round into South Street was designed with wedge-shaped rooms to take the curve, although Barratt did not approve of their shape. Most had three bedrooms, a few had four, and in 1897 the *West Briton* noted that these 'convenient and substantial houses, with gardens in front and behind, are let out at £9 and £12 a year, according to size'.[35]

Schools and churches

An example of ecclesiastical work gained through Trevail's connection with Layland Barratt was the restoration of St Austell Wesleyan Chapel, now St John's Church, where great emphasis was placed on the installation of heating apparatus.[36] A rostrum and electric lighting was designed at this time and later, in 1892, Trevail added new windows, seating and a magnificent ceiling. Francis Layland Barratt undertook to finance the restoration of the front of the chapel, having already helped with raising funds to pay for other renovations. He demanded a good deal of personal attention for his money, bearing in mind the low cost and often 'got restive', as Trevail put it, if his letters were not answered by return of post. Still the two men remained on easy social terms and dined together at the Hotel Cecil when they were in London and their correspondence was full of political discussion.[37] Bishop Gott had a small chapel built at Trenython seating 30 to 40 people, designed in a totally different style from that of the 17th century house, although this may have been the wish of the Bishop, since the new gatehouse described earlier is in the same style, stuccoed walling with black timber in a mock Tudor finish.[38] At Truro Wesleyan College Trevail designed a small isolation hospital in 1894 and his work for St Mawes School started in 1890 although the building has a date stone of 1894.[39] At Fowey Board School Trevail designed extensions for boys, girls and infant classrooms to the rear in 1894.

The grand plans for tourism, the educational and public health crusades, the municipal activities, together with a vast load of architectural commissions of all kinds that Trevail carried out in the early 1890s, and which we have described in previous chapters, would surely have been more than enough to satisfy the ambitions of any normal man. But not, of course, Silvanus Trevail. In the following chapters we shall see how his superabundant talents, energy and creativity drove him onwards to conquer new fields of public service and professional practice.

Left: *Wesleyan Chapel, St Austell, now St John's Church, interior renovation and new facade, 1886–1892.* Right: *Trenython Chapel, Tywardreath, for Bishop Gott.*

Ten
Resurrecting the tourist plan

In Chapter Seven we saw how Silvanus Trevail, despite the resounding success of the Atlantic Hotel at Newquay, met a blank refusal from his directors to carry on his grand plan to encircle Cornwall with hotels. Three of them, Mead, Rowe and Gatley, had Falmouth connections and they relinquished their option on the proposed hotel site at Falmouth, belonging to Lord Kimberley, to the directors of the Falmouth Hotel Company, who built on it. For them, Trevail had added a large flat-roofed annex to the landward side of the Falmouth Hotel, as mentioned in Chapter Seven, and also drawn up plans for a four-storey entrance portico.[1] He then received the consolation of a commission to design their new hotel.

The Pendennis Hotel and Boarding House, as it was called, was a modest affair, in line with his original proposals for a chain of hotels. He appeared to recycle plans, since

Pendennis Hotel, Falmouth, now known as the Royal Duchy Hotel.

earlier drawings of the Pendennis, entitled 'The Gyllyngdune Hotel', are virtually the same as those for 'a proposed hotel' for 'The Tourist's Hotel Company Ltd of Cornwall', seemingly a forerunner of the Cornish Hotels Company. With 34 bed-rooms and costing £10,000, built in the so-called 'Queen Anne' style, it opened in the summer of 1893 but closed down again in the winter, long-staying guests being trans-ferred to the Falmouth Hotel nearby.[2]

The Housel Bay Hotel and Maenheere

In January 1893, while work was in progress on the Pendennis, Trevail forged the next link in his chain by forming the Housel Bay Hotel and Boarding House Company to construct a hotel on the Lizard coast, with views of mainland Britain's most southerly point. For the Chairman he chose R G Rows, his influential County Council colleague and prominent religious and political leader in the area. The Secretary was Alfred Hamilton Jenkin, a later steward to the vast properties of Lord Robartes, on whose land it was built, the latter providing the road to the hotel. James Wickett of Redruth, mining adventurer, director and later Chairman of Cornwall's largest public house chain, the Redruth Brewery Company, was a major investor, as was his brother, Charles, the then Chairman of the Brewery.[3] The contractor was Arthur (later Sir Arthur) Carkeek, responsible for some of Trevail's largest projects.

Built of bluish-grey local stone with granite dressings, the 28–bedroomed Housel Bay Hotel was smaller than the Pendennis and cost about half as much, with an issued capital of £5,400. When it opened in June 1894 its owners expected it to emulate the success of the Atlantic Hotel, but within two years reports circulated that it was 'some-thing of a financial failure'. One problem was the steadfast refusal of its Chairman to apply for a liquor licence, and when the brewer James Wickett took over in later years as Chairman it moved into profit.[4]

Housel Bay Hotel built by Arthur Carkeek in 1894.

Whenever Trevail designed a building in any locality it was a fair bet that he would pick up other commissions nearby, and on this occasion he drew up plans for 'Maenheere' for John Roberts, a silver merchant in London and Paris who had returned home with his French third wife. A five-storey, six-bedroom house, built of local stone and granite, it was dubbed 'the bedstead' because of its four tall chimneys rising like posts at each corner with an iron-railed balcony between them. At the foundation stone ceremony, Trevail spoke at length in praise of the setting, 'quite as beautiful and less variable in climate' as the south of France.[5]

Rivalry at St Ives

For the floor tiles of Maenheere Trevail used the same pattern, made by his friend Henry Dennis of the Ruabon Terracotta Works in North Wales, as in his next hotel venture, the Carbis Bay Hotel, a few miles from St Ives. As part of the first stage of his original plan, Trevail had in mind a site at 'upalong', well above the picturesque but odoriferous port. The Tregenna Castle Hotel nearby, a private mansion converted by the GWR, already provided superior accommodation for 'men of means and title' but there seemed scope for a hotel that catered for the middle classes. The *Redruth Independent* enquired 'Why could the Cornish Hotel Company not build one?'[6] When, however, the directors of that company refused to proceed, a local consortium secured the site and built the Porthminster Hotel there. Its Chairman was Edward Hain, shipping magnate, Mayor, County Councillor and later MP for the area and another former mayor, J M Nicholls, was a Director, while the Town Clerk Edward Boase acted as secretary.[7]

Trevail had already designed Treloyhan, an imposing mansion the size of a hotel, for Hain not far from the Porthminster site. Twin-gabled, mullion-windowed, surround-

Treloyhan, St Ives, built on the surface workings of Wheal Margery.

ed by formal gardens and shrubberies, the main staircase in its grand oak-panelled hall the same as one in Lord Robartes' home at Lanhydrock, restored by Coad of Liskeard after a disastrous fire. It might have been copied by Lang, the Liskeard contractor for the restoration, who also built Treloyhan.[8] Some years later Trevail designed attractive rustic stables and a cottage in the grounds of Treloyhan, with granite dressings and clay tiled roofs, the latter an unusual feature in a region dominated by slate, and possibly imported as ballast on Hain's ships.[9]

A year after Trevail designed Treloyhan for Hain, he drew up plans for a five-bedroomed, twin-gabled residence nearby, built in coursed stone with granite trim for Captain Thomas Row Harry, another prominent St Ives man and several times Mayor of the town.[10] Another local design of 1893 was Draycott Terrace, a group of gabled houses with stuccoed fronts and cast-iron filigree balconies, commissioned by Henry Rouncefield, owner of seine fisheries.[11]

Draycott Terrace, St Ives, built as holiday lodgings for families.

The Porthminster and the Carbis Bay Hotels

Given Trevail's close association with Hain, it comes as something of a surprise that, although Hain retained Lang, the Liskeard contractor who built Treloyhan, to construct the Porthminster Hotel, he did not chose Trevail as the designer. Instead he commissioned another Liskeard man, the architect John Sanson.[12] Possibly Trevail did not become involved because he was already setting up a company to build a rival hotel. He had now lost two excellent sites, at Falmouth and St Ives, due to the caution of the Cornish Hotels Company directors, and he was determined to proceed with his plan to build a chain of hotels. He decided upon a site a couple of miles along the coast in what he called 'a charming position just above the sands of Carbis Bay'.

This was in fact the former location of copper and tin deep-mining activity, some of it under the sea, and photographs of the 1890s showed a bleak valley scarred with mining tips and shafts, with just a few new villas dotted about, not the pleasant wooded cove it later became. Trevail loyally described it as 'a wild and untrimmed site of natural beauty' and it is true that, with the arrival of the Great Western Railway line to St Ives, which passed through Carbis Bay, the valley had become a popular spot for Sunday school tea treats and bank holiday picnics. In 1878 William Payne developed four acres of ornamental pleasure grounds, and Mr Williams' Tea Gardens opened near the beach in 1890,[13] and those who frequented the valley may well have been upset when the hotel was built just above the beach.

*Carbis Bay
Hotel, architect's
drawing 1894
(Family papers).*

The hotel, Trevail admitted, was only 'a small edition of the Atlantic Hotel', with 21 bedrooms. The Porthminster Hotel, although it cost about the same as the Carbis Bay, between £7,000 and £7,500, had 38 bedrooms with a veranda on each floor allowing guests to 'savour the balmy atmosphere'. It also boasted a novel feature: a dark room for the fashionable hobby of taking holiday pictures.[14] The Carbis Bay Hotel, like Trevail's previous venture at Housel Bay, did not come up to expectations as far as profits were concerned, and later he confided to his friend George Hicks that he had always regretted losing the Porthminster site due to the stick-in-the-mud attitude of the directors of the Cornish Hotels Company. The Porthminster had stolen its thunder by opening a month earlier in 1894, much to Trevail's annoyance, and a storm later washed away the bridge across a stream that gave access to his hotel. In the summer season, hotel guests who sought peace and quiet might have been irritated by the revelry on the beach immediately below, but in 1898 John Payne was advertising new pleasure grounds with swings, hobbyhorses, skittles and an alpine railway.[15]

Other seaside homes

Apart from his hotel developments, and other commissions that followed from them, Trevail was also designing properties elsewhere along the coast. Yet another of his attempts at creating a vast seaside complex was a planned estate looking westward from Newquay harbour towards Fistral Bay. Fifty villas, 24 large semi-detached residences and over 500 terraced houses of varying sizes were to line wide boulevards called Trelawney, Treffry, Trevelyan, Trevanion and Trevose, linked to a Grand Esplanade fronting the bay, with pride of place taken by a palatial hotel.[16] As we shall see in Chapter Fourteen, Trevail built the hotel but the rest of the scheme never left the drawing board.

To the east of Newquay, Trevail designed 'Lamorna', a six-bedroomed home with a large frontage in Trevelga Road (later Lusty Glaze), overlooking the sea. His client was John Vivian and the development took place on what was a portion of the Stephen's estate mentioned in Chapter Five.[17] At Perranporth, Trevail drew up plans for a minor extension, not built, to a house constructed from fish cellars, on the Droskin, an elevated position above Perranporth beach. Commanding magnificent views, it had been acquired by Thomas Henry Pill, a Perranporth miner who had made money in America. 'Droskyn Castle' as he called it, was in keeping with its title, a battlemented residence with a square castellated tower of local stone, finished by dressings and string courses of a finer material.[18]

On the south coast at Mevagissey, Trevail designed in 1892 a fancifully castellated house with a commanding view, Polpier. The house was completed within a year for Dr Monro Grier and included a waiting room and surgery. Over three years later Trevail was still asking for payment of the commission of three per cent. Receiving no reply, he wrote again, adding a bill for £26.25 to cover travelling expenses and extra sanitary plans, explaining that he needed money urgently to pay the considerable costs of his duties as Mayor of Truro. In a further letter, he said he was 'sorry to do or say anything that would have the semblance of urging', but that the cost of three years' credit on the bill amounted to £3.75 at five per cent interest. Dr Grier's response was to suggest that he was thinking of building a hotel, the inference being that Trevail might design it for him. Trevail did not take the bait, instead informing Grier that 'It is an easier matter to erect hotels than it is to make them pay afterwards as no doubt Mr Hain has found in his venture at St Ives'. Grier then sent him a cheque for £6, which Trevail banked the same day, and was possibly all he received, as that is the last record we have of any dealings with him.[19]

Polpier Mevagissey, for Dr Monro Grier in 1892.

A little earlier, in 1889, Trevail had designed additions to a historic coaching inn, the 'Red Lion Hotel', in the centre of Truro. He later raised the height of the building, adding mock Tudor storeys to a classical facade. However despite, or perhaps because, Trevail was a member of a syndicate of local councillors, including Thomas Chirgwin the Mayor, John James and Joseph Rogers who financed the scheme, it met with fierce opposition from other councillors. Roberts accused Trevail of deliberately misleading the council about the size of a gable projecting at the rear. Buck claimed that Trevail was full of 'gas and verbosity' and 'deliberate lies' about the project. Trevail always, his opponents argued, condemned other architects if they did not explain to laymen what their plans entailed, and yet he was practising precisely the same subterfuge himself. Trevail was characteristically unrepentant. His honour had been impugned, he said, and if the Town Surveyor was not competent enough to spot the size of the projecting gables on his plan, then Trevail was under no obligation to point it out himself.[20] Pevsner, in his survey of Cornish architecture, thought Trevail had 'terribly treated' the frontage, but at the time the *West Briton* felt he had 'materially improved it', and when it was pulled down in the 1960s to make way for a retail store, there was a public outcry.

When the summer season of 1894 got under way the *Royal Cornwall Gazette* predicted that it would be 'full of promise, thanks to the admirable hotels with which Cornwall is supplied, largely through the energy and enterprise of Mr Trevail'.[21] As we have seen this promise was not realised in terms of profitability despite Trevail redoubling his efforts to promote tourism. He organised a group of thirty volunteers from different parts of Cornwall who fed him with news of the weather, which he collated to increase awareness of the mild climate. 'Cornwall must soon come to the front as one of the most picturesque and health-restoring holiday grounds of Europe,' commented a leading tourist trade magazine, 'and this will be largely due to the energy, conviction and propaganda of Mr Silvanus Trevail, who has devoted years of labour and unlimited exertion in organising sanitary and other reforms in order to have his county better and more fully appreciated.'[22]

Fine words, but did Silvanus Trevail fully share this optimism about future growth? His hotels were getting noticeably smaller: from 60 bedrooms at Newquay down to 34 at Falmouth, 28 on the Lizard and 21 at Carbis Bay. On the face of it he might have seemed to be sharing the caution of the directors of the Cornish Hotels Company. However, as we shall see in Chapter Fourteen, his next hotel ventures were on a more lavish scale than ever before.

Eleven
A crowded Mayoral year

Silvanus Trevail was not a man to do things by halves. Time and again we notice how, whenever he started a new venture, he determined to make it the biggest, the best, the most successful that Cornwall had ever seen. His year as Mayor of Truro from November 1894 was no exception, and even the manner in which he was elected was out of the ordinary. He was the first Mayor of Truro who was not a member of the Town Council.[1] What made it more surprising was that he had been a constant thorn in the flesh of some of his fellow councillors and had just been defeated in the council election. According to some, that was because of his continued refusal to canvass for votes, or even because of his rivals' 'manipulation' of the electorate 'with beer'.[2] According to others, it was because he had advocated imposing a heavy burden on ratepayers for expenditure to cure Truro's appalling sanitary problems.[3]

Despite this setback Alderman Heard, doyen of Truro council and proprietor of the *West Briton*, proposed Trevail for mayor. 'There has never been in the history of Truro,' asserted Heard, 'anyone who has worked harder ... a man of great imagination, large administrative ability, indomitable perseverance, great public spirit, pluck, zeal, energy and desire to be useful.'[4] Not everyone in Truro shared his opinion. Councillor Jennings, who had acted as treasurer for the testimonial fund set up for Trevail the railway hero (described in Chapter Nine), spoke of his 'peculiar temperament ... sometimes he waxes a little warm ... if stroked the wrong way he throws up sparks.' Councillor Hearn, elected alderman to replace Thomas Chirgwin after his sudden death in the previous September, proposed Councillor E Roberts for Mayor and accused Heard of 'playing politics' to elect a Liberal Party candidate. Councillor Bullen, temporary Mayor after Chirgwin's death, was sparing in his praise for Trevail but admitted that 'whatever his faults he is a giant for work'. The Tory *Royal Cornwall Gazette*, while agreeing that Trevail had many excellent qualities, commented that he 'lacks a sense of humour, is contrary, and fated to be in troubled waters'.[5]

Inevitably, the most ferocious opposition to Trevail's nomination came from arch-enemy Henry Buck. He had taken over the role of Chairman of the Finance Committee in 1889 after Trevail was defeated in the council election and had continued in this post ever since. He was particularly resentful of the way in which Trevail repeatedly claimed to have radically improved the town's financial position. Trevail, asserted Buck, was fond of taking credit for others' achievements. Trevail possessed energy, Buck accepted, but it was 'more often a curse than a blessing'. Moreover, Buck remarked, Trevail had been rejected by the electors of both the East and West Wards of Truro by over 100 votes and any attempt to foist him on the town as Mayor overrode the wishes of the electorate and was a piece of 'Liberal electioneering trickery'. Both Heard and Trevail were well-known Liberals and Buck was a Tory. In the end, however, Trevail's opponent Roberts withdrew. Roberts, Truro resident for a quarter of a century, Bible Christian and superintendent of the Prudential Insurance Company for Cornwall, was an honourable man who had no appetite for an unpleasant fight. And so the Council elected Trevail by twelve votes to nine.[6]

The Trevail-Buck war of words continues

Previous chapters have recorded some of the stormy exchanges between Buck and Trevail in Truro council chamber from 1886 to 1889 that continued on a wide range of issues, from provision for technical education to the choice of a railway route from Truro to Newquay. This intense animosity was resumed as soon as Trevail was re-elected as Truro Councillor in November 1891. They managed to pick a fight on the ownership of grass in a cemetery, a missing book borrowed by Trevail four years earlier, the forcing of a lock on a document cupboard and ventilation of the council chamber. Their main bone of contention, as current and former chairmen of finance, was the state of the town's accounts, where Trevail accused Buck of 'fencing' by dodging his questions, of 'twisting' figures, of neglect, oversight and getting the accounts into arrears, things which Trevail claimed, he had never have done himself. Buck, in turn, resented Trevail's 'very indecent manner' and complained of his 'tremendous heat'. In reporting their bickering, newspapers resorted to such headlines as 'Mr Trevail and Mr Buck at loggerheads again', referred to 'unseemly squabbling' between the 'old opponents' and urged the Mayor to 'put his foot down to stop the undignified running battle'.[7]

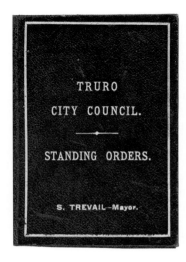

Trevail's copy of Truro City Council Standing Orders, drawn up by himself (Family papers).

Clearly a sizeable minority opposed the choice of Trevail as Mayor and from the very first meeting Buck and others seemed to be spoiling for a fight, to make his year as Chairman of the Council as difficult as possible, with slanging matches over a whole new range of trivia such as the dates and times of committee meetings, paving stones outside the Royal Hotel, and lost or missing documents. To try to reduce time wasting, Trevail composed a new set of standing orders for council procedure, which Buck and his supporters objected to as giving Trevail dictatorial powers. Goaded by the opposition, Trevail would lose his temper and order Buck to leave the chamber, only for Buck to refuse and for Trevail in turn to threaten to vacate the chair.

When Trevail asked for more meetings to get through a growing backlog of business, Hearn, who often sided with Buck, suggested that the avoidance of 'long-winded orations' from the Chairman would solve the problem. In March 1895 Buck carried his fight with Trevail into a wider arena by opposing him for re-election to the County Council in a campaign that even the *Royal Cornwall Gazette*, which tended to agree with Buck's views, criticised for its 'personal animosity' against Trevail. But when Trevail triumphed by a three to one majority, he was attacked by the same newspaper for 'crowing over' Buck at public meetings and 'kicking a man when he was down.'[8]

Moments of Mayoral glory

If Trevail's chairmanship of the council was marred by bickering and outbreaks of his own fiery temper, other events in his mayoral year of office were much more to his liking. There was always more than a touch of the showman about Trevail, and he revelled in functions where he took centre stage, receiving accolades from all quarters, and several such occasions presented themselves in the course of the year. For he had now reached the height of his fame. 'Few men are better known in Cornwall,' commented the editor of the *West Briton* on Trevail's election as mayor: 'As Chairman of the Sanitary Committee of the County Council he has done more than anyone else to improve conditions, and Cornwall is also indebted for the part he played in "The Battle of the Railways" in 1894'.[9]

The hero's welcome that rewarded Trevail for his role in this affair, described in Chapter Nine, was one of the first triumphal ceremonies of his mayoral year in February 1895, followed by the laying of the foundation stone by John Passmore Edwards in May for the Free Library that Trevail designed in Truro, to be discussed in Chapter Thirteen. To celebrate this occasion, Trevail lined the streets with flags and bunting and organised a procession of soldiers, firemen, police, Rechabites and Oddfellows, county and Truro councillors, mayors of Cornish towns, Justices of the Peace, members of school boards and teachers. Passmore Edwards was lavish in his praise of Trevail, commending his 'organising capabilities, indomitable energy and steam engine power ... you have among you a man of genius'. The following day Passmore Edwards opened Camborne library, also designed by Trevail, and made further references to him in ceremonies in that town.[10]

In addition, Trevail attended the many functions that every mayor was expected to honour with his presence: meetings of charitable organisations, church services and funerals, the tea of the Methodist conference at Truro School, dinners of the Cabmen of Truro and the Uniform Staff of Truro Railway Station, Masonic assemblies and balls. He was also invited to mayoral dinners outside Cornwall in London, Liverpool, Carlisle, Wrexham and Tunbridge Wells.[11] The most elaborate occasion was probably his own Mayoral Banquet, 'the biggest thing in Mayor's dinners ever known in these parts,' according to the *Royal Cornwall Gazette*. The hundreds of guests included Lord Robartes, the Bishop of Truro, the Lord Mayor of Liverpool and the Mayors of Winchester, Exeter, Torquay and Plymouth as well as those of Cornish towns. The meal was interspersed with no fewer than forty-two speeches and toasts, not to men-

Truro Free Library, later had the Central Technical Schools added to the rear.

tion a number of impromptu interventions and orations by the Mayor himself.[12] A fitting climax to an eventful year, it led a leading local government journal to conclude that, 'In his Mayoralty, Mr Trevail had given every satisfaction'.[13]

Trevail was asked to stand again as Mayor but declined, and Roberts was elected, supported by Rogers who, in an obvious allusion to Trevail, predicted that the new Mayor's 'tolerance, tact and discretion were just as necessary as a superabundance of energy and ability'. John James, often an opponent of Trevail, then proposed a vote of thanks to him as 'a perfect champion among men' with 'large powers of organisation', and Councillor Johns echoed the words that Heard had used when proposing Trevail for Mayor a year earlier by commending his 'indomitable pluck and energy', and 'exceptional local knowledge'. Trevail, in his reply, did not hesitate to continue his attack on Cornwall's failure to address the drainage problem which, he claimed, was 'driving people out of Truro'.[14]

A year later, Roberts refused to carry on as Mayor, and Trevail told an acquaintance that he himself would have to be careful until after the election date, 'to avoid being Mayor as I hear that they have my name on their list again and I must be on the spot and on the alert or they may have me into it again before I can get out'.[15] Who could blame Trevail for not wanting to take up the burden again, which occupied so much of his time? In any case he was up to his neck in County Council work. In January 1896 he had declined an invitation to visit the Plymouth librarian W H K Wright, who had been so helpful in Trevail's design of libraries, because he had to attend a County Council finance meeting at St Austell. 'At one time,' he wrote to Wright, 'I felt I could hardly undertake too much local government work which gave great satisfaction, especially Sanitary Reform,' but now he found it 'white slavery'.[16]

Another reason for not wishing to be Mayor was that mayoral duties also cost a good deal of money, and he was trying to collect as much as possible from commissions. For instance he asked a wealthy client, J R Collins of Bodmin, for an advance of £30. 'I really want the money,' wrote Trevail 'to meet the heavy demands upon me when bills are coming in from all quarters.' In another letter, written on the same day, he tried to obtain payment from Dr Grier of Mevagissey, although this was like getting blood out of a stone, as we saw in Chapter Ten.[17]

His heavy mayoral commitments had not, however, curtailed his involvement in other matters such as public health and railway access. At the mayoral banquet the principal guest, W H Watts, Lord Mayor of Liverpool, had upset some of those present by complaining that Cornwall had not made the most of its opportunities and criticised its growing dependence on tourism, saying that he spent his holidays elsewhere because he was put off by its poor sanitation. Had Trevail put him up to this? For at that time he was fighting a losing battle against Buck and others in trying to push through a scheme to improve Truro's notorious drainage system.[18]

On the railway front, though, Trevail's success in backing the North Cornwall Railway (NCR) scheme was beginning to look like a hollow victory. Once again the NCR supporters failed to match their enthusiasm with hard cash, and the Great Western Railway's rival, the London and South Western Railway, was also unwilling to finance it. In Truro council, Buck delightedly claimed that the Buck-Rogers project for a direct Truro-Newquay line would now go ahead after being 'thrust aside by the short sightedness of those who never ought to have put their fingers in the pie and know nothing about it'. Trevail retorted that there was 'complete justification' for his idea but, ominously, was not appointed as an official member of the sub-committee that looked into the question of reviving the Buck-Rogers scheme, although he acted as an ex-officio member.[19]

Leading architectural commissions

Somehow, on top of his enormous load of municipal duties, Trevail still found time to carry on his architectural practice. Apart from Camborne and Truro libraries, described in Chapter Thirteen, another educational commission was for extensions to the Camborne School of Mines, built in 1882 (not by Trevail) between Fore Street and Market Place. His additions comprised a second entrance, Principal's room, balance room, laboratory and furnace room. On the first floor a secretary's room was placed on the corner with an attractive oriole window, and a lecture room was built above the laboratory. With these facilities it was claimed that the school offered 'the best accommodation for teaching technical subjects in Cornwall'.[20]

During his mayoral year, Trevail was also occupied with some ongoing projects in St Austell. He continued work there for Francis Barratt in Tregarne Terrace and Moorland Road, described in Chapter Nine, and for another client he designed a rear extension

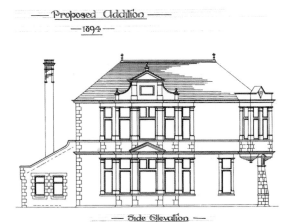

Top left: *Camborne School of Mines, as seen from Trevithick Road (CRO: AD396/628).*
Top right: *Public Rooms, St Austell, opened in 1896.*
Bottom left: *Fowey Church vestry. The access steps inside the church were also by Trevail.*
Bottom right: *Trebarwith Bridge built in 1896 for Lord Wharncliffe.*

with kitchen facilities at Sydenham Villa.[21] An important project was the St Austell Public Rooms, which cost over £3,000. As was so often the case with buildings in which local councils were involved, progress was slow. Trevail had drawn up plans for an extension to the St Austell Union workhouse to make room for the newly formed Town Council to meet, but the cost was felt to be too great and after much discussion the council agreed to take space in the newly built public rooms. Clad in dark stone with granite dressings around large arched windows, the ground floor was occupied by a drill hall, storeroom, kitchen and meeting room, as well as a space for the town's fire engine. Above was a large hall like the nave of a church, with a stage and wide balcony at one end and a smaller balcony at the other, together with offices and cloakrooms. Sir Charles Graves-Sawle, an important local landowner, opened the public rooms in August 1896.[22]

At Bodmin, Trevail was dealing with J R Collins, mentioned earlier. Originally Collins asked Trevail to design a new building to replace his property, St Nicholas House, to be variously named Palazzio Raffaelo or Villa Angelica, and bombarded Trevail with notes about alterations and critical comments on Trevail's drawings. Eventually a more modest project seemed to have been decided upon, which in part may have been added to the older house, as evidence of lifting the roof may be seen on the rear wing. Collins arranged for the building stone to be brought from Margate Wood quarry nearby.

At St Fimbarras church, Fowey, he cut an opening between the west wall and the churchyard for a new vestry, adding its entrance steps inside the church.[23] In Truro he was still involved as a director of the Truro Public Baths Company along with his fellow Councillors Joseph Rogers, Alfred Blenkinsop, Hugh Rice and others.[24] Another project near Truro was at Chacewater Board School. Originally built as a National School in 1847, William White first extended it in 1861, then James Hicks in 1878. In 1894 Trevail made a multiplicity of suggestions for further additions which culminated in two new blocks for a classroom and a cloakroom.[25] Finally, towards the end of his mayoral year, Trevail was planning work on a road and a bridge on the north coast at Trebarwith, near the site of his next hotel, the King Arthur's Castle Hotel, to be discussed in Chapter Fourteen.

Twelve
Trevail in the world of commerce, banks and shops

One of Silvanus Trevail's defining characteristics was a willingness to exploit any commercial opportunity that came his way. We have already described how he formed his own companies to finance hotel development when others failed to back him, carried out an unspecified assignment for the Tangye's company in America, and became a Director of Truro Baths. He also sought to take advantage of other possibilities, however far-fetched or trivial they might appear. This, moreover, was not simply a feature of his early life when he might have been anxious to augment his income, but continued when he had become a well-established professional man.

For instance, in paying a bill to a whisky supplier in Kilmarnock in 1896, he offered to 'make a speciality out of pushing your whisky on a graduated scale of commission' among his acquaintances. To show how influential they were, he mentioned that he would like to visit the distillery, but only after a trip that he had to make to Rouen 'at the special invitation of the Mayor to meet the President of the French Republic'. Apparently the firm were not impressed, for a few months later he was requesting samples of whisky at reduced rates from Johnny Walker and Sons.[1] He also acted as an insurance agent, not only to insure the buildings he designed, but also for life assurance policies for his clients. The firms with which he was involved included the Royal Exchange Assurance and the Midland Fire Insurance and he complained to the former that although he tried to 'push business your way, other companies offer more favourable commissions'.[2]

Another opportunity that presented itself in the same year arose from the unexpected death in January 1896 of his rival James Hicks, the Redruth architect. Hicks had built up a lucrative local practice through his position as land agent for Lord Clinton, developing an estate of prestigious houses on Clinton's land south of Redruth.[3] In letters to local leading and business acquaintants Trevail, while regretting the loss of his professional colleague, also enquired, 'Who succeeds Hicks as Lord Clinton's agent? When and by whom will it be decided?'[4]

Trevail always took a keen interest in Cornish mining and his correspondence contains many references to its declining fortunes. In 1881 he descended to the bottom of

Dolcoath, the deepest mine in Cornwall and walked seven miles underground. 'It was so hot I had to strip,' he told his sister, and said he would not repeat the visit 'except on business.'[5] Despite his interest in mining, however, he never seemed to speculate in any mining venture, unlike many of his acquaintances. However, in 1896 he became involved in two local industries that were prospering when metal mining was in decline, namely china clay extraction and granite quarrying.

China clay producers had revolutionised the refining and drying of clay slurry, and Trevail spotted an opportunity to apply their processes to imported guano, which was imported in liquid form and widely used as a fertiliser to raise yields in agriculture. Trevail persuaded Parkyn and Peters, clay merchants at Burngullow near St Austell to experiment with slurry from the Native Guano Company of London, in which he had acquired shares and become a Director. He asked the London firm to pay the 'trifling expenses' of shipping 'a couple of hogsheads of sludge' to Cornwall. The Cornish methods, he informed them, would reduce drying costs by 80 per cent.[6]

Unfortunately the clay producers found that guano dried much more easily than china clay and did not need the sophisticated technology they had developed. However, in 1902 he was able to be of service to the guano company, confiding to his sister that 'I succeeded in pulling off an agreement that will be worth many thousands of pounds and lengthening my period of office with £100 per annum for many years to come'.[7] He did not specify what this coup was, but it involved Chichester Corporation.

Yet another outside venture that Trevail bought shares in was the development of Kit Hill quarry on the east side of Bodmin Moor. The area had been mined and quarried for centuries, but after the East Cornwall Mineral Railway opened along the north side of the hill, the quarry developed rapidly to provide stone for major civil engineering projects in Plymouth and elsewhere.[8] Typically, Trevail was brimful of confidence about its future. The granite was 'excellent' with easy access to Devonport, and profits of 20 per cent to 30 per cent a year were predicted. He also forecast that 'the glass business' as he called it, would be lucrative.[9] He expected to become a Director, and tried to persuade acquaintants like Conybeare the politician and Henry Dennis the terracotta manufacturer to join him.[10]

Trevail's banks

As an architect-developer Trevail was closely involved with Cornish bankers, and he did not fail to get a share of the many commissions for bank design that occurred in the 1890s. A flurry of mergers and acquisitions, as well as some failures, had concentrated the banking system in the hands of a few large regional chains, which had a branch in every town and competed with one another to attract customers by erecting imposing buildings in prominent central sites. Trevail designed or produced plans for a dozen Cornish banks and his main clients were the Truro-based Cornish Bank, run by the Quaker Tweedy family,[11] and the Devon and Cornwall Bank, which had its head office in Plymouth. He began work on his first commission for the D and C Bank in 1890 in Truro, where he linked a new structure on the corner of Lemon Street and Boscawen Street to their existing office next door, designed by Henry Rice of Liskeard.[12]

Although Trevail used similar materials of Bath stone and granite, he made no

Top: *Devon & Cornwall Bank, Truro, a large extension to the building on the right.*
Bottom: *Cornish Bank, Helston, only half the height Trevail originally designed.*

attempt to integrate his design with that of his distinguished predecessor, either in style or elevations, giving the impression of two separate buildings although they were internally joined. The upper floor contained six bedrooms, since bank managers were expected to live 'above the shop' in those days with their apparently numerous children. In a contemporary report it was described as 'one of the principal architectural adornments of the city ... the largest as well as the most complete and convenient bank premises in the county.[13]

While work was in progress for the Devon and Cornwall premises in Truro, Trevail was designing a building for the Cornish Bank at St Columb. It was built on the site of a former butcher's shop, coach house and stables, acquired for the bank by Henry Whitford, an important local attorney.[14] As ever optimistic, Trevail's original designs show a classic granite facade of three storeys, with 12 bedrooms, but the bank reduced this to two storeys and seven bedrooms. John Colliver, the builder, signed the plans and he, as we shall see, constructed other Trevail banks, although the Bank originally announced the contractor as Thomas J Smith of St Austell, who built Trevail's extensions to the Red Lion Hotel, Truro.[15]

The building now functions as Lloyds TSB Bank, and further along Fore Street is the Miners' Bank, which was acquired by the Consolidated Bank and later by Barclays Bank. The design for this building has been credited to Trevail by a local guide-writer, but we have found no evidence to support this, and the date of construction, 1873, seems too early for him.[16] At around the same time, Trevail was commissioned to add a storey to the branch of the Devon and Cornwall Bank in Chapel Street, Penzance, to give more space for the Manager, but instead the Bank built new premises in Market Jew Street, designed by James Hicks.

'Ancient lights' at Helston

Meanwhile, Trevail had become involved in one of the most troublesome of his banking projects, the Cornish Bank on an oddly shaped piece of ground opposite the Guildhall in Helston. Unusually, the Corporation invited him to a special meeting to discuss the project, at which the Bank amicably agreed to give up some footage to ease access to the top of the town.[17] Trevail then completed alternative designs for a two, three and four storey structure but two years elapsed before work began on the smallest option.[18] The west side of the building is the most impressive, with a vast pillared banking hall window looking straight down Coinagehall Street, its surprisingly delicate pillars echoing those of the Guildhall.[19]

Unfortunately the bank was 3 feet 6 inches higher than the building it replaced and the owner of the premises opposite objected to a loss of 'ancient lights', although, according to Trevail, only one small window in the basement was affected. Trevail then had to produce detailed plans and elevations, not only for the Bank, but also for the former building and for the complainant's property. The case went to the Chancery Division of the High Court in London, and the Bank had to bear the cost of accommodating expert witnesses for five days before it was settled.

The Judge only awarded £50 to the complainant, but legal costs came to over £900, and the case always rankled with Trevail. Later, when President of the Society of Architects, he referred to it in his presidential address, calling for local courts of appeal to be set up to try such cases. Many expensively prepared schemes, he claimed, 'lay in pigeon holes' because businessmen 'buttoned up their pockets at the smell of a claim', to the detriment of localities, architects and ratepayers.[20]

Trevail's next design for the Cornish Bank was mercifully less problematic. A two-storey structure on the site of a dwelling acquired by the bank in Newquay, it had a drawing room and five bedrooms on the upper floor. Constructed by John Colliver in 1894, it stood opposite the Commercial Hotel, and the building line had to be moved back by order of the local board.[21] Plans also exist for premises for a branch of the Cornish Bank to be included in his design for the Fiddick and Michell building in Camborne, to be discussed later in this chapter. However, it was the Devon and Cornwall Bank that actually occupied these premises when the Camborne building opened in November 1894. The manager's accommodation included seven bedrooms.[22]

The 'Red Bank' at St Austell

A time-consuming project was the design of a large building in St Austell costing over £4,500 for Coode and Shilson, well-known local attorneys and bankers. It contained their legal offices, a banking hall, shops and a committee room for meetings of Cornwall County Council committees.[23] It was dubbed 'the Red Bank' because it was externally clad in unrelieved terracotta, Trevail's first use of that material since his extension to Laninval, the Bodmin home of Henry Dennis, a terracotta manufacturer. Built on an awkward irregular shape, between two roads leading steeply upwards, it had to be set back from the road to ease access to the railway station and the east of the town at the request of the local council. But they still objected when entrance pillars project-

Coode & Shilson banking and solicitors offices in St Austell. Popularly known as the 'Red Bank'.

ed nine inches onto the pavement and Coode-Shilson contested this in a legal dispute that rumbled on for years.[24]

Coode and Shilson were also sticklers for detail, making regular visits to the site and checking on the cost of every item, from cupboards and partitions to mantles and grates and generating numerous telegrams, letters and revised drawings and plans.[25] The site, according to Trevail, was 'very troublesome' and terracotta, unlike Bath or Portland stone, could not be trimmed to size in situ but had to be fitted together like a gigantic, three-dimensional jigsaw puzzle. Coode and Shilson took a particularly keen interest in all contracts with suppliers, including the heavy bill for terracotta from Henry Dennis, and Trevail had to persuade them of Dennis' integrity: as a County Magistrate, Deputy Lieutenant and County Alderman for Denbighshire, Trevail assured them, Dennis was 'not likely to run away or break faith'.[26] Could they perhaps have got wind of the fact that Trevail was receiving a secret commission from Dennis for the use of terracotta, as we discover from the correspondence of his assistant, Cornelius, after Trevail's death?

Trevail worked on the assumption that his building had to impress the public from all angles and so installed gables on all three sides. Although it is mainly viewed from the west, a walk up either of the roads to the north and south reveals equally impressive facades. The west front, especially when lit by the setting sun, adds a splash of colour to the town,[27] but the 'Red Bank' has not pleased everyone. A L Rowse called it 'so grotesque with its minarets and roofscape as to be comic, except that it is beyond a joke'. Despite this criticism from such a well-known son of St Austell, it has been designated as a listed building.

The autocratic management of the Devon and Cornwall Bank

While occupied with the long drawn out Coode-Shilson project, Trevail also engaged in alterations to the St Austell branch of the Devon and Cornwall Bank, comprising new windows and internal renovations.[28] More importantly, he embarked upon another lengthy involvement of four and a half years in the design of a Devon and Cornwall branch at Falmouth.[29] Learning from the extra work required on Coode-Shilson plans when the local council made him move back the building line, Trevail made a prior agreement with the Falmouth authorities to do the same. If he thought his problems were over, however, he was much mistaken, because of the variety and conflicting nature of instructions he received. Despite competition from Cornish builders, the contract went to Ambrose Andrews of Plymouth, who made the lowest tender for £2,783. Andrews then appointed W H Dunstan of Falmouth as Clerk of Works, and N Robins, the Devon and Cornwall manager in Falmouth, also took a keen interest in work in progress. The General Manager A H Pridham, although based in Plymouth, and having many other West Country banks to deal with, kept an eagle eye of every detail, seeking to reduce the cost down to his target of £2,500.

Trevail was caught in the crossfire between these parties. Robins was eager to secure the best furniture and fittings, Pridham was anxious to keep everything that was not in the public gaze to the bare essentials, and disputes arose over tiles in the lavatory and on the floor of the strong room, mahogany dadoes in the manager's office and lettering on the mosaic entrance flooring. The design of gas mantles, grates, railings, and the brass letter box, the curvature of the banking counter, the size of the clerk's desk, the need for hot water and a speaking tube also involved a lot of discussion. Dunstan, for his part, kept Trevail informed of the minutest variations in the work force, reporting in one instance that it contained '4 masons and plasterers, 3 carpenters and 2 labourers, with 2 painters and glaziers and 3 plumbers needed', and noted that 'the stone carver has not been lately'.[30]

Through his interventions, Pridham succeeded in reducing the cost to £2,650, half way towards his target. But despite this the building, according to Peter Laws, late President of the Silvanus Trevail Society, was the most distinguished of Trevail's banks. Trevail then played his part in delaying completion by failing to present the final accounts for well over a year. Andrews, after many applications for payment to Trevail ('I want the money' was how he started one letter) wrote directly to Pridham who was much put out by being pestered by a local builder, but Trevail was too busy with other projects to attend to the matter.

One of these ventures was work on the St Ives branch of the Devon and Cornwall Bank. Its premises there had been converted from a draper's shop by Trevail in 1897 by adding a new granite front, bank vaults and banking hall. Three years later he was involved in internal alterations, and also railings, since the manager complained repeatedly of fishermen outside 'talking and singing until past eleven o'clock' and was afraid they would soon be 'kicking the doors and striking matches etc'. The manager, J Square Paige, was also a man who demanded instant attention: on one occasion he sent a telegram to Trevail at midday demanding to know why he had not received a reply to one despatched earlier that morning.

118

Paige was convinced that Trevail failed to give specific instructions to the local contractor, Thomas Glasson, builder and undertaker of Carbis Bay, but the latter would not move without the most detailed specifications for every task, and refused to carry out operations such as cornices on ceilings or joinery work on the grounds that they were

Top: *Devon & Cornwall Bank, St Ives, from a re-vamped draper's shop in 1894.*
Bottom: *Devon & Cornwall Bank, St Agnes, built 1899.*

'quite new' to him. Trevail, for his part, was often slow in responding and no doubt irritated the diligent Mr Paige by informing him that he was about to make a trip abroad or visit some important acquaintance in London or elsewhere. Pridham, the General Manager, also intervened in his customary fashion, and Trevail, as usual, kept everyone waiting for his final accounts.[31]

Three commissions for the Devon and Cornwall Bank were completed after Trevail's death by his assistant, Cornelius. At Newquay, Trevail designed a large bank for the Devon and Cornwall Bank on the corner of Bank Street and Beachfield Avenue, with manager's accommodation to the rear as well as above. John Colliver was the contractor, having made the lowest tender of £2,495, beating Andrews and W H Lethbridge of Plymouth and others.[32] Another commission for the Devon and Cornwall Bank was premises at St Agnes on the corner next to the Miners Institute. It is not clear from the documents that survive whether this involved the design of a completely new building or the conversion of an older property. Cornelius continued to supervise the completion of work at both St Agnes and Newquay.[33]

In April 1901 Pridham asked Trevail to visit a possible site at Fowey owned by Treffry and occupied by the Fowey China Clay Company to obtain an offer from Treffry for the lease of the site if it was suitable. Delays by the Bank allowed the Cornish Bank to pip them at the post and Trevail then investigated a number of other possibilities including the Globe Inn, The Sailors' Rest, Collingwood's restaurant and a site on Albert Quay, which the Bank agreed upon. By October 1902 Trevail had produced a large number of drawings and the final plans were approved by the council in June 1903 and specifications were written out by Cornelius.

The premises, constructed by Thomas Battershill of Truro, who had worked on other Trevail buildings, consisted of three storeys with seven bedrooms, faced with granite, yellow terracotta and brick, and had a back garden leading to a landing stage on the Fowey river. The site posed problems however. As he confided to his sister, 'dry rot has got into the floors, they will all have to come out at an expense of £60 or so for which I may be held personally accountable'.[34] It opened after Trevail's death and Cornelius was bold enough to disagree with Pridham on a number of issues. Whether this was the reason why he received no further bank commissions is not known.[35]

Some Trevail shops

A glance above the modern fascias of Cornwall's main shopping streets reveals many ornate Victorian and Edwardian frontages, some of the finest of them designed by Silvanus Trevail. While bankers emphasised classical symmetry and order, shopkeepers favoured a flamboyant architectural vocabulary to attract middle class customers for fashionable clothing and household wares. In newly prosperous St Austell, for instance, a guide-writer of 1893 had marvelled at 'the people smartly dressed and altogether unprovincial in appearance, in costumes that rivalled Bond Street or Piccadilly', but contrasted them with the town's gloomy architecture and cramped thoroughfares.[36] A decade later, another guide praised its 'well-tended streets, while all the important shops, lighted with electricity, present a smart and well-to-do appearance'.[37]

Below left: A shop in Fore Street, St Austell, for Henry Hodge, seedsman & nurseryman.
Below right: Burton's premises, Truro, for a china and glass showroom and warehouse.

Some Trevail-designed buildings that contributed to this transformation of St Austell have already been mentioned in Chapter Nine, including the Liberal Club and Hawke's three-storey showroom. Trevail's designs for the neighbouring shop of the seedsman, florist and nurseryman Hodge were considered 'very colourful, with accommodation on three upper floors'.[38] In 1898 the electric works of Veale and Company in Menacuddle Street were extended to provide new workshops, rest rooms, offices and stores. The Veale family were pioneer electrical contractors and Veale became a Director in Trevail's King Arthur's Castle Hotel Company.[39]

Apart from St Austell, Truro was Trevail's most lucrative town for retail commissions. As a Councillor he took an active interest in its commercial affairs, and in 1888 he proposed that hawkers and farmers who, he claimed, paid no tolls but took trade away from rate-paying shopkeepers, should be banned. As always, he was opposed by Buck and Jacobs, this time under the banner of 'Free Trade', but he won the day.[40] Trevail's Truro buildings already described included Samuel Polkinhorne's warehouse in Prince's Street of 1888; the new front to the exchange in Boscawen Street, where a coffee tavern was installed; the Post Office at High Cross; Martin's stores and stabling on Lemon Quay and alterations to Prince's dining rooms, run by a well-known local confectioner and caterer C E Tregonning.[41] All except Polkinhorne's warehouse have been demolished.

Although Trevail's great rival James Hicks rebuilt an old store belonging to Edward Burton, a long established china merchant in St Nicholas Street, it was Trevail who in 1890 designed premises for Burton in King Street facing the Cathedral. Although the frontage was only 24 feet, it extended 115 feet to the west to the waterway called The Leats. At some stage, Trevail also altered a building for Burton at High Cross, next to the old Assembly Rooms, known as Burton's Furnishing Warehouse. For a fellow Town Councillor, Arthur Laverton, Trevail drew up plans for attractive red brick premises in River Street. Designed as for a wine and spirit merchant, Nankivell, the frontage gave no idea that it went back 130 feet to The Leats, where railed, hand-pushed trucks took casks into storage from the roadside delivery carts.[42]

Trevail's retail developments in other towns in Cornwall included a post office and shops in Honey Street, Bodmin in 1884, discussed in Chapter Four,[43] and another post office and two shops for J T Perry in 1903 at Bude. This post office was on the corner of Villa Road and Court Lane (now Strand). The land rises sharply in Villa Road, and the design compensated for this by raising the rear half of the building, with internal steps to reach the back part.[44] The shops lay at an angle to the Globe Hotel, designed by Trevail for Walter Hicks, to be described in Chapter Fourteen. Two larger commissions in Camborne were those for Fiddick and Michell, mentioned earlier in this chapter, and for the Vivian Brothers. Fiddick and Michell's shop and offices, a three-storey building on a curved site in Commercial Street, included the premises of the Devon and Cornwall Bank already referred to. Built in granite and polyphant, the upper floors were in red brick with Bath Stone trimmings, with a Dutch gable over the centre of the three large bay windows.[45]

One of Trevail's finest designs was that for the Vivian Brothers'.[46] Carefully worked out plans enabled the drapery business to continue running on part of the site while the

*Vivian Brothers
store, Camborne,
an architect's
drawing 1897
(Family papers).*

new, large and elaborate building was erected. Vivian's then moved into the finished part of the new building so the old one could be knocked down, making room for the second stage. All this was not accomplished, however, without a good deal of acrimonious correspondence. John Vivian JP and James Francis Vivian, commission merchants of Dunedin House, London, who conducted a large business in Johannesburg and South Africa with Cornish miners who worked there, were used to replies by return of post. When Trevail, as was his wont, did not respond, they bombarded him with telegrams and letters: 'Life is short, may come to an end before plans arrive' was one, 'what is in the wind – are you ill?' was another.

To complicate matters, they were afraid of an 'ancient lights' case because of the height of the building. They had purchased the adjoining premises to the west to avoid litigation, but were concerned that the owner of the property to the north might make a claim. As in the case of the Helston bank, Trevail had to prepare detailed plans and elevations of all the buildings involved. The Vivians constantly complained of the loss of sales because of the building work, and were equally determined to limit the construction cost, including the architect's fee, to £2,750, even if it meant using cheaper materials than terracotta. In the end John Colliver the contractor received £3,029 and Trevail's fees would have added another £150, and Colliver complained bitterly that the work had cost him considerably more. There followed the by now customary lengthy delay caused by Trevail's dilatoriness in completing the certificate necessary for Colliver to receive his final payment, together with the inevitable ill feelings generated between builder and clients, who were not at fault. In the end, however, everybody seemed satisfied except for the unfortunate Colliver, and Trevail prepared a drawing of the new stores, which the Vivians were proud to display on their letter headings.[47]

Trevail's last major retail commission was a large building of three floors for the Public Benefit Boot Company, a chain store otherwise called Lennard's, on a promi-

Top: *Public Benefit Boot & Shoe Company, King Street, Truro (CRO: AD396/580).* Bottom: *Blackford's premises, Truro, where the roof was lifted to make an extra storey in 1903.*

nent site on the corner of Boscawen Street and King Street, Truro.[48] Thomas J Lennard was not a man to be trifled with and when Truro Council asked him to set back his shop by 12 feet he instructed Trevail 'not to sell an inch'. When the Council made what they called 'a liberal offer' of £380, Lennard demanded not a penny less than £600 and threatened to go to arbitration. Trevail advised him that the Council were 'stupid enough to suppose they can act with impunity' and that it would do them good to be taken down a peg or two. The first year of the new century was taken up by this dispute, after which work proceeded, although delayed by Trevail's absences in Paris and Bristol. The builder was W E Blake of Plymouth, whose tender was £2,287 for Bath stone or £2,257 for terracotta. Trevail chose terracotta and Lennard was always on the look out to cut down on items like bars to windows and parapets.[49]

Just before his death Trevail drew up plans for Oscar Blackford's, the printers who were using the 'Great House' in Prince's Street. These premises had once been the home of some of Cornwall's most illustrious citizens including the Husseys, Sir Francis Bassett and Henry Sewell Stokes, the Cornish poet and county administrator. Trevail had the roof lifted by building on top of the existing parapet walls and inserted skylights, altering the second floor layout from five small rooms to one large compositor's room. The project was largely overseen by Cornelius and completed in 1904.[50] Plans have also been found for a factory for N Gill and Sons, leading Truro traders, to accommodate cabinet makers, polishers and upholsterers, next to the City Hall. Other plans exist for premises for Anthony A Buckingham, but no building has been identified. Finally, two Truro shops often erroneously attributed to Trevail must be mentioned. Firstly, a small but picturesque mock-medieval shop on the corner of Boscawen Street and Cathedral Lane was the work of Trevail's former assistant and successor Cornelius in 1904. The white tiles had to be used to avoid an 'ancient lights' dispute, and it is now a listed building. Secondly, the flamboyant red brick and terracotta West End Stores on a corner site in Prince's Street with its great semi-circular upper-storey windows on both sides, was enlarged and partly rebuilt by Cornelius in 1908.[51]

This outline of Silvanus Trevail's business interests underlines – if any emphasis is needed – his incredible energy, the diversity of his architectural skills and his passion for pursuing commercial opportunities, no matter how small. His designs for banks, warehouses and shops have not perhaps received the recognition they deserve. This is partly because some of the best of them – for instance the imposing stores designed for the Vivian Brothers in Camborne – have been demolished, and partly because of their cramped position in streets of nondescript buildings. The 'Red Bank' of Coode & Shilson in St Austell is an exception: it cannot fail to catch the eye, although not all residents were pleased to see it. On the other hand few if any passers-by in the main street of Falmouth give a second glance to a bank which Peter Laws, late President of the Silvanus Trevail Society, called Trevail's finest banking design. In the following chapters we discuss the buildings upon which Trevail's architectural reputation mainly rests: the libraries, technical schools and hotels that stand alone in prominent positions in town centres or dominate the cliff tops of Cornwall.

Thirteen
Passmore Edwards and
Silvanus Trevail

One of Trevail's most prestigious as well as financially rewarding clients was the Cornish philanthropist, John Passmore Edwards. Born into a modest family at Blackwater, between Redruth and Truro, Passmore Edwards worked as office boy in Truro and journalist in Manchester before making a fortune as a publisher in London, devoting his wealth to the provision of over sixty hospitals, children's homes, working-men's institutes, public libraries and technical and art schools, a third of them in Cornwall. Trevail was his most favoured designer in Cornwall, second only to the London architect M B Adams in England as a whole.

Trevail's first commission was the Institute at Hayle, commemorating the benefac-

Hayle Institute opened by John Passmore Edwards in 1896.

tor's father. An ambitious design costing £3,000, the original plans included a reading room, library, lecture hall, classroom and laboratory for technical education as well as a sailors' rest room, recreation room, gymnasium and skittle alley. It was built by John Symons and Sons, who came from Passmore Edwards' own village, and a public holiday was declared to celebrate the laying of the foundation stone in September 1893. The site consisted of reclaimed land filled with industrial waste from Harvey's, one of Cornwall's leading engineering firms, and solid concrete foundations were needed to support the heavy stone exterior with its granite dressings, intended to give an effect of 'boldness and solidity'. Although work was completed in just over a year the Institute was not officially opened by Mrs Passmore Edwards until April 1896, when the occasion was marked by processions, a military band and a public luncheon.[1]

Public libraries, technical and art schools

Trevail's subsequent work for Passmore Edwards apart from one hospital, consisted of public libraries usually also containing technical education and art classrooms. Although a series of parliamentary acts from the mid 1800s had empowered local authorities to levy rates to finance Free Libraries, progress had been slow in Cornwall, as indeed in many other areas. One reason for this was that local councillors who built the libraries were often the principal ratepayers who footed the bill. In 1885 Trevail started the ball rolling in Truro by heading a subscription list (with £20) to finance a library and after a good deal of opposition, one was opened the following year in the existing public rooms. Penzance was not far behind commissioning a design for a new library building from Hemmen and Timmins of Birmingham.[2]

Most towns in Britain waited for a philanthropist like the Scottish-born industrial magnate Carnegie to provide the funds for a library, and Cornwall was fortunate to benefit from Passmore Edwards' offer of £2,000 to any town that built one. As a shrewd businessman, however, he tested local enthusiasm by restricting his gift to the building alone. This meant that local residents had to pay for building land, which could cost upwards of £500, together with several hundred pounds' worth of furniture, fittings and books, as well as meeting maintenance and staffing costs once the library was in operation. Five Cornish towns – Penzance, Falmouth, Camborne, Redruth and Truro – were doubly fortunate when another Cornish exile, Octavius Ferris, for many years headmaster of a large school in Manchester, left £10,000 to be divided between them to help finance libraries.[3]

Penzance had already begun construction as we have seen, and the other towns got off to a quick start. At Falmouth the Borough Surveyor W H Tresidder designed a library, technical and art schools, while James Hicks drew up plans for a library in Redruth, and Trevail was commissioned to design one in Camborne. The wealthy landowner G C Basset offered the lease of a site in Camborne at a low rent and Trevail's design appeared in Passmore Edwards' publication *The Building News* in April 1894, the contractors being Symons and Sons. On an awkward corner site, Trevail designed an asymmetrical structure with a square tower, Tudor mullioned windows and high pitched Dutch gables. In May 1895 Passmore Edwards officially opened the building in one of his periodical grand tours. Although the ceremony passed off well with mutual

Camborne Free Library, for John Passmore Edwards, opened in 1895.

congratulations between architect, benefactor and councillors, relationships later became strained when as one of their economy measures, the Council cut Trevail's commission. Instead of receiving £105 he had to settle for £70 so as not to offend Passmore Edwards who had become involved in the dispute, and who did not like to be troubled with petty squabbling.[4]

During this visit Passmore Edwards also laid the foundation stone for a Free Library at Truro. The Council had purchased a site from J D Enys, an important landowner, at a reduced price of £725 and it was hardly a surprise when Passmore Edwards informed them that Trevail was his preferred architect as he had been a prime mover in the creation of the original public library. Trevail acted as president of the Cornwall Library Committee from 1894 handing over to Enys in 1896.[5]

At the foundation stone ceremony Passmore Edwards praised Trevail in the glowing terms that were discussed in Chapter Eleven, but some of his fellow councillors were more critical including John James and of course, the perennial enemy Henry Buck. They enquired why Trevail had received a commission of £100, that is to say 5 per cent on a building of £2,000, when the construction contract was only for £1,717. Trevail who was then Chairman of the Council, threatened to have Buck ejected for 'brawling' and was technically in the right, since the final costs including gas heating exceeded £2,000. Indeed rumours spread that the total expenditure was over £3,000 and although this was an exaggeration, Trevail had difficulties keeping within the Passmore Edwards and Ferris bequest allowances and advised his mentor on such matters, the Plymouth librarian H K Wright, that he could 'hardly see where the money is to come from'.[6]

Despite these problems the library, built by M Clemens and T Battershill, was officially opened on the 30 April 1896, a year after the laying of the foundation stone. Described as an 'artistic and pleasing emanation from the brain of Mr Silvanus Trevail, FRIBA', reports of the ceremony also referred to other Trevail designs nearby such as the Post Office and Burton's shop which 'added importance to the locality'. Criticism of Trevail's spending continued but he was able to produce accounts that revealed that he had kept within his expenditure limits and even paid for items normally charged to the council. These included the foundation stone, the memorial stone and brass tablet, erection of platforms for the ceremonies and a silver key presented to Passmore Edwards, as well as for repairs to adjoining buildings, Trevail having maintained that it was customary for councils to pay for such items.[7] The niggardly amount of £200 was all that the Council allocated for books and a bazaar was held to raise more money, at which Sir Edwin Durning-Lawrence, MP for Truro, spoke of 495 English public libraries with their four million books. Cornwall's institutions never came anywhere near this average of 8,000 books.[8]

Municipal parsimony

Camborne and Truro were far from being the only councils that exercised extreme economy, for the dying years of the nineteenth century were not a propitious time for financing large municipal projects. Many Cornish towns were struggling to make ends meet because the continued collapse of the once prosperous mining industry deprived them of potential benefactors. The Passmore Edwards Library at Liskeard for example designed and built by Symons and Sons, was only allocated £70 a year for running costs and paid the miserly salary of £14 per annum to their part-time librarian.[9] Ironically St Austell, one of the towns that could have afforded a library because of the wealth generated by the rapidly growing china clay industry, did not take advantage of Passmore Edwards' generosity. Unfortunately, while urban ratepayers supported the idea of a library, in the rural districts where the mineral wealth lay, hardly a voice was heard in favour. Later some of them changed their minds and Trevail informed Passmore Edwards they 'deeply regretted being behind other parts of Cornwall' and were willing to provide a site for a library if Passmore Edwards would repeat his offer: but he did not.[10]

St Ives: a commission that got away

St Ives provided a rare instance of a library project that Trevail lost to another architect. James Hicks of Redruth was the Council's first choice and he visited several proposed sites in July, but did not approve of them, before accepting a location in the Market Place in August. No progress seemed to be made, however, and at the end of November the council received a 'suggestion' from Passmore Edwards himself that Trevail should submit plans 'in competition with Mr Hicks, the best set of plans to be accepted'. In December the Council secured another, apparently more suitable, site but a few days later, on Christmas Day, the Mayor received a letter from Passmore Edwards requesting that Symons and Sons of Blackwater should get out plans.[11]

An unexpected turn of events then occurred. Hicks, a comparatively young man, died suddenly in early January 1896 and Trevail, apparently not knowing of the intervention of Symons, may well have thought that the commission was his, but heard nothing from the Council. Correspondence of January shows him appealing for help from two influential councillors and past mayors, Edward Hain and Captain Harry, for whom he had designed substantial residences, as we saw in Chapter Ten.[12] Trevail reminded Harry that he had designed 'the best Board School in Cornwall' (the Stennack school) for them at St Ives and that Sir Charles Reed, former St Ives MP and Chairman of the London School Board, had praised it 'as good as any in the whole of London'. Trevail also told Harry that he 'expected something definite' from Hain on the matter, but we have found no Trevail plans, nor any sign of a council meeting where Trevail's name was mentioned. In the end the library was designed and built by Symons and opened in 1897. The site finally chosen had been donated by T B Bolitho the banker, landowner, and local MP, and Trevail later advised Passmore Edwards, when considering locations for a library at Launceston, 'not to make the blunder of choosing the wrong site' as at St Ives, which 'only had eleven feet of frontage'.

Building problems at Bodmin

Bodmin Free Library with Science and Art Schools, for John Passmore Edwards, opened in 1897.

An example of Trevail's intervention in the choice of an architect occurred at Bodmin. After the councillors secured a site at a nominal cost of £100 from Lord Robartes of Lanhydrock, they were about to select an architect when Passmore Edwards informed them that Trevail was his choice, a decision they felt obliged to accept but not without ill-feeling. As leaders of Cornwall's county town they wanted a library to rival Truro's, and Trevail obliged with one in what he describes as 'Gothic style with Dutch Renaissance features ... a bold gable and corner window, giving a very picturesque and

quaint effect'. Although he economised by using stone from Robartes' quarry obtained 'on exceptionally favourable terms', he assured the Council that the window dressings and mullions of Bath stone would be 'the admiration of everybody'. The upper floor would be maintained by the County Council as accommodation for technical and art classes so as to be 'no burden on the rates'.[13]

During his visit to Cornwall in October 1895 to open his libraries at Camborne and Redruth, Passmore Edwards had expected to lay the foundation stone at Bodmin, but the councillors were still arguing about sites and so this ceremony was not performed until April 1896, when Trevail marred the occasion by attacking a political opponent Leonard H Courtney, MP for Bodmin: 'He looks after number one, Passmore Edwards looks after those who cannot look after themselves'.[14] However when Courtney was principal speaker at the opening of the library in May 1897 Trevail steered clear of politics.

As often happened Trevail identified local historical figures to whom Passmore Edwards could pay tribute in his speeches, and whose descendants might be persuaded to contribute to the costs. On this occasion he mentioned, among others, Sir William Molesworth of Pencarrow, Secretary of State for the Colonies in 1855.[15] Disaster struck later though when the Bath stone mullions far from being the 'admiration of all', began to collapse. An ill-tempered correspondence dragged on for years about responsibility for repairing the stone between Trevail and Samson Trehane the builder, the Bath Stone Company, the Borough Surveyor E J Oliver (who also acted as Clerk of Works) and the Town Clerk Edyvean. In the end Edyvean won the case.[16]

Delays at Launceston

Trevail got off to another uneasy start at Launceston, where Passmore Edwards seemed to leave it to him to inform the local Council that he was to be the architect. Trevail passed the news on to an acquaintance, John Kittow, auctioneer and surveyor, agent for the influential Coode and Carlyon families and prominent Launceston councillor. If he expected Kittow to inform the rest of the Council, he was disappointed, for Kittow replied that there was 'sure to be heartburnings among councillors' and advised Trevail to take the unusual step of announcing his appointment as architect by a notice in the local newspaper. Having done this Trevail received a stream of offers of sites. After considering locations at Northgate and James Corner, the Council following a stormy public meeting, agreed on one at Westgate only for the owner to withdraw his offer.[17]

The search continued with site meetings at an old sheep market, the property of a local landowner L C P Wise; some adjoining shacks known as 'Noah's Ark Cottages', suggested by Kittow and a property in Castle Street, favoured by the incoming Mayor William Proktor and the Town Clerk Claude Hurst Peter. Another location costing £500, was recommended by the retiring Mayor, T P Trood, and belonged to Councillor Thomas B Hender who, in turn, offered some other less expensive properties.

Each new site involved extra work for Trevail: surveys, sketch plans and meetings with councillors who pointed out minor discrepancies in his plans, since the building committee comprised a group of self-appointed experts who cut costs by cancelling such features as a bell turret and extending technical and art classrooms at the expense of the library space. They also tried to use building money for other purposes, and Trevail had to send them a curt telegram ordering them not to buy furniture with the 'building gift'. His patience, never strong, was at breaking point and he informed the Mayor that he was turning down lucrative commissions because of the time spent on dealing with their alterations. The mayor's reply was cool: 'I very much regret our library difficulties are such a strain on your intellect. I only hope it will not be permanently injured'.[18] Passmore Edwards was drawn into the dispute. Noting that 'it is now more than three years since I proposed to provide a library building for your town', he warned that he would withdraw his offer if the council did not guarantee to raise £500 for books and equipment.[19]

This seemed to do the trick. A site at Northgate was chosen, building commenced and the Council eventually raised £1,000. The contractor, William Burt, was soon complaining to Trevail that Kittow, Proktor and other councillors were inspecting his

progress on a daily basis and correcting what they claimed were errors in his work. Then Burt fell ill leaving his inexperienced son in charge who refused to proceed without instructions from Trevail on every detail. Trevail, however, was not available since he had embarked on one of his lengthy health cures.[20]

Construction costs exhausted the £2,000 allocated and Trevail had also promised to ask for a further £350 from Passmore Edwards for a chemistry laboratory which the latter refused. At last in April 1900, five years after the library project was first discussed, it was completed with the help of substantial contributions from the descendants of the locally born Professor J C Adams to whom the building was dedicated. For months afterwards the builder and his wife wrote a series of plaintive letters to Trevail, complaining that the venture had cost him both his health and his savings. But although Burt had been of great help to Trevail in keeping him informed of local affairs, he never received a reply.[21]

The Central Technical Schools for Cornwall

The Passmore Edwards library that Trevail had designed for Truro differed in one important respect from the others that we have described: it did not incorporate rooms for technical or art classes. The City's Councillors, encouraged by Trevail, believed as Truro was the seat of Cornwall's Cathedral and county council, it should possess a building that would make it a centre for scientific education. In October 1895, seven months before Truro's library was officially opened, Trevail had secured a promise from Passmore Edwards for £5,000 for this purpose, but had asked the donor to 'keep dark' about the magnitude of the sum since as we shall see, it was not nearly enough to satisfy Trevail's ambitions.[22]

Trevail set about gathering financial support in London from a number of Guilds, the Local Government Board and the Department of Education, as well as from Cornwall County Council, Truro Council and as many private donors as he could find. Already in October 1896 he was able to inform Passmore Edwards that he had been favourably received by the Secretary of the Drapers Guild which had recently granted £10,000 for technical instruction in South Wales and given the People's Palace to Londoners. He also approached the Guilds of Goldsmiths, Ironmongers and Fishmongers. Two months later his illness was reported, 'caused by four very cold all-night railway journeys to secure a gift of £500 from the Honourable Drapers Company'. Truro Council passed a resolution of thanks for his 'continuing exertions' and the *Royal Cornwall Gazette* praised him as 'a guarantee of energy and work'.

Yet as always he met with opposition from some Truro councillors, with the old enemy Henry Buck to the fore. Buck, while noting that Trevail would 'make a bit out of it', doubted whether any other Truro ratepayers would benefit. Robert Dobell, the Town Clerk, who was familiar with Trevail's financial methods, pressed for more detailed accounts. Trevail nevertheless persuaded the Council to borrow £530 from the Public Loan Board to buy more land from Enys that Trevail valued at £1,100. He then received a setback on finding that a grant scheme of the Department of Education had been discontinued. He solved this dilemma however with the aid of the Truro MP Durning-Lawrence and the St Ives MP T B Bolitho. Together they managed to obtain £1,000 on the pretext that Truro council had gone ahead with the project, unaware that the grant scheme was coming to an end because they had been misled by a schools inspector from London.

A centre for agricultural education

To administer his project Trevail set up an executive committee, with himself as Chairman and a handpicked group of what he called, in a letter to Passmore Edwards, 'the best people'. They would, he asserted, provide 'the key to success' which was shown when he met leading members of the County Council Technical Instruction Committee. Having already co-opted them onto his own executive committee he had no difficulty in persuading them to give £600 to the Truro schools fund. Once more though, he asked them to keep this amount a secret while he went after some more 'handsome promises'. One avenue he explored was investment in agricultural education. For decades Cornwall's farming leaders while agreeing on the need for an agricultural college, had always disagreed on its location. R G Rows, powerful Chairman of the County Council Technical Instruction Committee was suspected of accumulating government funding to build a centre in the west, which led to 'battles royal' with wealthy landowners and influential county councillors in the east including Tremayne, Digby Collins and John Dingle of Callington.[23]

Trevail cleverly resolved this impasse to his own advantage by setting up the Truro schools as a centre for agricultural training among other subjects. He secured grants for farming-related equipment and for scholarships for farm students awarded by the county. He also appointed an agricultural scientist Dr James Clark, as Principal of the schools at a salary of £300 a year, and Clark acted as peripatetic lecturer on farming subjects, paid for by the county. Rows was reluctant to build up agricultural education in Truro, but the east Cornwall councillors supported Truro's claims since they stopped him from accumulating capital to set up his own fully-fledged farm college. In addition Trevail benefited from a donation of £200 from J C Williams, and Digby Collins also made contributions to the Truro schools fund.

Trevail faces his critics

Trevail, moreover, achieved all this while he was conducting a running battle with his opponents on both Truro Council and the County Council. E Lawrence Carlyon, perpetual thorn in his side on Truro Council, argued that Trevail's executive committee rarely met, that it was packed with his cronies, that Trevail was 'riding roughshod' over all opposition and acting as his own paymaster, approving expenditure which increased his own commission as architect. When the Truro Mayor, J Rogers, tactfully suggested that Trevail might co-opt Carlyon to his committee to see for himself that all was above board, Trevail replied that such a move would lead to his instant resignation. This would have brought the whole project to a standstill, since Trevail alone understood the complex state of the finances.[24]

One of Trevail's fiercest critics on the County Council was E W Rashleigh, Chairman of the important General Purposes Committee. In addition to issues raised by Carlyon and others on Truro Council, Rashleigh asserted that Trevail had never been properly elected as Treasurer as well as Chairman of his own executive committee, that the committee was not entitled to offer training paid for by the county, and that the County Council itself was at fault in not auditing Trevail's accounts.[25] An enquiry was conducted into these allegations by the Chairman of the County Council but, ironically, Trevail could no longer defend himself as a County Councillor because he had resigned in order to avoid a very similar problem of overlapping responsibility. As Chairman of the Public Health Committee, he would have been dealing with projects that would increase his own income as newly appointed architect to the county asylum. He was, however, loyally supported by former colleagues on the Technical

Central Technical Schools for Cornwall in Truro, showing carving of Cornish trades.

Instruction Committee, and apart from deciding to audit his accounts the enquiry cleared Trevail on all other counts.

As some compensation for these traumas, Trevail's designs for the Truro Technical Schools had been selected for an exhibition of 'the most prominent Architects' Drawings' at the Royal Academy, a month after the laying of the foundation stone in May 1897.[26] Because of legal errors by Truro Council and inaccurate estimates by the builder John Colliver, construction of Truro Technical Schools was delayed for months. Councillor Blenkinsop, honorary secretary of Trevail's executive committee was soon complaining to Trevail of sleepless nights caused by the latter's cavalier attitude to money matters. The always-optimistic Trevail tended to treat vague promises of financial support as cash in the bank, assuring Blenkinsop that he had amassed £16,200, thus, apparently, more than trebling Passmore Edwards' original gift for the project. In any case Trevail maintained 'Number One', that is, Passmore Edwards, would always foot the bill in the end.

Constructed of Plymouth limestone with Bath stone dressings in what Trevail called his Tudor Renaissance style, the building included organic chemistry, botany and physics laboratories, a metal workshop, a school of art and a museum. The very title engraved in stone on its facade, Central Technical Schools for Cornwall, upset Truronians and non-Truronians alike. Some Truro ratepayers feared it would be a perpetual burden, a white elephant, too big for Cornwall let alone Truro. Councillors from the rest of Cornwall resented county funds being channelled into Truro. When the schools opened in October 1899 however, the Chairman of the County Council, the Earl of Mount Edgcumbe, called them 'the keystone of John Passmore Edwards' work' in Cornwall and thanked the many donors, but without mentioning Trevail, without whom the money would not have been raised. Soon, though, Trevail was able to announce with pride that over 500 science and a similar number of art students had enrolled 'all without the ratepayers of Truro having to put their hands in their pockets for a single sixpence'. The *West Briton* commented, 'For this state of affairs, too much praise cannot be accorded to Mr Trevail, who laboured noon and night'.[27]

In a personal letter of congratulation R G Rows called him 'a distinguished man of Cornwall'. In view of all he had gone through to achieve this, we can perhaps excuse Trevail's crowing over his detractors, 'a small number of small men', as he called them, who had fought so hard to thwart his construction of the greatest educational complex that Cornwall had seen. Rows must have had mixed feelings about the success of the agricultural classes, however, since they effectively halted all attempts to set up a separate farming centre. As far away as Launceston, where attendance at technical classes was extremely poor, the sole exception was the agricultural course of Dr Clark, the principal, with an enrolment of 42 students, a record for Cornwall.[28]

The Bowring Library, Moretonhampstead

Trevail's reputation as a designer of libraries and technical and art schools led to a similar commission from another public benefactor at Moretonhampstead in Devon. The library was a gift to the town from Thomas (later Sir Thomas) Benjamin Bowring, whose family had developed the wool trade there and who ran a shipping company

Top: *Bowring Library, Moretonhampstead, Devon, a gift from Thomas Bowring in 1901.*
Bottom: *Moretonhampstead, Devon, Nurses Home endowed by George Wills in memory of his wife, Lucy.*

with agencies in Newfoundland, San Diego and New York. Bowring was an acquaintance of two of Trevail's clients, Sir Robert Harvey and John Parkes of Dublin (the latter to be discussed in Chapter Fifteen). Like those businessmen he was a stickler for detail, bombarding Trevail with letters, cards and telegrams, on one occasion five in the same day, demanding 'prompt attention' and the utmost economy.[29] The library again in the 'Tudor Renaissance' style, was built by Harry Goss at a tender of £2,510 and decorated with yellow terracotta from Ruabon. The first floor contained art and science classrooms, and on the ground floor the library space was reduced to make way for a billiard and recreation room at the request of the Town Council. Bowring also reduced the book provision from 4,000 to 2,000 although by 1906 it contained only 1,400 volumes.[30]

Progress was held up by the reluctance of a lady to sell an 'old shanty' she owned which allowed a more regular shape for the site. Further delays occurred because Bowring seemed to spend as much time abroad on business trips and cures at spas as Trevail himself, but the library was completed early in 1903 three years after planning began.[31] Drawings by Cornelius dated December 1903 exist for an extension apparently not built. Trevail seldom let a design in a new locality go by without picking up further commissions, and on this occasion he secured one from a local resident of Moretonhampstead, George Wills, for a home for nurses given to the town in memory of his wife Lucy. Trevail produced plans for a double-fronted house, consisting of a parlour, kitchen and scullery with three bedrooms on the first floor. The plans were approved in May 1903, but it was left to Cornelius, his assistant, to continue work after his death five months later. Cornelius had to deal with what he considered 'unreasonable objections' from J Sampson, who owned a shop and bakehouse next door, and who complained, *inter alia*, that gables were overhanging the pavement. It was completed in March 1905.[32]

The Plashet Grove library in London

The next commissions that Silvanus Trevail carried out for John Passmore Edwards were a library and a hospital in East Ham, London. In 1898 he designed a library on the recreation ground of Plashet Grove in East Ham, the foundation stone of which was laid in November by T McKinnon, Chairman of London County Council, on behalf of the donor. Another of Trevail's Tudor Renaissance style buildings, it was faced in Ruabon red brick with Bath stone dressings. The front archway was supported by two columns of Plymouth marble surmounted by a magnificent four-dialled clock, presented by T L Knight, Chairman of East Ham District Council, its Cambridge chimes given by W H Savage, the former district engineer and surveyor, who also acted as Clerk of Works. The contractor, James W Jerram, was an experienced builder although he had difficulties caused by the late delivery of Bath stone and poor quality wood for the rafters. Trevail was on one of his health cures in the autumn of 1898 and was seriously ill the following February but the library was opened in September 1899 by the Right Honourable Herbert Gladstone MP.[33]

In the same month that the library opened the District Council launched an appeal for funds to build a hospital.[34] The population of East Ham had risen from 1,700 in 1851 to over 80,000 and a hospital was needed according to the Council, to cope with the 'sadly frequent accidents' among the 'toilers with limited wages' who made up the bulk of the residents. Passmore Edwards offered £4,000 towards the building if the committee could find a suitable site.[35] W H Savage the former Surveyor, was a member of the appeals committee and had earlier drawn up plans for a hospital, which were possibly not suitable for the new site at Shrewsbury House. Savage generously sent his own plans to Trevail, advising him to keep construction costs within Passmore Edwards' budget, but not to let the latter know because they did not wish to 'appear half-hearted'.

Trevail apparently took his advice, because at Christmas 1899 he sent out a four page greetings card with a general view of his design for 'The Great Cornish Philanthropist's Latest Gift to London: Passmore Edwards Hospital, East Ham'. A ground plan by Trevail was also featured and on the back was an illustration of Passmore Edwards' 'last gift to Cornwall', the Central Technical Schools for Cornwall at Truro. Although the East Ham building was small with only 20 beds, Passmore Edwards did not want it called a 'Cottage Hospital' like the one designed for him by James Hicks in 1895 at Liskeard. Lady Tweedmouth laid the foundation stone in July 1900, and Jerram was again chosen as

John Passmore Edwards East Ham Public Library, now used by the Superintendent Registrar.

the builder with Savage acting as Clerk of Works. Construction proceeded without any important difficulties apart from problems with heating equipment, but the cost of the building rose from the original contract for £5,140 to £6,158.[36]

The Newton Abbot Library and Technical Schools

Towards the end of the year 1901 Silvanus Trevail embarked upon his final commission for Passmore Edwards, a library at Newton Abbot. The donor had originally thought of giving a hospital to the town in memory of his mother who was born there, but on meeting Councillor Parker of Newton Abbot at a Masonic dinner in London, he was persuaded to present a library instead. This gift inspired Devon County Council to build adjoining science, art and technical schools also designed by Trevail, on an important corner site. The foundation stones for both buildings were laid on the same day in October 1902; that for the library by Passmore Edwards himself, and for the schools by the Earl of Morley, Chairman of Devon County Council and a prominent local landowner. The contractors for the entire project were Harry Goss, followed by Francis Watts and extra foundations had to be laid because the site was in an old river bed.

The buildings were again in Tudor Renaissance style, of grey limestone with yellow Ruabon terracotta mouldings. Plans exist for an L-shaped, three-storey building but the rear wing was omitted and Trevail was asked to send his drawings to G Bedford, the art master of the School of Art at Torquay to see if he could suggest improvements. Passmore Edwards gave £2,500 for the library and the final contract price, which was

Newton Abbot Public Library designed by Trevail, together with the adjoining Technical and Art Schools.

supervised after Trevail's death by Cornelius, came to £2,800 including a lift. The library contained the unusually high number for the West Country, of 6,000 books including 1,000 donated by the Great Western Railway from its own Institute and another substantial gift from a local mill owner. The County Council paid £2,700 for the schools, augmented by public subscriptions of £1,200, and the buildings were opened in September 1904 by the Lord Lieutenant of Devon, Viscount Ebrington.[37]

The Passmore Edwards legacy

It seems likely that in the absence of the generosity of John Passmore Edwards, and in some places that of Octavius Ferris, the Victorian libraries and technical and art schools that add a touch of architectural distinction to so many Cornish towns would not have been built. They are lasting tributes to the ideals of a great Cornishman and one of the most celebrated of Victorian Britons, portrayed by the painter George Frederick Watts in his Hall of Fame alongside poets such as Tennyson and Browning and artists like Millais and Rosetti.[38] Yet sadly Passmore Edwards finished his adventures in library construction in Cornwall disillusioned by the way in which so many local councillors looked a gift horse in the mouth.

He did not mind councils using his buildings to house technical and art classes, in fact in his speeches he often spoke of the need to prevent Cornwall from lagging behind in these subjects. Indeed, he seemed to be in agreement with Trevail's opinion, expressed in a letter to him, that technical instruction was a better use of space than 'novel reading or gossip'.[39] He did object most strongly to the frequent misuse of them for other purposes. For example, in opening Camborne Library he had boldly proclaimed that books were just as necessary to the residents as 'the pavements on which they walked and the gas that lighted the streets'.[40]

Yet to cut costs Camborne Council closed the newsroom. Liskeard council let the ground floor of their library to the post office and also as we have seen, paid only a miserly sum to a part-time librarian. At Bodmin they relied on gifts of books because they spent all their funds on Queen Victoria's Jubilee celebrations, and initially opened only one classroom because they had not attempted to form art classes. When St Ives Library was opened, Alderman Jenkyn asserted that it would attract those 'who resort to street corners and even worse places', but Councillor Faull feared that 'it would not be attended like it ought' although 'all would come right in the end'. His initial prophecy was fulfilled when municipal officers used one part, with band practice in another, and the library confined to just two rooms. 'Did Mr Passmore Edwards give this building to the town,' asked one resident, so that 'the residents should derive only such a meagre benefit.' The endless delays and disputes caused by Launceston councillors, together with news of the misuse of his buildings by other councils, dismayed Passmore Edwards. 'Had I known a few years since what I know now,' he wrote to the mayor of Launceston, 'I would have spent less on Cornwall and more in London.'[41] The Mayor sent a copy of this letter to Trevail who made some of these complaints known to the press,[42] and Launceston was the last Cornish town to benefit from the generosity of John Passmore Edwards.

Fourteen
Seaside problems and Newquay riots

Towards the end of his mayoral year in 1895 Silvanus had been contemplating his most ambitious tourist project to date; the King Arthur's Castle Hotel at Tintagel on land belonging to Lord Wharncliffe. It would be, he assured the Earl, 'of incalculable benefit' in raising the rentable value of the surrounding estate, just as the Atlantic Hotel had increased the value of Treffry's land at Newquay. However, when Trevail laid his proposal before the Board of Directors of his Cornish Hotels Company they turned it down. William Trethewey, the original Chairman, had died and John Jose who succeeded him was in poor health, and refused even to visit the proposed site. Then he too died. Another of the Directors, Major John Mead, a prominent Penryn businessman, took over, and proved to be even more risk-averse than his predecessors.[1]

An undercover operation
Trevail decided to go it alone, but in great secrecy, for he was convinced that the 'Cornish Hotels Squad' as he called the Board, would acquire land at Tintagel to prevent him from having access to a water supply. He also feared that the Falmouth Hotel Company, headed by J C Daubuz, the Truro banker and smelter, would buy up the small Wellington Hotel at Boscastle and expand it into a rival. It was no easy matter to keep his dealings dark since he had to negotiate with Wharncliffe's agents, persuade the farmer tenant to relinquish the site, secure water from a local source and engage solicitors and bankers (Bolitho and Company). In these matters he was lucky in having the help of his mentor George Hicks who agreed to become Chairman of a new hotel company, and he found another powerful backer in Robert Harvey. Both men had made their fortunes in the complex and sometimes treacherous business world of Latin America, and perhaps enjoyed the clandestine nature of this enterprise.[2]

Not surprisingly the 'Atlantic Turks', another of his descriptions for the Cornish Hotels Board, got wind of his operation and summoned him to a board meeting to explain his actions. Still needing time to complete his arrangements, Trevail employed a Machiavellian ruse to hoodwink them. He tendered his resignation and apologies for not attending the meeting in a letter that he addressed to the Secretary of the Board. He

was technically correct in that all letters on board matters were addressed to the secretary, but since he still occupied that post himself the letter remained unopened. When the Chairman wrote to ask why he had not attended the meeting, Trevail feigned surprise and sent a copy of his original letter, but this time addressed to the Chairman. By now he had completed his transactions, but he later had a good deal of trouble getting the outstanding salary and expenses due to him from the Cornish Hotels Board.[3]

The new hotel Trevail announced, would equal the Atlantic Hotel in size with 61 bedrooms, but surpass it in the splendour of its facilities. It was to have lifts and electric light in all rooms (which the Atlantic Hotel lacked) as well as running fresh water and hot and cold sea water baths. In his publicity Trevail exploited the historical appeal of the site to the full. It would, he claimed, stand on the very spot where Tennyson had composed his Arthurian odes while looking down on the supposedly royal palace below. Adorned with medieval tapestries, stained glass windows and archaic interior plasterwork, it would have a gigantic Round Table with place names for Queen Guinevere, Sir Mordred, Sir Lancelot and the other Knights. The guests would be summoned to dinner by a 'trumpet, instead of a common dinner gong'.

Less lavish though was the stark battlemented exterior. Trevail was anxious to keep expenses down. The site itself had only cost half that of the Atlantic hotel at Newquay and he advised his assistant Cook to cut out the circular windows if necessary in order to keep the building budget within £11,000. 'With stone on the site and "slapdash" cement face walls we shall build cheaply,' Trevail told him.[4] The expense of paying for water from the mains supply would be avoided by using local sources for drinking water, with seawater for baths and lavatories.[5]

King Arthur's Castle Hotel, Tintagel, opened in 1899.

Some early environmental protests

It would hardly have come as a shock to Trevail when the public announcement of his plan caused an uproar among the literati and intelligentsia of Cornwall, led by Arthur (later Sir Arthur) Quiller-Couch, together with the best-selling novelist Joseph Hocking and the maritime historian and guide-writer Arthur Norway. These early environmentalists were beginning to rebel against what they called the 'monster' hotels, 'barrack-like' boarding houses and 'jerry-built' villas that were springing up around the coast. The idea of a large hotel 'grinning down in derision', as one of them put it, on the noble ruins below incensed them still further.[6] In one of their first acquisitions, the National Trust purchased Barras Head nearby to stop further development. Trevail was untroubled by this since it also stopped rival hotels being built and he publicly announced his own contribution to the Trust. (It was actually paid for by his new hotel company). Lord Wharncliffe on the other hand was far from amused. He sent Trevail a cutting from a journal, *The Atheneum*, that alleged that the hotel would ruin the environment, and commented, 'I am sure that your scheme is universally reprobated and I wish with all my heart that it could be abandoned.'[7]

Trevail seemed to revel in this notoriety: 'Some people must have something to grumble about,' he told John Thomas, one of his major prospective shareholders.[8] He assured all doubters that shareholders were rushing forward to invest in the £15,000 in shares and £5,000 in debentures that he offered, even announcing that he was oversubscribed. In fact, his records contain lists of potential subscribers with important names crossed out.[9] He also admitted privately to Hicks that profits were unlikely to reach Atlantic Hotel levels 'for some years to come'. As the date of the share launch approached, he became uncharacteristically apprehensive and advertised repeatedly in the press. Hicks and Harvey allayed his fears by doubling their contribution to £1,000 and £5,000 respectively, with Harvey also offering to buy up unsold shares. In the end applications rolled in and Trevail was able to announce with satisfaction that some applications would have to be returned as the share issue was over-subscribed. Among his loyal supporters were Lord Robartes (a leading shareholder of the Atlantic Hotel) with £2,000, and Francis Layland Barratt, T B Bolitho and J E Veale the St Austell electrical contractor with £1,000 each.[10]

In the spring of 1897 Trevail invited tenders for the construction of the hotel, Arthur Carkeek was chosen and King Arthur's Castle Hotel opened with a celebratory luncheon in June 1899, chaired by George Hicks. Following a post boy's complaint that after taking travellers to the hotel, he had to find accommodation for their horses in other hotels in the village, a carriage house and stabling were built a short distance away. To provide power for the hotel an engine was at first placed inside, but it proved too noisy and not big enough, so an engine house with caretaker's accommodation was added on a slope below the hotel in December 1899.[11]

The Headland Hotel, Newquay

While Trevail was advertising for contractors to build his hotel at Tintagel, he was also seeking tenders for another hotel in Newquay which was to cause even more controversy. He made no bones about the fact that it was a deliberate attempt to beat the

Atlantic Hotel by erecting 'the largest hotel in the west ... twice the size of the Atlantic, in a better position and better appointed'. His 'better position' was in full view of the Atlantic's directors and guests, and it was to stand five storeys high, be 300 feet long and lavishly decorated with red Ruabon terracotta columns and pediments. Like the King Arthur's Castle Hotel it would boast an electric lift and electric light in all rooms. 'Without such facilities,' Trevail announced, 'no modern hotel worth its salt was complete,' knowing full well that the Atlantic possessed neither. The cost was estimated originally at £25,000 including £4,000's worth of terracotta, but rose towards £50,000 as he installed luxurious furnishings from Heal's of London, expensive carpets, costly kitchen equipment, a tennis court and a croquet lawn.[12]

To finance the venture Trevail formed the Headland Hotel Company with himself as Chairman. Since it was in direct competition with the Atlantic Hotel in which many of his usual subscribers were already heavily involved, he probably found it necessary to look elsewhere for funds. He confided to Hicks that Layland Barratt would only put in £250 plus a similar amount from his mother. Two of his new Directors were City of London acquaintances with business addresses near his own, Harman Mackenzie and Martin Fradd from Sherborne Lane, and the Secretary was William E Pearce of Tokenhouse Buildings, the same location as that of Preston, for whom Trevail designed a house in Newquay to be discussed later in this chapter. Others were Bernard Strauss, mining speculator and prospective parliamentary candidate for the mining division of Cornwall, and C A V Conybeare, whose earlier victory in that constituency, aided by Trevail, was described in Chapter Five. The Great Western Railway took up £2,000 in debentures.

Trevail was worried that the Atlantic Hotel's Directors would do their utmost to thwart his plans for the Headland Hotel and he, in return, showed no loyalty to them, as indicated when a fire broke out on their premises. Although no longer directly connected with them, he still acted as their agent for the Royal Exchange Assurance Company and he informed the insurers that the fire had been entirely due to the 'carelessness and incompetence' of one of the directors, Charles R Gatley, who had struck a match to illuminate the source of a gas leak in a dark place. As a result their compensation was greatly reduced.[13]

The 'Newquay riots'

Unfortunately, although he had broken his link with the Atlantic Hotel, Trevail was still associated with them in the public's mind, and became the scapegoat for the series of events that led to the 'Newquay riots', which were in fact triggered off by the Atlantic management without his knowledge. In 1897 they walled in part of the Headland round their hotel, and a crowd, claiming that this deprived them of their customary rights to dry their fishing nets or graze their animals, pulled down the wall, sang Rule Britannia and God Save the Queen, and then dispersed. In the Newquay Regatta of that year the Atlantic Company was pilloried as 'The Cornish Land-Grabbing Company'[14] and Major John Mead, the Chairman, probably had enough trouble on his hands already because he had married into the Harvey family, the famous Cornish engineers, who were losing money hand over fist. He had to sail to South Africa in the

Headland Hotel, Newquay, completed in 1900 by contractor Arthur Carkeek.

summer of 1897 to sort out their operations there, and for whatever reason, he made no further attempts to enclose the land surrounding the hotel.

However, when a notice, coloured in 'flaming red', appeared a little further along the headland to the west, announcing the erection of a new hotel, it was indeed like a red rag to a bull. Flushed by their victory over the Atlantic management, a crowd ripped up the new hotel foundations as soon as they were laid, threw the workers' tools and shed over the cliff and when Trevail stormed down from Truro to inspect the damage, pelted him with rotten apples and stones, bruising his back and striking him on the ear.

The irony was that Trevail, unlike the Atlantic Hotel directors, was perfectly within his rights in developing his part of the headland. Taking the ringleader to court he proved that he had 'not taken an inch of unenclosed land' and that his company held a 999-year lease from Treffry. Trevail knew that he had the law on his side and visited Newquay again to identify the culprits. He got the magistrate Gully Bennet to sign 55 summonses to the 'savages', as he called them in a letter to his sister Laura. 'I expect it will mean the treadmill for some of them,' he added, 'as one of the policemen guarding me was rather badly injured in the arm ... I am getting letters from all over the county congratulating me on the stand I made against the blackguards from Lord Mount Edgcumbe downwards.'[15] The magistrates charged 22 rioters with malicious damage and eleven with assault and condemned them all for a 'wicked and wanton attack on a pioneer of the Cornish hotel movement who has been of immense benefit to Newquay'. Meanwhile, two of the Atlantic Hotel directors had been up in the Bude, Tintagel and Boscastle area looking for a site for a hotel that would compete with Trevail's. They did not go ahead and build one, perhaps wisely, as we shall see later.[16]

Delaying tactics by Newquay council

The 'Newquay riots' are one of the best-known episodes of Trevail's life, described in detail in books and radio and television programmes. Yet it was not the riots that seriously held back Trevail's plans but the delaying tactics of the District Council, chaired by the wealthy Michael Williams, High Sheriff, County Councillor for Newquay, Chairman of Newquay Mercantile Association and Director of the North Cornwall Railway. After wasting a good deal of time and public money disputing Trevail's use of public or private land, the council had to back down. 'It would be difficult', commented the editor of the *St Austell Star*, 'to find a person in Newquay who would attempt to justify this treatment'. For apart from raising numerous objections about drainage and rights of way, one of the councillors, J Cardell Oliver, had alleged that Trevail had made a killing by acquiring a lease from Treffry and selling it at an inflated price to the new company he had formed. Oliver had to write what the *St Austell Star* called a 'most abject withdrawal' of these false accusations to Layland Barratt, who had loyally sprung to Trevail's defence. Nevertheless the rumours persisted, forcing Trevail to hold a meeting of directors to refute the allegations.[17]

In the face of these obstacles Trevail was in a militant mood as his letter to his contractor showed. Addressed to 'Major-General Carkeek, RE' from 'Field Marshal Silvanus Trevail', it detailed train times and rations to be issued for the '3rd Division of the 5th Army' to be assembled on Newquay Station from Helston, Hayle, Truro and Tintagel (he did not seem to trust local labour) to await the 'personal orders of the Commander in Chief' before marching through the town to the Headland Hotel site like colonial conquerors entering a rebellious tribal stronghold. Addressing the crowd attracted by this spectacle, he warned them that any further opposition would not stop his project, but merely prevent the employment of local men.[18]

What really rankled with Trevail though, was what he saw as double dealing by some prominent Newquay men to hold up the construction of his hotel while forging ahead with the erection of one of their own. This was the Victoria Hotel, erected by John Ennor, a District Councillor, on land belonging to the important Liskeard contractor Thomas Lang and designed by another Liskeard man John Sanson, architect of the Porthminster Hotel at St Ives. The Chairman of the Victoria Hotel Company was none other than the all-important Michael Williams, although he claimed that he was only following the advice of other councillors, including the Company's Secretary Councillor G C Bullmore, who had played a leading part in delaying progress on the Headland Hotel.[19]

With fifty bedrooms and costing £30,000, (compared with the Headland's £50,000) the Victoria was less luxurious than the Headland, but with a direct lift down to the beach it was a formidable competitor. Although work on it started after Trevail had begun the Headland, because of the delays caused by the Council it opened ahead of Trevail's hotel, which was not completed until July 1900. To add to Trevail's annoyance the Victoria Hotel advertised itself in the *ABC Railway Guide* as the biggest in Newquay, when, as he pointed out to the editor, the Headland was 'double the size' (as indeed was the Atlantic).[20] He was even more irritated when Newquay Council, having held him up because of their supposed concern to protect open spaces for local residents, did nothing to improve access to the surrounding cliffs: 'Not a penny spent on the roads, footpaths, fences or lighting,' he complained, and quoted in a letter to the press a visitor staying with him who described Newquay's roads with their 'ruts and cobbles' as no better than those of a Yorkshire village.[21]

Some uncompleted hotel commissions

Despite the erection of two large hotels, the final years of the nineteenth century were a time of disappointment for Trevail as a tourist developer. Ambitious schemes for seaside estates were largely unsuccessful, as we shall see, and three hotel projects that did not materialise were for the Isles of Scilly, Guernsey and Exeter. At St Mary's on the Isles of Scilly, the daughters of the late Captain and Mrs Frank Tregarthen were running a small hotel, and in 1895 Trevail was involved in plans to remove some private dwellings nearby in order to build a larger establishment. T Dorien-Smith of Tresco, leaseholder of the Duchy of Cornwall, and his Penzance solicitor, A G Jenkin, were interested in the project and Trevail persuaded the Great Western Railway (GWR) to take up £1,000 in debentures, but the GWR only agreed if the hotel cost at least £7,000 plus £5,000 for furnishings. Although this was quite small fry for Trevail, even so he was doubtful if it would pay. 'Will this be too ambitious?' he asked Jenkin, who was to be the Company Secretary. Jenkin was slow to respond, Dorien-Smith grew impatient and threatened to consider 'other applicants' and the venture petered out.[22]

In May 1899 Trevail told his sister of a visit to Guernsey, where he was entertained in great style with a government yacht placed at his disposal by his 'good friend H Austin Lee CB, Chief of the British Embassy in Paris'. Poor Trevail, usually a good

Centre portion of the Grand Hotel, Guernsey, never built (CRO: AD396/654).

sailor, was seasick all day while steaming from island to island with 'rocks and breakers enough to turn a fellow inside out'. The purpose of the visit appeared to be a hotel project, for Trevail papers contain plans dated 1898 for a 'Grand Hotel' at St Peter Port on Guernsey, to be financed by a company with £60,000 in shares, mostly subscribed by Guernsey bankers and a Director of the London and South West Railway Company that was linked to the island. The building was to cost £44,000, plus £8,000 for land and was to be designed by 'a well known architect'. Trevail told his sister that his host wanted him to join him in 'a big thing there, but I have not the money as I tell him, so shall be obliged to forget it'.[23]

Designs by Trevail also exist for a large half-timbered building, to be called 'The Great Western Hotel' on what he described as 'a commanding site more convenient to travellers than the Rougemont Hotel', near Exeter railway station. To be fronted by 'some acres of ornamental ground' it would have stood where the present Great Western Hotel is situated. Unusually in Trevail's ventures the Great Western Railway Company itself did not appear to be involved in its finance, and the principal investor seemed to be Walter H Harris of Tunbridge Wells, Chairman of Harrington Hotel Co Ltd, ex-Sheriff of London and proprietor of the Red Lion Hotel at Henley on Thames. The project did not go ahead,[24] and a 'W Harris' was one of the investors that Harvey had promised to find for the King Arthur's Castle Hotel, but who failed to subscribe.[25] If this was the same Harris, he possibly backed out again.

Two other Trevail hotel designs were actually constructed, not for one of his own companies but for Walter Hicks, owner of Cornwall's second largest chain of hotels and public houses (after the Redruth Brewery Company), who came from Trevail's own village of Luxulyan. Both hotels were modest in size; the Ship and Castle at St Mawes cost £2,900, plus £800 for land and £750 for furniture from Maples of London, while the Globe Hotel at Bude cost under £3,500. Work started in October 1899 on the Ship and Castle, a symmetrical three-storey building with a twin-gabled frontage and heavy stone facing. Delays in the arrival of stained glass windows, railings and stairs held up completion until the end of 1901.[26] Erection of the Globe began in early 1903 as a three-storey building with a large gable and stucco walls, with Ruabon terracotta dressings on the front and part of one side. Again progress was delayed, this time by the need to rebuild adjoining walls and by damaged terracotta finials. Cornelius took over supervision after Trevail's death and the hotel did not open until 1905.[27]

Other coastal developments

Amid all these controversies Trevail had not been idle in pursuing other plans for tourist properties, although only with limited success. In 1896 he had produced outline drawings for an estate on the heights above his Carbis Bay Hotel for William Backwell Tyringham, comprising about 50 detached or semi-detached villas and a terrace of nine houses. Only one road (later called Headland Road) with a group of one large and two smaller three-storey dwellings was actually built.[28] In the same year he also planned a terrace of four three-storey houses with half-timbered gables at Fistral Road, (now Headland Road), Newquay, for personal investment. This resulted in another quarrel with Newquay council on the laying of drains although as he remarked, they had not

Top: *Ship &
Castle Hotel, St
Mawes, opened
about 1900 by
Walter Hicks of St
Austell Brewery.*
Bottom: *Globe
Hotel, Bude, for
Walter Hicks of St
Austell Brewery.*

Fistral Terrace, Newquay, a personal investment for Trevail in 1896. (Family papers).

objected when John Ennor constructed houses nearby. Trevail also had to allay the fears of one prospective customer, M L Macleod of Newquay, about hooliganism by local youths.[29]

At Polzeath five miles from Port Isaac on the north coast, Trevail produced a large coloured plan in 1896 for Lord Robartes' property at Pentireglaze, for 56 semi-detached villas and nine terraced houses set in pleasure grounds facing the sea along projected roads entitled 'Esplanade Drive' and 'King Arthur's Drive'.[30] This was another scheme that did not leave the drawing board, nor did one for Lord Wharncliffe at Trebarwith with sites for 15 detached and 16 semi-detached residences north of the track leading down to Trebarwith Strand. A complication here was that two of the plots would be expected to share the extra cost of £160 for a projected new bridge across a river at Trebarwith Strand.[31]

The north coast schemes were triggered off by hopes that the long-awaited railway along the north coast towards Padstow was finally on its way. In September 1897 the landowner Charles Prideaux-Brune of Prideaux Place was anxious to offer building plots on the west side of the line for the hoards of newcomers who, according to some enthusiastic promoters, would be flocking there to buy a house. On the 30 September his agent William Coode wrote to Trevail asking him to lay out an estate, but that if Trevail was too busy he would apply to someone else. Trevail swiftly agreed but a fortnight later had not come to Padstow as promised and Prideaux-Brune was 'getting uneasy about the delay', especially as sewers had to be laid under the track of the railway line.[32]

Top: *On board the 'Norse King', Trevail, centre, leaning on the railings (Family papers).*
Bottom: *Trevone Bay Hotel, not enough backers were found to finance the project (CRO: AD396/614).*

Two weeks later Trevail stayed with the landowner, and on thanking him for the hospitality offered in his 'delightful ancestral home', enclosed 'photochromes' of North Devon, North Wales, Switzerland, Northern Italy and Venice. Noting that the Honourable Mrs Prideaux-Brune was 'fond of scrap-collecting' he offered to send her his 'Norwegian Collection' of his 1897 trip as soon as it returned from loan elsewhere. He possessed, he informed Prideaux-Brune, 'upwards of 30 volumes of photos and scraps' of places he had visited, and a 'standing arrangement' to see every new coloured photo and take his pick. Prideaux-Brune wrote in December to say that he was pleased with the Norwegian Collection and also with the layout of the estate, but found the railway company 'very difficult to move' about getting sewers under the line.

After the arrival of the railway the population of Padstow, which had been in decline, grew rapidly but Trevail's planned estate was yet another that did not get off the drawing board.[33] About the same time Trevail produced a plan, possibly for Prideaux-Brune's own use, showing a proposed extension of the North Cornwall Railway, indicating other land in the parishes of Padstow and St Breward also owned by Prideaux-Brune, and marking the names of those occupying the land.[34] Another large project that came to nothing as far as Trevail was concerned was a complex of 125 detached villas and a three-storeyed, half-timbered gabled hotel on the coast at Trevone, west of Padstow, planned for three landowners Robson, Tredwen and Bartlett.[35]

Newquay was becoming a popular watering place for the well-to-do and Layland Barratt who had homes in London, Devon and Cornwall, asked Trevail to find him a house for three months near the sea in Newquay. Trevail offered Quay House but Barratt said it was too small. He wanted at least ten bedrooms plus one for a manservant, together with stabling and sleeping accommodation for two men outside.[36] A Newquay property almost of this size that later became a hotel, was Bon Air designed by Trevail in 1900 for Edward Oxenford Preston, a trader with half a dozen branches from Swansea and Bristol to Edinburgh. As mentioned before his headquarters were at 4 Tokenhouse Buildings in London, the same address as some of the Headland Hotel directors and it seems likely that it was through this link that Trevail gained his commission. As Trevail had already found in his work for captains of industry, they were hard taskmasters, and extensive correspondence records Preston's many amendments and reductions in details of bells, lights, window sashes, fanlights and paint colours. Although referred to in Trevail's correspondence with his builder as 'Preston's Bungalow' it was in fact an attractive two-storey, seven bedroomed house with half-timbered gables and a wrap-around balcony in colonial style with fine stained glass windows in the central hall.[37]

At Truro, although not on the coast, considered itself a tourist resort accessible to passenger ships, Trevail added rooms to the Royal Hotel. During his mayoral year Trevail had engaged in one of his frequent arguments with his enemy Councillor Buck, on repairs to the pavement outside the hotel[38] and sets of alternative plans exist for extra accommodation in 1898, including a billiard room and two floors of bedrooms. However, only some of the bedrooms were built, above two shops to the right of the main doorway.

WEST ELEVATION

*Bon Air,
Newquay, now
demolished
(CRO:
AD396/528).*

The tourist bubble bursts

The final year of the nineteenth century and the opening year of the twentieth witnessed a boom in construction of the hotels, villas and terraced boarding-houses that still dominate stretches of the Cornish coastline to the present day. Hotel accounts of the period suggest that promoters aimed at net profits of at least 10 per cent a year to cover a dividend of 5 per cent on ordinary shares but, as Trevail wrote to a supplier of furniture at the end of 1901, 'the past two seasons have been disappointing in the hotel world owing to the [Boer] War, increases in taxation and withdrawal of dividends'.[39]

In Cornwall, this reduction in demand coincided with a glut in the supply of accommodation and as a result few hoteliers met their financial targets. The Falmouth Hotel Group reported a net profit of only 5 per cent per annum, after expenditure of £10,000 on an extension.[40] The Fowey Hotel, also greatly increased in size, noted a decline in occupancy although it maintained a 5 per cent dividend.[41] The Coverack Headland actually made losses, and did not go ahead with its planned extension.[42] The Victoria Hotel at Newquay only paid a dividend of 4 per cent.[43]

Trevail was in no way exempt from these problems, indeed he fared worse than some of his competitors, having spent more lavishly than most of them on luxurious furnishings and fittings. Although the Headland got off to a promising start, with a net profit of 8 per cent in its first six months of trading, it slumped to only 2 per cent for the first full year while costs mounted. Bertini, the London hotelier and one of the Directors, had installed an expensive cooking range which had to be replaced. The manageress threatened to leave unless her salary was raised to £100 a year and Trevail exhausted his slender reserve fund to meet her claim. Carkeek the contractor, after waiting 18 months for his final payment of £1,500, threatened to take legal action and one of the Directors dipped into his own pocket to pay him £500 on account. When three years later in 1903, Carkeek had still not received the balance, he took the Company to arbitration.[44]

Matters were even worse at the King Arthur's Castle Hotel. Its costly modern cooking range proved to be a disaster and had to be replaced at a cost of £500, and since the reserves were exhausted a Director purchased £500 of preference shares to pay for it. Veale of St Austell resigned as Director in 1901 after undisclosed problems with Headley the Manager, and Trevail persuaded Harvey to take his place on the board.[45] As we saw in Chapter Twelve, Veale's electrical firm had earlier gone into liquidation. Trevail had always enjoyed easy relations with Harvey, and stayed with him in his Devon home. When the promised profits turned into losses, Trevail soon encountered a different side to Harvey, now Sir Robert and High Sheriff of Devon, who showed that he had not made a vast fortune by putting up with failure.

In the final months of Trevail's life the annual profits of the Carbis Bay Hotel increased in 1902 by 16 per cent and those of the Headland by 83 per cent.[46] He was trying to boost occupancy by appealing to the 'commoner people at smaller rates'.[47] This was to no avail for King Arthur's Castle Hotel and at an Extraordinary General Meeting of the Company in June 1903, the Hotel Company went into liquidation and later sold at Exeter to the Padstow developer Nicholls for £13,505,[48] perhaps a quarter of what had been spent on it. Silvanus Trevail's career as hotel developer that had begun in a blaze of glory a dozen years earlier with the overnight success of the Atlantic Hotel, seemed to have ended in failure.

Fifteen
Public and private health problems

After spending the best part of a decade, as a Truro Councillor and Mayor, attacking what the *West Briton* called 'The Great Sewerage Question',[1] Trevail had little to show for his efforts. Whenever he tried to press ahead with a solution councillors always objected to making a 'rushed decision', following the time-honoured tactics of appointing sub-committees and sending delegates to inspect other schemes. In 1895 they held a competition, adjudicated by a London expert Baldwin Latham, among sanitary engineers all over Britain to devise a scheme. When Trevail moved to adopt the prize-winning plans of the London-based Santo Crimp, costing an estimated £10,000 (but £70,000 with flood water drains) he came once more up against a brick wall. Councillor Roberts claimed another scheme, costing a third of this amount would suffice. Councillor Rogers outdid Roberts advocating one for under £1,000. Councillor Hearn quoted a supposedly old adage: 'Never do today in the matter of drainage what you can put off until tomorrow.'[2]

Trevail's old enemy Henry Buck had introduced another delaying tactic, by persuading the Council to wait for the results of a new septic tank system that was being tried out at Exeter. When Trevail said he had visited Exeter and was not impressed, Councillor Dorrington went there and returned to announce amid great cheers from the Council, that adopting the Exeter scheme would save thousands. Trevail dismissed Dorrington's and Hearn's opinions as 'worthless' since they knew nothing about such matters. As always Trevail had made himself the master of the subject, corresponding regularly with Baldwin Latham and Santo Crimp and lecturing the councillors at length on the fine details of alternative systems. His repeated warnings of the dangers of disease infuriated Buck who accused him of 'gloating over typhoid'. Truro's real problem, Buck maintained, was not the state of its health which was 'in every way satisfactory', but the gloomy predictions of Trevail himself. Their troubles would only end, Buck argued, when Trevail 'vanished from the scene – which God provide for very soon'. And so the dispute went on with the Council pursuing yet another chimera, a bacterial treatment by 'coke breeze'.[3]

The county 'Health Crusade' continues

Meanwhile, as Chairman of the County Council Sanitary Comm-ittee, Trevail maintained his harsh criticisms of other Councils' lack of progress in providing the drainage systems that we discussed in Chapter Eight. Launceston Urban and Rural District Councils, St Columb and West Penwith were still, like Truro Urban and Rural District Councils, refusing to send him detailed reports

To the Electors of the Eastern Ward
OF THE CITY OF TRURO

LADIES AND GENTLEMEN,
If it be your pleasure to re-elect me to a seat on the Council, I shall be willing to exert myself in the interest of this city in the future as I have always done in the past.
Yours obediently,
SILVANUS TREVAIL.

Truro, 26th October, 1898.

Your Vote and Interest is desired on behalf of MR. TREVAIL at the Election to be held at the TOWN HALL, on **Tuesday, 1st November, 1898,** between the hours of 8 a.m. and 8 p.m.
The ballot paper may be marked as below:

TREVAIL..
Silvanus Trevail, Lemon Street, Truro, Architect. X

Printed & Published by Lake & Lake, Ltd., Truro.

1898 Election card. Trevail realised he had to make some effort to get elected (Family papers).

of infectious diseases. In speeches in Launceston and Liskeard and outside Cornwall (for example at a meeting of the Midland Cornish Association), he once more rammed home the allegation that towns that advertised themselves as health resorts but spent not a penny on their sanitary systems were asking for trouble. Again, in his address for re-election to the County Council he argued that if Cornwall could make people feel that they could come without fear of infection, this would be one of the best invest-ments that the County Council could make.[4] Yet his untiring efforts met with little recognition although rare messages of support came from Dr Adams of Bodmin asy-lum and from a Cornish doctor practising in England, W Dale James who wrote, 'no one in Cornwall can appreciate the value of Mr Trevail's Health Crusade'.[5]

Silvanus Trevail might have carried on his work as County Councillor and Chairman of the Sanitary Committee for years to come, had he not been forced to make a difficult choice. An opportunity arose to become the official architect for the county asylum at Bodmin, which was planning large-scale extensions involving over the forthcoming years a budget 'upwards of £100,000'.[6] Here was a chance to design on a scale greater even than his libraries or hotels, and of course earn a good deal of money.[7] The question was, would he be allowed to continue as a leading member of the County Council who ran the asylum and be their employee as well?

He outlined his dilemma to County Councillor John W Dingle of Callington and to Lt Col Tremayne, Chairman of the Asylum Committee, as well as to an official of the Local Government Board in London who had to approve his appointment. Never one for false modesty, he explained that he was the best man for both jobs. As FRIBA and Vice President of the Society of Architects he had an unrivalled knowledge of Cornish contractors, building practices and materials. As Chairman of the Sanitary Committee, 'for five years I have practically done the work of the County Sanitary and Medical Officer by full and general supervision of the Sanitary Administration of the County'. However, although the County Council was willing for him to continue the dual roles, and Trevail assured Tremayne that the Local Government Board were 'straining every nerve' to allow him to remain a councillor, in the end the board decided that he had to choose between the two posts. He pondered long over the question of where his duty to Cornwall lay; his decision was to take the position of architect.[8]

His resignation from the County Council came as a shock to many of his admirers and detractors for a variety of reasons. Some Truronians, like Buck, were no doubt afraid that it would mean that he would spend even more time in Truro Council lambasting his colleagues on sanitary matters. They were right, for Trevail soon threatened to take the Council to court as a private citizen if they did not get on with their schemes. After re-election to Truro Council in 1898 he continued to condemn, at great length and in considerable detail every scheme they proposed as inadequate and unworkable.[9]

Others regretted the absence of his forceful interventions at the county level. 'Despite his little peculiarities,' commented the *Royal Cornwall Gazette*, 'no one did more for the County ... now he's no longer there to keep Medical Officers of Health up to their duty, what will happen?'[10] Meanwhile, the disastrous consequences of the inaction of some councils were soon evident. For years F R Ray, editor of the *St Austell Star* and a Liberal County Councillor, had supported Trevail's strictures on the poor state of the water supply in mid-Cornwall, and in particularly the 'deplorable state of health' in St Columb rural district which had 'stubbornly declined to adopt the Infectious Diseases (Notification) Act, and treated the County Council and its Chairman with little short of contempt'. Now, Councillor Ray contended, they were paying the price – a fatal outbreak of typhoid at Wadebridge that threatened to spread throughout the rural district. 'If ever the Sanitary Committee ... and especially their late energetic Chairman, Mr Silvanus Trevail, needed any indication of the value of their persistent and praiseworthy efforts to improve the health of the County', Ray concluded, 'this was it.'[11]

The asylum building programme
Silvanus Trevail produced, in minute detail, plans of the many areas of the buildings for the asylum, as the hundreds of surviving blue prints and drawings testify. Every one of them had to meet the exacting and sometimes fickle requirements of the Cornwall County Council Visiting Committee, and then be scrutinised and approved by the Lunacy Commissioners and the Secretary of State in London. Not all of this time-consuming work was fruitful. He laid plans for farm buildings for £3,000 and a bailiff's residence for £1,000, but after 15 alterations were made by the Visiting Committe, and a further delay of six months occurred when yet more amendments were made, these projects were dropped.[12]

Despite these problems Trevail was delighted to receive the congratulations of the Asylum Committee when his plans for the main project were accepted by the Lunacy Commissioners without referring them to their own architect, apparently 'a most unique experience'.[13] Later that year the district auditor disallowed 12 items of expenditure and surcharged the trustees personally for making these payments without authorisation from the Secretary of State. Trevail was kept waiting for six months for an enquiry to be held into this matter, and then a date was chosen that coincided with a meeting of the Society of Architects over which he presided.

In 1901 tenders were invited for extensions and additions 'comprising separate detached blocks for sick and infirm, recent and acute, chronic, epileptic and other classifications of patients, together with assistant medical officer's residence, waiting rooms, recreation and dining-hall, kitchens, offices, staff quarters, workshops, stores,

Top: *The Assistant Medical Officer's entrance at the Cornwall Lunatic Asylum. The wording 'Lunatic Asylum' has been removed from round the Dutch gable.* Bottom: *Artisans' workshops at the Cornwall Lunatic Asylum.*

boiler house etc according to drawings, specifications etc prepared by Mr Silvanus Trevail, FRIBA, architect of Truro and Palace Chambers Westminster'.[14] The lowest tender received was from Pethick Bros of Plymouth for £87,973 and this was accepted. Trevail was pleased, because he had estimated the budget at £105,000 which worked out at £220 per bed, whereas a similar hospital in Croydon had cost £320 a bed. Nevertheless, Colonel Tremayne, Chairman of the Building Committee, still thought the cost was excessive. For this work, Trevail was to receive a commission of £2,000, according to the editor of the *West Briton*.[15]

Trevail produced some distinguished designs for the 250–bed asylum complex, later known as the Foster Building. Built of Plymouth limestone with rich red terracotta decorations, its composition contained subtleties, such as different architraves and varying the spacing between windows so as to avoid monotony.[16] The first stage was completed in July 1901 and the full programme was due to be finished 'within about three years'. When Trevail died two and a half years later only some £30,000 of his estimate of £100,000 had actually been spent[17] and his successor Cornelius did not reap the full benefit of the vast amount of work already undertaken, for the scheme was handed over to the London architect John Kirkland. Cornelius complained that he spent a good deal of time on asylum matters after Trevail's death 'all out of pocket'.[18]

Other architectural commissions

In the final years of his life Trevail was also busy with many other commissions in addition to those for Bodmin asylum and the libraries, banks, shops, hotels and seaside residences described in earlier chapters. One project was for James Muir at Tregenna House in Michaelstowe, a substantial granite, ashlar and local stone mansion north of Bodmin. Trevail drew up alternative designs for a new porch entrance at what had been the rear of the property, which actually faced the road, with an archway into the old hall.[19]

Another small-scale project of 1896 was a two-storey aisled conservatory for John R Daniel of Polstrong, Camborne.[20] In May of that year he designed a new conservatory at North Hill, St Austell, for J E Veale the electrical contractor whose workshops he later designed. The extension had elaborate and intricate glazing bars forming arched windows on two sides and the front elevations and a roof with a glass lantern ventilator.[21] Also in 1896 he received one of his few commissions in the Penzance area, Poltair Terrace for A C Jenkin, a local solicitor. Eight houses were built at right angles to Madron Road, Heamoor, each with a bay window to the principle bedroom and the main room on the ground floor below, a better class of dwelling than Moorland Road, St Austell, with granite surrounds to doors and windows rather than red brick. Later in

Poltair Terrace at Heamoor, a terrace of eight houses built in 1896.

the same year he created a new facade to Ashleigh, St Columb, for Miss Martyn, moving the front wall forward about five feet and adding bay windows to the ground and first floors. The old walls thought to be of cob were lost when the new wall was built, the sidewalls possibly faced with random rubble to match the extended wall.

Also in 1896 he added a classroom and cloakroom to Chacewater Board School,[22] mentioned in Chapter Two, built by Moyle and Mitchell at an estimated cost of about £450; Trevail was asked to install 'unclimbable' iron railings around the school.[23] In the following year the work already referred to in Chapter Nine at Witherdon, Beaworthy, Devon was carried out for Hugh Carlyon, who had changed his name to Spry.[24] The building work was carried out by William Burt of Launceston at a cost of £2,500 and a

Top: *Ashleigh, St Columb, a new facade and extended front rooms in 1896.* Bottom: *Witherdon House, Beaworthy, Devon, extension and new facade started in 1872.*

new water heating system was installed by the Launceston ironmonger William Proktor who, as mayor of that town, was involved in the planning of Trevail's Launceston library.[25]

A smaller but troublesome commission that dragged on for years was the design of Chyvelah School near Threemilestone, Truro. Since 1894 a reluctant Kenwyn School Board had been pressurised by the Department of Education in London to provide Chyvelah with a school. Having selected a site and drawn up plans which were approved by the Education Department, the Board received a letter from Coode & Shilson, the solicitors, objecting to the location and offering an alternative which meant further site visits and plans. It was September 1896 before tenders for the school were requested and Moyle and Mitchell were again accepted as builders for an estimate of £640. Slow progress continued to be the order of the day however. 'Great complaints' were recorded at School Board meetings about the slowness of W H Moyle, the carpenter, and in November 1897 the Board imposed penalties under the contract.

The school opened in May 1898, although claims for extras presented by the contractors were still under discussion in June 1901, by which time the cost had risen to £670.[26] However, as soon as the school opened heating problems arose. The stoves were faulty, the children were unable to boil their kettles on them, coal tar and soot blocked the pipes, and the chimney stacks had to be raised, with chimney pots and hoods provided to prevent a down draught. While this work was carried out the school was closed for two months because it was too cold.[27]

Another project of 1896–8 was the addition of a new wing of three bedrooms with a billiard room below for the Thomas family who were leasing an eighteenth century house, Trewince, from the Spry family. John Thomas, the son of a Cornishman who had made money in the fruit and vegetable trade in London, was a large shareholder in

Left: *Trewince, near Gerrans, the new wing built in 1898 contained a billiard room.*
Right: *Market Place shop, St Austell, each floor only had space for one room.*

the King Arthur's Castle Hotel. The family wished to purchase Trewince but the deal appears to have fallen through.[28]

In 1898 Trevail designed a three-storey building on a small corner site at Market Hill, St Austell, for his important client Francis Layland Barratt, requiring the demolition of a tumbledown hairdresser's shop described by the *West Briton* as 'another revelation of what wretched character the old houses of the main streets of St Austell are'.[29] A much more important commission for Barratt was the development of workingmen's dwellings along Moorland Road, described in Chapter Nine.

From 1895 to 1898 Trevail was responsible for Truro British School, later known as Bosvigo School, to hold 450 'babies', infants and older boys and girls. In November 1896 he had written to E R Robson FSA of Westminster, architect for all the British Schools: 'Hip hip hoorah! I am today surprised with a cheque for £20' from the Truro School's managers. This was the remainder of the commission of £45 for the British School after promising them £25 as a contribution to their building fund. Despite his generosity, by the end of the following year the managers had fallen out with him over the state of the building. They complained that partitions between the rooms were 'like a pig's ear', that no partition had been erected in the infant's room, that Trevail had failed to attend the meeting to discuss their complaints, nor had he been to the site to inspect them. 'If you cannot settle your dispute with the contractor we must call in an expert,' they threatened. They also protested to the local Medical Officer of Health about the 'monstrous sanitary arrangements'.[30]

Also in Truro the foundation stone of the Mission Church of St Andrew, was laid in July 1899, on a small site in Charles Street, by Mrs Bolitho of the banking family of Trewidden, Penzance. Costing around £600, it was built by John Colliver 'in the style of the thirteenth century with lancet windows, moulded corbels and a gable surmounted by a bell cote'.[31] In 1897 Trevail also supervised the building of Truro High School for Girls for its architect, Robson of Westminster, mentioned earlier.[32]

Significant among Trevail's later commissions was Laninval, near Bodmin, the home of Henry Dennis, who came from that town, but prospered as a mining and railway engineer elsewhere, becoming Chairman or Managing Director of many companies. They included the Ruabon Coal and Coke Company in North Wales, which produced among other items terracotta and facing bricks. He was also a large shareholder in

Laninval, near Bodmin, for Henry Dennis who owned the terracotta works in Ruabon.

Bodmin Gas Company. Dennis' new house was of unrelieved terracotta, but the kitchen of the old house was used until Trevail made further extensions in 1903, when a large wing was added. This provided a billiard room, dining room and new kitchens. A serving hatch from the kitchen to the new dining room was removed from the plan by Dennis, as he did not wish the servants to hear the guests' conversation. Dennis probably intended his house to be a showcase for the use of terracotta and, after Trevail's first association here with the product in 1895, he used it to conspicuous effect during the remainder of his career in such buildings as the 'red bank' at St Austell, the Headland Hotel at Newquay and the Devon and Cornwall Bank in Falmouth.[33]

Some irksome proposals

Some of Trevail's later commissions proved troublesome and on occasions fruitless, and we may wonder why, with an established reputation, he bothered to take them. Perhaps he wished to keep in favour with influential local families. One such project at Bodmin was a house for Miss M S Collins, daughter of John Bassett Collins, several times Mayor of Bodmin. Trevail was not unacquainted with the rigorous requirements of the Collins family, having designed St Nicholas House for J R Collins, referred to in Chapter Eleven.

Considering that Miss Collins specifically required a 'modest residence, plain but not pretentious', often reminding Trevail that 'ladies purses are not very deep', the demands that she, aided by her cousin the Reverend E V Collins of Blisland, made upon his time were inordinate.[34] Even before the building started Trevail produced at least five alternative designs, and over the years from 1897 to 1900 his bulky correspondence file is full of requests for economies, counterbalanced by instructions for additions. The reductions usually affected the servants' quarters, the extras involved Miss Collins' own rooms. Progress was also delayed by Trevail's own absence on one of his health cures, with Miss Collins politely anxious about his well-being and also about the date of completion. Even in the early days of the project, Trevail had expressed his fears that 'the cost will exceed my first estimate of £750' and eventually it rose to £1,300. St Guron's, as the house was called, was built in an attractive setting near the parish church with a fine staircase leading from a central hall.[35]

Two projects that proved both time-consuming and unproductive were for the Reverend Charles W G Vivian and Gilbert H Chilcott. In April 1900 Trevail visited Vivian at Lapford Wood, Devon, to discuss a gardener's cottage and produced a very elaborate plan with not only a downstairs WC but an upstairs bathroom, facilities not always enjoyed by many greater houses. After Trevail's death Cornelius wrote to Vivian asking if he intended to go ahead but it seems the project had been dropped.[36] As for Chilcott, he wanted to rent a home in Truro but, after rejecting Lord Falmouth's terms as 'so exorbitant', acquired land at the top of Mitchell Hill, north of the town, now known as Bodmin Road, to build his own. Unfortunately for Trevail, Chilcott regarded himself as something of an amateur architect making sketches of alternative elevations and room plans and plaguing Trevail with suggestions for the size, shape and layout of the building and questions about water pressure.

He wished for a home with a frontage of 100 feet but insisted it should be 'nothing

St Guron's, Bodmin, Miss Collins had at least five different sets of drawings.

showy with no extras' and cost no more than £900 plus £300 to lay out the garden. As usual, Trevail designed something more expensive and Chilcott, after consulting with an architect friend (probably Henderson, the Truro engineer and architect) replied that Trevail's ideas would cost too much. Months of dithering ensued during which Chilcott requested reductions, while at the same time insisting upon costly features: slates had to be fixed with copper nails and project over the edge by four inches, inside walls and ceilings had to be soundproof, sash windows were to be added. Trevail managed to escape Chilcott's interference for a time, his assistant informing Chilcott that Trevail was 'in a distant part of London' and could not be reached. Finally, after a full set of much revised drawings had been completed Chilcott wrote that he wished to 'drop the idea of building; I wish to get the thing off my mind'. We may imagine that Trevail fully shared his feelings.[37]

In 1900 Trevail had discussed plans for another house, which although it materialised did not live up to his expectations. His client was a Dublin ironmaster John Parkes, an acquaintance of Edward Hain of St Ives. Trevail probably envisaged another important mansion like Hain's 'Treloyhan', for he wrote to his sister, 'I have a large mansion to build,'[38] and on the back of one of Parkes' letters he noted 'my Dublin client who will be spending something like £20,000 upon this residence.' His hopes were soon dashed though, when Parkes informed him that he was having problems with the settlement of his father's will and asked for a small house costing no more than £4,000.[39]

Not surprisingly, the estimated cost of Trevail's designs exceeded £4,000 despite Parkes attempts to reduce expenditure, and a tender of £5,198 was finally accepted.[40] The house, called Woodside, was erected in Shrewsbury Road in a fashionable new quarter of Dublin (the British Embassy and other Consulates are nearby). It was built

Woodside, Dublin, for iron manufacturer, John Parkes in 1901 (Photograph by R. Lyle).

in rich red brick and decorated with yellow Ruabon terracotta. It contained eight bedrooms, only one less than in Treloyhan but had much smaller grounds without Hain's stables and outhouses. Trevail made a surprising number of trips to Dublin, some of them lengthy, to design the house and supervise progress. He said they were needed 'to get a better picture of Dublin, its buildings and materials' but post cards and letters sent to his family show that he was extending his visits to picturesque parts of Ireland. 'I am racing about from point to point,' he wrote to his sister, visiting Tralee and Limerick, sailing up the river Shannon, then on to Sligo, Enniskillen and Dundalk. In Dublin he was the guest of Sir Thomas Drew. He seemed to get on well with Irish people who spoilt him, urging him to take extra helpings of food. 'I always joke good humouredly with them and am not stiff or starchy as they say many English are.'[41] After Trevail's death, Cornelius dealt with the final stages, involving many disagreements about costs with the local builder Joseph Pemberton, and the project was not completed until August 1904.[42]

In addition to the astonishing workload we have described, Trevail appeared to have arbitrated or acted as a professional witness in several disputes, for example in 1901 at Silverswell Chapel in the case of Higman versus Lee at St Austell, and also at Manaccan.

Personal health problems

As he grew older, Silvanus Trevail's concern about the state of the public's health, which as we have seen existed even as a young man of twenty-three, was more than matched by a preoccupation with his own. In December 1896 he apologised for his absence from Truro Council, saying he was in 'excruciating pain'. A week later he was said to be making progress,[43] but soon he fell ill again as a result of the overnight journeys he made to London to secure funding for Truro Technical Schools, referred to in Chapter Thirteen. In the summer of 1897 he interrupted his heavy work schedule to attend a naval review at Newcastle on Tyne, and then sailed on the SS *Norse King* to Bergen and Trondheim for a few weeks. He thought the Review 'a great success', but unusually did not seem to enjoy himself very much in Norway. 'I shall be very glad to be back', he wrote to his sister.[44]

He was beginning to become anxious about being overweight and started to weigh himself on the scales that used to be placed on railway platforms for use by passengers. He embarked upon a diet and his weight declined steadily from 16stone 6lbs in July 1898 to 15stone in October, a period which included a lengthy spell abroad from August to October to take the waters at Marienbad. His rest cure was preceded, however, by a crowded schedule of visits to Ostend, Ghent, Brussels, Waterloo, Louvain, Aix la Chapelle, Cologne, Coblenz, Frankfurt and Nuremburg. ' When I came here,' he wrote to his sister, 'I was completely run down and in a much weaker condition than I had imagined myself to be.' This was due to 'a fatty growth over my heart which would have ended fatally if I had not taken the step to remove it. I think I am benefiting by the waters though slowly and have the violent pains still in my stomach ... I am restricted very much in diet.' He asked his sister not to worry their parents by telling them of his illness.

He announced that he was spending 'a month or more' at Marienbad but less than a week later he was off to spend a day at Karlsbad 'for a change', and just two weeks after arriving in Marienbad he set off for Prague. A month later, at the beginning of October, he was writing from Budapest 'All well and feeling better every day'. While in Marienbad he had lost 4¼ lbs in weight by taking long walks and bicycling for an average of seven miles a day. Then, on his journey home he also stopped in Vienna, Linz, Salzburg, Munich, Stuttgart, Karlsruhe, Strasborg Metz, Paris and Rouen.[45] It is not clear whether he continued his rigorous exercises and diet in these cities. Probably not, because he was soon overweight again and in January 1899 his doctor told him he had a very bad abscess in his back which required an immediate operation. He was admitted to a private patients hospital at Woodside, Plymouth, where Dr Swain, according to Trevail 'the best surgeon in the West of England' operated upon him.

According to the *West Briton*, the abscess was ' the sequel to a slight accident which Mr Trevail met with in London'. Perhaps this is what he informed the newspapers, but he had a different story for his sister: the abscess resulted from a fall as a child when a lady had removed a chair from behind him on which he was about to sit. He was having 'a very painful time,' he wrote to his sister. He could not sleep at night but was cheered by many kind enquiries including one from Colonel Tremayne, Chairman of the Bodmin Asylum Committee. He also received a bouquet of flowers from 'an awfully nice young lady' whom he 'saw a great deal of at Marienbad'. Within a month he was well enough to attend a meeting of the County Nursing Association.[46]

He was now following a diet laid down for him by Dr W E Yorke-Davies of 44 Harley Street. It started rigorously enough with a tumbler of hot water at 7 am and breakfast consisted of tea with no milk, sugar or cream and toast with no butter. However, this was accompanied by steak, chop, kidney, chicken, tongue or boiled fish.

A light lunch of 'beef, mutton, chicken etc' had to be fat-free, but wine or whisky was allowed. A late salad tea was followed by a dinner of soup and meat with wine and black coffee.[47] The diet seemed to be working for, although he had intended to make a return visit to Marienbad in the autumn of 1900 for another period of exercise and massage, he went instead to Paris for the Exhibition, in the company of George Hicks and Coneybeare. He appeared to be in good health and spirits. 'I would not have missed the Exhibition for anything ... Paris is as gay as ever ... Mr Coneybeare and myself are doing Paris very thoroughly,' he wrote to his sister from the top of the Eiffel Tower. Hicks was feeling the pace however: 'poor old Hicks is particularly beaten. He could not stand the excitement.'[48]

As time went on he became increasingly depressed about the state of his health and in letters to his sister Laura he expressed his fears that he had not long to live. Again, in a letter to the *West Briton*, in promising to reward Truro's soldiers returning from the Boer War, he cautioned 'if we live to see the Boer War finished.'[49] Then a new honour seemed to give him a fresh lease of life: he was unanimously elected President of the Society of Architects.

Sixteen
Presidential glories and personal tragedies

Throughout his life, as we have seen, Silvanus Trevail accumulated an increasingly prestigious series of architectural prizes and honours. His professional ability was recognised early in his career by membership of the Architectural Association in 1874, followed by election to the newly founded Society of Architects in 1885, and he soon became a member of its council. Fellowship of the Royal Institute of British Architects came in 1893, and three years later he was unanimously chosen as Vice President of the Society of Architects. In 1897 a selection of 'the most prominent Architectural Designs hung at the Royal Academy, London' included drawings and ground floor plans of the Central Technical Schools for Truro in a volume published in Leipzig, Berlin, Zurich, Paris, Brussels, Amsterdam, Rome, Barcelona, Stockholm, St Petersburg, Melbourne, Sydney, Adelaide and New York.[1]

By this time he was living in considerable style, not only in Truro, but also in London where, he told his acquaintance Thomas Bowring, he spent 'about half' of his time.[2] In 1897 he had an office in Sherbourne Street, then moved a short distance to 9 Bridge Street in 1899 and to Palace Chambers, Westminster, in 1900. He spent a good deal of time and money furnishing his apartment and office there with such luxuries as a Turkish carpet and bronze gazelier.

In October 1901, after being re-elected four times as Vice President, he was unanimously elected President of the Society of Architects, which had a membership of nearly 600. The *Royal Cornwall Gazette*, not always an admirer of his actions, generously applauded his triumph. 'There is not a Cornishman living who ought not be proud that the same ability, pluck and courage which Mr Trevail has exercised in local and County affairs ... has led his fellow professionals to elect him to the highest pinnacle in their power'. The *West Briton* was no less appreciative: 'That he would some day make a name for himself was always an easy prophecy, but the destination he has attained is almost beyond what could have been hoped.'[3]

Just as in his days as Mayor of Truro, Silvanus Trevail enjoyed to the full the pomp and ceremony of his presidential role, taking centre stage in visits to branches of the Society throughout Britain, giving and receiving banquets, and making speeches on architectural matters which achieved national coverage. His opening address as President was reported in the *London Daily Mail*, *Daily Express*, *Evening News* and *Evening Standard*, *Financial News*, *City Press*, *Court Circular* and *Building News*, and also in the *Birmingham Mail*, *Scarborough Gazette*, *Glasgow Daily Record* and *Mail*, *Bristol Observer*, *Devon and Exeter Gazette*, as well as in the leading Cornish papers.

An advocate of town planning

A major theme of his presidential addresses was the need for town planning. His visits to Chicago and New York had preceded the age of the skyscraper and he did not seem impressed by the grid system on which American cities were laid out. He would probably not have approved of later developments there, either, since he disapproved of buildings designed to give as much flat wall space as possible for 'advertising atrocities'.[4] As we know, he was only too keen to cover his own buildings with Ruabon terracotta. What he admired were the 'magnificent boulevards, new thoroughfares and monumental work' of Paris, Brussels, Rome, Berlin, Dresden, Vienna and Budapest. On his visits to these cities he would have witnessed the flowering of what came to be known as Art Nouveau or Jugendstil. He also respected the 'magnificent municipal buildings' of Birmingham, Liverpool, Manchester, Leeds, Sheffield, Newcastle, Glasgow and Edinburgh.

Even when speaking in the heart of London, he was not afraid to contrast these places with London's 'wretchedly narrow and insignificant streets ... dilapidated, rickety and ramshackled properties'. This he asserted was in no way the fault of architects: it was entirely due to a regime that placed 'all sorts of incongruous blocks of government offices dotted about in all sorts of inconvenient positions, shapes and sizes.[5]

While some London papers supported these criticisms, the *Daily Mail* published a 16-line poem defending the capital's buildings: 'cockneys view its civic slums with pride, nor wish to follow in the wake of France, or see our dear old city Yankified'. Trevail as ever delighted in the controversy he had created, deriding a 'small minority' who 'sacrificed great improvements to retain Ye Olde Curiositie Shoppe just as it was in Dickens' day. The advancing civilisation of our time demands that such old rookeries and purlieus should be swept away and something notable take its place'. In a lantern lecture of 150 slides to Society members he compared 'miserable' English buildings with views of the Champs Elysées, Unter den Linden, the Ringstrasse in Vienna and the Boulevard Andrassy in Budapest.[6] The *Royal Cornwall Gazette* loyally supported his disapproval of a city that 'gave foreigners and colonial visitors a beggarly idea of the Metropolis'.

Trevail used his presidential addresses to press for other reforms that he had advocated for years such as alterations to the 'Ancient Lights' laws that had cost his clients so dearly at Helston. He also attacked 'the evil results of the leasehold system ... one of the last relics of feudal times' that encouraged property developers to build cheap because their building would revert to the landowner at the end of the lease.

Another bee in his bonnet was the practice of unqualified builders and developers who styled themselves 'architects' and, he argued, gave his profession a bad name. Journals such as *The Builder* and *Building News* contained detailed drawings that could easily be copied and he canvassed members of the Society and of the Royal Institute of British Architects to stop this practice.[7] He even persuaded the Society to pass a resolution demanding legislation that debarred architects, surveyors and engineers in public employ from competing for other work, undercutting architects in private practice. In these matters though he was ahead of his time, and it was many years before the action recommended was taken.

Presidential banquets and festivities

When Trevail entertained he did so on a lavish scale. His annual dinner of December 1901 was reported to be 'the most successful gathering hitherto seen'[8] and in the following months he attended among many other engagements, the inaugural dinner of the Bristol Cornish Association, invited 'the aged of Truro' to a high tea, and sat at the Chairman's table at the annual dinner of the London Cornish Association. Speaking to the Mevagissey Mercantile Association, he cautioned them to be careful of building more hotels, the last three or four years' experience being 'not satisfactory ... the [Boer] war had a great deal to do with it'. Again in London, he addressed the Institute of Clay Workers, castigating the government for the lack of instruction given in modelling and design in clay compared with continental countries.[9]

In between these engagements he presided over Society of Architects' dinners which, as the *Building News* noted, 'were organised on a much larger scale than had previously been attended'. The *West Briton* praised the 'energy and thoroughness with which he carries out everything he faces in hand ... every detail was arranged, the selection of guests representing every strand'. However, it commented on a dinner in 1902, 'if there is one fault it was the length of the toast list, no fewer than 27 speeches'. Trevail's love of rhetoric had not deserted him and he made several contributions himself. The *Building News* also remarked that his toast lists 'were swelled to abnormal proportions.[10]

Poster for Dedication of Bells Ceremony (Family papers).

The death of Jane Trevail

Trevail's triumphs in his social and professional life were, however, marred by a series of personal tragedies. His satisfaction at achieving the presidency was tragically overshadowed by the death of his mother Jane in March 1902. He later said that his heart was so stirred at her funeral by the respect that was paid to her memory that he resolved to bestow upon the parish a gift that would be 'a delight to the parishioners for all time'. Two months later when visiting Luxulyan, he met the Reverend R Sinclair Kendall who was inspecting the bells and bell tower which had fallen into a sorry state. Only two bells were still intact and the framework and ropes were so dilapidated as to be unusable. Trevail had the four old bells recast into three and added three new ones.

LUXULYAN PARISH CHURCH.

DEDICATION

OF THE

NEW PEAL OF BELLS

The New Peal of Bells, the Gift to the Parish of

MR. SILVANUS TREVAIL,

Will be Dedicated on

TUESDAY, October 14th, 1902.

The Dedication Service will begin at 3.30 p.m.

The Bells will be Dedicated by Venble. | The Sermon will be preached by Venble.

Archdeacon Du Boulay | Archdeacon Cornish.

The Collection will be given to the Church and Tower Restoration Fund.

Ringers from beyond the Parish may have the use of the Bells from 9.30 a.m. till 1 p.m., on application to Mr. Alfred Phillips, Captain of the Tower.

A PUBLIC LUNCHEON

Will be held in the Vicarage Grounds at 1.30 p.m. and

A PUBLIC TEA at 4.30 p.m.

During the Evening a Magic Lantern Exhibition

Will be given in the Board School.

At which a very fine show of Views from different parts of the world will be given, and also, it is hoped a Set of slides illustrating the Coronation of King Edward the Seventh, at Westminster.

It is intended to end the evening with a Short Concert if time permit.

ADMISSION TO THE SCHOOL ROOM, SIXPENCE.

ROBERT SINCLAIR KENDALL, Vicar of Luxulyan.

BAKER & SON, Printers, St. Blazey.

Silvanus took immense pains to design a memorial that would please his father and the rest of the family and remain 'for a thousand years after we are all gone'. He visited churchyards and cemeteries throughout Cornwall and in London, and inspected crosses erected for William Coode, Thomas Drew and J B Collins in Cornwall. On the day of the dedication of the bells, 14 October 1902, a luncheon was held in a tent in the Vicarage gardens where the people of Luxulyan surprised Trevail by presenting him with a magnificent illuminated address of thanks, framed in gold and edged with the Trevail crest, masonic arms, Celtic knots, and illustrations of the bells in the tower and the new Trevail family cross that he had designed and erected.[11]

He was very proud of his memorial design, taking it on his travels and showing it to all his friends, acquaintances and clients including Frank Bond, past High Sheriff of Berkshire. 'It will be, I am sure', he wrote to his sister, 'the prettiest and most interesting monument in Cornwall'.[12] The details for the sides of the cross, all different, were copied from what Trevail considered to be the best Celtic examples in Cornwall, namely at St Neot, Cardinham, St Mabyn, Lanivet, St Columb and Padstow. The base had four sides to record the lives of his mother, his father, his sister Laura and himself. In addition he designed a new top for a sundial in Luxulyan churchyard which dated back to 1687.

Silvanus later produced a booklet containing designs and details of the bells and the cross and of the dedication service, together with the names of all the school children present and newspaper reports of the day. This was to be presented to every school child in the parish and inscribed with their name; he intended to send it to 'all the great national libraries',[13] but he died before it was published and it was his sister who signed the booklet after his death.

For several months, however, Silvanus had become increasingly concerned about the state of his father's health. John Trevail had suffered an earlier collapse in 1886 and, as Silvanus had written to a friend, 'for 13 nights I had no sleep nor my clothes off as I was by his bedside nursing him. Now he is strong and hearty at 82'. But this letter had been written in March 1901[14] and two years later John Trevail was sinking into a deep depression. Silvanus visited him often and asked his sister to 'find people to take his mind off' his worries, some of which seemed imaginary. Trevail too was in a melancholy state, which was not improved by a stay in Devon with Sir Robert Harvey, who was also according to Trevail 'in terrible distress' about the recent tragic losses of his elder son, aged eleven, his wife and his younger boy aged nine. Trevail asked his sister to tell his father about Sir Robert's suffering in the hope that it might 'assuage his grief'. These events increased his own forebodings about his own mortality. He wrote on more than one occasion to his sister Laura about the booklet and memorial stone, saying 'if I should live to see it finished' and 'Whether I live to see it done or not, life is so uncertain'.[15]

Presidential duties

Nevertheless Trevail launched himself into his duties as President of the Society of Architects. In July 1902 he took members of the Devon and Exeter Architectural Society on a visit to Truro's new stone railway viaducts, Waterfall and Victoria Gardens and the cattle market, as well as Kenwyn Church, the Royal Institution, the Cathedral and of course some of his own designs, including the Passmore Edwards Library and Technical Schools and St Mary's Wesleyan church.

He planned the visit of the Association with the same meticulous attention to detail that characterised his other activities. He entertained them to lunch and tea in his own home in Lemon Street, which he had greatly extended and was anxious to show off. He had combined two houses, numbers 80 and 81. His own room, dining room and break-fast room were on the ground floor, and on the first floor was a drawing office with a smaller office behind, a sitting room, a drawing room and a bedroom, with a library over the kitchen annexe. He had given a great deal of time and thought to the design of

Opposite page top: The Trevail Family Memorial erected in Luxulyan churchyard after Jane Trevail's death.
Opposite page bottom: Memorial booklet given to all Luxulyan school children (Family papers).
Left: Devon and Exeter architects on their tour around Truro in 1902 (Family papers).

his home and a large number of drawings and water colours exist showing in great detail such features as a frieze above the picture rail, dado panelling and the position of paintings on the walls. He planned his drawing office in similar fashion, with plans showing the position of furniture, some old, some new and designed by himself. When completed he had many photographs taken of the room settings some including himself.[16]

A printed programme of the Exeter Association luncheon showed a choice of every imaginable variety of meats, sea fish, shell fish and desserts, washed down with the finest hocks, clarets, moselles, burgundies, champagne and liqueurs. The meal was punctuated with nine speeches and toasts, three of them by the host. After which the party sailed down the river Fal to Pendennis Castle, Falmouth and returned for tea, followed by a perusal of 'Mr Trevail's collection of interesting and valuable books of photos and curios' before leaving about 8 pm. The following month saw Trevail in Berlin, and on his return journey through England he made business trips to Bristol, Clevedon, Exeter, Lapford, Newton Abbot, Totnes and Plymouth. In September 1902 he made another lengthy trip to Ireland, ostensibly to oversee Parkes' house in Dublin, but spending much time elsewhere.[17]

Top: *Devon and Exeter Architectural Society luncheon menu, 1902 (Family papers).* Bottom: *Dining room at 80–81 Lemon Street, Truro, soon after the renovation in 1901 (Family papers).*

The deaths of John Trevail and George Hicks

At the end of his first year as President he was unanimously re-elected for a further year, but this recognition of his untiring work for the Society was again marred by another personal blow: the death of his father in December 1902. For Trevail, the last few months of his father's life had been a particularly harrowing time as his behaviour became more and more irrational, troubled by problems which his son thought were imaginary. A month after the dedication ceremony for the bells he took a severe chill and was moved to the Cottage Hospital at Liskeard.[18] Silvanus travelled up and down every day, sometimes staying overnight if his father's condition worsened, until he died.[19]

In addition to the booklet about the church bells given to Luxulyan schoolchildren, they also received a medallion about the size of a 5p piece. On one side was the words 'Speed the plough. John Trevail 1820 –1902', together with a design of a ploughman, and on the other 'No plough, no bread' with a man scything corn, copied from a Canadian coin that John Trevail had brought back from his travels in Canada. According to Trevail's cousin Charles, John's favourite saying was 'No labour, no bread'. John Trevail was remembered as belonging to the 'old yeomanry who farmed their own estates, independent, self-reliant, original'. Attendance at his funeral was said to be the largest ever known in Luxulyan.[20]

In January 1903 he received another great shock: a telegram announcing the death of his friend, mentor and loyal supporter in his hotel ventures, George Hicks of Newquay. An old friend of John Trevail, Hicks had proved himself to be a trusted ally in Trevail's turbulent relations with Newquay councillors and residents. He had stood by Trevail when, uncharacteristically, the latter had panicked about a lack of financial support for the King Arthur's Castle Hotel at Tintagel. Hicks had attended Jane Trevail's funeral and the dedication of the bells at Luxulyan and paid visits to John Trevail, indeed he was the last person to see him alive, and he was present at the funeral.[21] Silvanus wrote Hicks' obituary for the *Western Morning News* and told his sister that he would attend Hicks' funeral if he was well

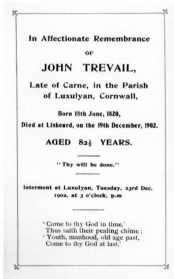

In Affectionate Remembrance
OF
JOHN TREVAIL,
Late of Carne, in the Parish
of Luxulyan, Cornwall,

Born 18th June, 1820,
Died at Liskeard, on the 19th December, 1902.

AGED   82½ YEARS.

"Thy will be done."

Interment at Luxulyan, Tuesday, 23rd Dec.
1902, at 3 o'clock, p.m

'Come to thy God in time.'
Thus saith their pealing chime ;
'Youth, manhood, old age past,
Come to thy God at last.'

Top: *'Speed the plough' tokens minted as a memorial to John Trevail (Private collection).*
Bottom: *Service for John Trevail (Family papers).*

enough. For now it was his turn to fall ill. He missed a meeting at the end of January of the Society of Architects because he was confined to his bed at Palace Chambers, Westminster with bronchitis and congestion of the lungs. He was also absent from two of the first three meetings of Truro Council in January and February, and only attended the third against doctor's orders, suffering from 'an acute attack of neuralgia'.[22]

Trevail was now spending much time perusing photographs of 'worthy contemporaries ... too many of them, alas, dead'. In a letter to John Enys, landowner and colleague on several municipal undertakings, he listed a great number of them, finishing 'and heaps, heaps of others'.[23] Even a few days spent in the Berkshire home of his 'dear friend Sir Warwick Morshead' with 'a valet and footman in constant attendance' did not lift his spirits . Writing of this visit to his sister Laura, he confided that he felt 'very tired, and it will take very little' to give up 'active business life'. He was also filled with regret about what he now saw as past extravagances, and upset that his father, on his deathbed, had said he had the reputation of 'spending money as fast as I get it'.[24]

A final flourish

Yet at the end of February 1903 Silvanus seemed to have bounced back to form again, speaking at the annual banquet of the London Master Builders Association 'with his old vigour'.[25] In the following months he embarked upon a series of presidential and professional journeys punctuated by trips abroad. In March he attended Treffry's annual court dinner at Newquay and as one of Treffry's principal tenants he was called upon to toast the health of the Lord of the Manor. Some men, remembering the bitterness of past relations with Newquay Council might have used the occasion to pour oil on troubled waters, as some councillors were present at the dinner. Not so Trevail; he did not pull his punches and continued the attack, mentioned in Chapter Fourteen, on the Council's failure to develop Newquay as a tourist resort. Treffry, he proclaimed, had done Newquay the honour of introducing Cornwall's first 999-year lease for the headland, virtually giving away the best part of the land, worth upwards of £3,000. How, Trevail asked, had Newquay reacted? 'By spending not a penny on roads, footways or fences, provided no lamps or public lighting, nothing except four or five rough cart tracks 12 to 18 inches deep in mud'.[26]

In March 1903, he also made what the *West Briton* called 'one of his rare attendances' at Truro Council, intervening in an issue that was being discussed and 'boldly laid it down that if the corporation required extra land to widen roads they had to compensate the owners'.[27] Soon after that he was in London attending the annual dinner of the London Cornish Association presided over by Sir Robert Harvey,[28] and early in April he was abroad again: 'I am going over old ground that I visited in 1877', along the French Riviera, Switzerland and Italy. He made no mention of a health cure.[29]

During these trips he always kept in close touch with his professional affairs, instructing his assistant Cornelius to 'send a post card by 5pm every day even if nothing to report' and to 'make a blueprint of every tracing you do and send to me immediately.[30] He was still interested in local politics as was shown by his letter in April 1903 from Marseilles which was printed and posted on hoardings in Truro. Addressed to Trudgeon, proprietor of the Globe Hotel in the town who was standing for Councillor as representative of the Rate Payers Association, the letter said: 'The Truro papers have reached me here by which I observe you are a candidate for the vacancy created by the elevation of Mr Councillor Heard to the Aldermanic Bench. Allow me to congratulate you upon your public spirit in coming forward and to wish you as an independent all success'.[31]

The letter added that Trevail was about to move to the Riviera Palace Hotel at Monte Carlo where he would spend the next week or so. There he was impressed by the sight of '£500 changing hands per minute' at one of '40 or so gaming tables'.[32] Other places visited on this trip included Zurich, Genoa, Turin and Milan. At the end of April further news reached the *West Briton*: 'Mr Silvanus Trevail, whilst staying at the Schweizerhof Hotel, Lucerne, has been consulted by 'a wealthy American in regard to what remains to be done to complete the fabric of Truro Cathedral and its probable cost. At present no name can be given but the gentleman in question is likely to be Mr Trevail's guest before the summer is over'.[33] This was not the first time he had performed a service of this kind. A year earlier he had 'entirely through my own influence' arranged for a work of art valued between 700 to 1,000 guineas to be given to the Cathedral.[34]

Meanwhile the Truro Mayor Captain Henderson had died suddenly. Although aged 82 this came as a surprise to many, because of the 'energetic and lively manner in which he carried out his duties'.[35] 'There is only one person to fall back on,' pronounced the *Royal Cornwall Gazette*, 'Silvanus Trevail. But he is suffering from a severe bereavement: will he accept?'[36] He was also out of the country again for a lengthy period, but he sent a telegram from Genoa to Robert Dobell, Clerk to Truro Council, 'Deepest sympathy with the late Mayor's family'.[37] But he did not rush back, as he had done in the case of the missing Luxulyan bells. John James was unanimously elected Mayor.[38]

By May 1903 Trevail was back in London to give his most spectacular Presidential banquet, to which he invited over 120 guests from his large circle of influential acquaintances. Among them was Edward Hain, now MP for Penwith, Sir Robert Harvey, now knighted and Sheriff of Devon, and Thomas Bowring, benefactor of the Moretonhampstead library, all of these knowing each other well. Others included Lord St Levan, Viscount Clifden, Colonel C Prideaux-Brune, H Passmore Edwards (son of the philanthropist), J W Jerram, (connected with the East Ham library and hospital projects), and E O Preston (of 'Preston's bungalow', Newquay). Speaker after speaker praised his 'commanding personality' and 'marvellous powers' and Sir Walter Foster MP said he should change his name to 'Silvanus Prevail'. Trevail, buoyed up by this acclaim, announced his candidacy for election to the Council of the Royal Institute of British Architects.[39]

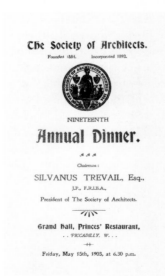

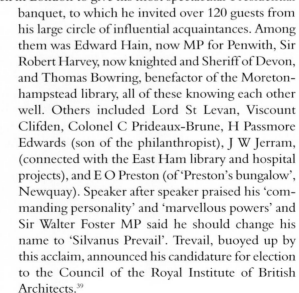

The Society of Architects dinner menu for 1903 (Family papers).

This was his last big Society function, although later in May he presided over a field day of the Society at Rochester, taking a party of over 60 ladies and gentlemen to the museum, Cathedral, castle and other sites.[40] In July the Prince and Princess of Wales visited Truro for the benediction of the Cathedral and Trevail attended the ceremony.[41]

The last months

In contrast to the praises heaped upon Trevail at his presidential banquet, one of those present, John Lanyon, later recorded his shock at how much he had altered: 'vigour and coherence of thought and presentation of language gone'. No one else seems to have remarked publicly on the change, but according to evidence given at the inquest by his assistant Cornelius, until that dinner he had 'seemed all right and very cheerful' but on his return to Truro he confided that he was very worried. Charles Trevail also testified that his cousin was very concerned about business affairs.[42] Nevertheless, he was soon off again on another trip to Ireland.

This seems to have been his last major outing. Thereafter, according to Cornelius, he only left Truro on half a dozen occasions, two or three times to Bodmin, once to London and once to Newton Abbot. The *West Briton* reported that 'His interest in Corporate matters seemed to have suddenly died out', as he had not sat on the magistrate's bench for a year. An old acquaintance who met him at Luxulyan in September was 'amazed at the change in Mr Trevail ... he bemoaned the estrangement from some of his former friends'.[43] Trevail was no longer doing any work according to Cornelius, although his letter book contains copies of correspondence up to October 30th 1903, addressed to Robert Edyvean, Clerk to the Asylum Committee, regretting delay in replying to letters.[44] He attended an October meeting of Truro Council but, possibly for the first time in his life, did not speak.

Early in November 1903 Silvanus Trevail visited the Royal Institution of Cornwall in Truro and viewed the progress in improvements to the building. According to Sir Robert Harvey he 'expressed his satisfaction' with them.[45] A few days later he received news of yet another death in the family, that of his Uncle Joseph who as Chairman of Luxulyan School Building Committee, had set Trevail off on his career by commissioning him to design Luxulyan school. He wrote to his cousin Charles promising that he would do his best to attend the funeral, 'if not prevented by what I am unable to control ... I am no better'.[46] On 7th November he set out for the funeral at Luxulyan at 11.30 in the morning in a frock coat and silk hat, and rode to the railway station where he bought a third class ticket, but only as far as St Austell. However he stayed on the train past that station and Lostwithiel and, whilst it was passing through the tunnel before Bodmin Road station, he made his way to the ladies' lavatory, put a gun to his head and shot himself.

Seventeen
What drove Trevail to self-destruction?

'Poor Trevail, dead, and by his own hand too!' wrote the editor of the *St Austell Star*, 'a pitiful ending to a life that was so big'.[1] At the inquest the coroner R P Edyvean took evidence from Trevail's assistant, Cornelius, and his cousin Charles. As Clerk to Bodmin Council and to the Asylum Committee, Edyvean had many dealings – and some disputes – with Trevail over the building of Bodmin library and the county asylum, and concluded that 'for a man of the disposition of Mr Trevail to suddenly exclude himself from contact with his fellow men pointed in itself to something being wrong. There seemed no doubt that business worries and pressure had wholly unhinged the poor man's mind, and that

Luxulyan Church.

at the time of the act he was totally irresponsible'. The jury recorded the verdict that the deceased committed suicide while temporally insane. The funeral took place at Luxulyan, where 'the little church was crammed full', the mourners included directors of his hotel companies, his contractor Arthur (later Sir Arthur) Carkeek and Cornwall's leading man of letters Arthur (later Sir Arthur) Quiller-Couch.[2]

The strange circumstances of his final act shocked Cornwall – picture postcards of his funeral were in great demand – and the tragedy has continued to fascinate authors of the mysterious and macabre ever since.[3] Two less sensational and more analytical interpretations by James Whetter and Henry Tregilgas are of particular interest in attempting to unravel the mystery of his death.[4] Whetter focuses mainly upon external influences: family deaths, professional and political disappointments and financial problems. He also hints at a relationship with a Mrs Masterman of London who was clearly close to him – 'hers was one of the three wreaths at his funeral'. Physical illness, Whetter adds, may have aggravated his condition. Tregilgas, in contrast, concentrates upon Trevail's internal mental state, suggesting that he, like Tregilgas himself, was a manic-depressive. This condition was not recognised in those terms at the time of Trevail's death, but it involves unpredictable mood swings from extreme elation, possibly coupled with reckless financial dealings and delusions of grandeur, to total apathy, even suicidal tendencies.

Family deaths and professional disappointments

These two sets of explanations are not mutually incompatible. External events such as the deaths in rapid succession of his mother Jane, his father John and his uncle Joseph were undoubtedly cruel blows, although the apparently mysterious Mrs Masterman turned out to be a relation of Jane's. With no wife or children of his own, Silvanus had only his sister Laura to turn to, but although she remained a loyal supporter and confidante, she could not help him with any of his work-related problems. In this context, the loss of John Trevail's advice and support on business matters was all the more crippling because of the death, shortly after, of George Hicks of Newquay. Hicks was in many ways a second father to Silvanus and his death so soon after Jane's and John's passing must have been a devastating blow, one that has not been recognised by previous commentators.

Architectural problems also clearly loomed increasingly large in Trevail's mind. Edyvean, the coroner reported at the inquest that he had written to Trevail about some extra costs of £60 (a trivial amount in an asylum building programme of £100,000), and had been surprised when Trevail was so alarmed that he hastened to Bodmin to discuss the matter. His sister Laura's papers show Trevail confiding about worries in other commissions including dry rot in the Devon and Cornwall Bank at Fowey, and the library and technical schools at Newton Abbot which were, 'worrying the life out of me'.[5]

This sort of difficulty would never have troubled the Trevail of old, who showed a cavalier disregard for such mishaps as a large cost over-run for the Truro Technical Schools, the disintegration of Bodmin library windows, or the collapse of a chimney. Indeed, it is tempting to think that he almost relished disasters so that he could demonstrate his skill in overcoming them. Only a year before his death he had delighted his audience at the dedication of the Luxulyan church bells with a story of how the Great Western Railway (GWR) had mislaid the clappers to the bells somewhere in England. Learning of this in Paris, he had immediately rushed back to London and the office of the general manager of the railway: 'soon about one hundred telegrams were despatched all over the system' and the clappers were discovered at Newquay. The GWR had also lost two consignments of Moselle for the dedication ceremony, he informed the congregation, but regretfully he had been less successful in retrieving them.[6]

Clearly, despite the loss of his mother, he was then still in his habitual imperious mode, triumphing over the obstacles put in his way by lesser men, just as when, calling himself 'Field Marshall Trevail', he had instructed his contractor 'Major General Carkeek' to march his army of builders through the streets of Newquay to demonstrate to the residents that he would build the Headland Hotel despite the efforts of rioters to pull it down. Nonetheless, he must have been aware that his tourist projects had not lived up to his expectations in later years. At the ceremony of the dedication of the Luxulyan church bells, his cousin Charles had praised Trevail's efforts to 'get visitors into the county and so turn the tide into one of prosperity'.

Hotel problems

Unfortunately, the tide was on the ebb as far as hotel revenues were concerned. Nothing had come anywhere near equalling the success of his first development, the Atlantic Hotel at Newquay (an immediate and continued money-spinner), but derided by residents as a white elephant – 'Trevail's Folly'. As we saw in Chapter Fourteen, a number of apparently promising hotel ventures in the Isles of Scilly, Guernsey and Exeter had never left the drawing board and none of the ambitious schemes for seaside estates, designed for landowners along the north coast, came to full fruition. Although Trevail blamed these problems on a general recession in the holiday trade caused by the Boer War, he might have felt he had lost his golden touch.[7]

It was not just in tourist development, however, that Trevail seemed to run out of commissions. By June 1903 he was in the depths of despair. 'I was never in a more unhappy or anxious period of my life,' he wrote to his sister, 'nothing new and heaps of expenses in all directions ... Prospects that seemed so bright twelve months ago seem now dashed to the ground. I had hoped to have close upon £20,000 worth of work in hand in London by now, but it has fallen through, and worse than that I have all the preliminary expenses to pay for my pains.' A few days later he wrote to his sister again

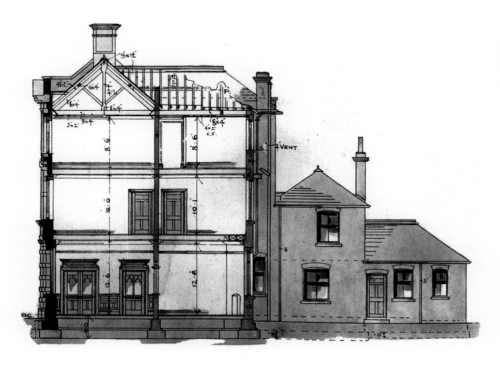

Devon & Cornwall Bank, Fowey (CRO: AD396/625).

about his 'trouble and anxiety ... I feel I must give up soon if matters don't improve ... night after night without sleep'.[8] What these abortive projects were is not clear, and there are no references in his letter books, correspondence files or family papers to other, unsuccessful, ventures in London.

He still had a considerable body of work to complete: about £70,000 of construction at Bodmin asylum, together with Newton Abbot Library and Technical Schools, Moretonhampstead nurses home, the Devon and Cornwall Bank at Fowey, the Globe Hotel in Bude, Blackford's premises in Truro, the house in Dublin and some more workers' cottages in Moorland Road, St Austell. But there seemed no new major project in the offing: no Passmore Edwards buildings, no banks, shops or hotels.

Perhaps the final straw was the bankruptcy of the King Arthur's Castle Hotel at Tintagel. He had taken over the chairmanship of the King Arthur's Castle Hotel Company after the death of George Hicks and in May 1903 he had to suffer the indignity of holding an Extraordinary General Meeting to wind up the Company.[9] Curiously, this event was never mentioned when the reasons for his suicide were discussed at his inquest. True, this would not have resulted in personal financial ruin, because although he acted as Chairman, Director or Company Secretary of his hotels, they were all limited companies and his own shareholdings in them were modest. Nonetheless, the collapse of the Tintagel company would have dealt a severe blow to his self-esteem as the acknowledged prime mover of Cornwall's tourist industry.

Political disappointments

Trevail's career in local government, too, ended in disillusion. In earlier days he had cherished high hopes of the new, more democratic structure of county and district councils and had made himself an acknowledged master of municipal administration. The continued refusal of Truro Council to deal with its notoriously bad drainage system, and the failure of some local authorities to take public health reform seriously when he was Chairman of the County Sanitary Committee had led to disenchantment with democratic processes. After some Newquay councillors obstructed the erection of his hotel while forging ahead with their own rival hotel in the town, he told a Newquay audience at the opening of the Headland Hotel, probably only half in jest, that benevolent despotism, not local democracy, was the only way to get things done.[10] As discussed in Chapter Eleven, he confided to acquaintances that he was growing tired of the increasing burden of local administration and that he sometimes escaped from Cornwall to avoid being press-ganged into another wearying session as Mayor of Truro.

These sentiments contradict an opinion, expressed at the inquest, that a major setback that preyed on his mind occurred when he was not chosen as Mayor of Truro in November 1902. 'His apparent disgust at not being chosen for Mayor' commented the West Briton, 'will be vividly in the minds of most readers'.[11] Did he secretly hanker after the honour? As mentioned in Chapter Eleven, he had refused re-election as Mayor for 1895–6 and avoided a further period of office in later years. He was not the only councillor to do so; discussing the elections for November 1901 the *Royal Cornwall Gazette*, while suggesting that John James or Trevail would be 'excellent' choices, commented that it was becoming difficult to find willing candidates.[12]

Of course Trevail's concept of an election was always one in which he remained aloof until asked to stand by public acclaim, and then returned unopposed without the need to mount a campaign. But he was well aware that, if this approach succeeded at county council level, it certainly did not work in local Truro politics. As mentioned in Chapter Six, he had been unseated back in 1889 when he had set off for Paris during the election period, leaving the way clear for opponents to accuse him of neglecting his constituents in order to indulge in frivolous pursuits.

These absences, he was well aware, were his Achilles heel. Back in 1898 he had told his sister how annoyed he was when the *Western Morning News* announced that he was about to make a lengthy trip on the continent when he did not 'want everyone to know I had left'.[13] Since then his non-attendance at council meetings had increased because of his commissions in Devon, London and Dublin, added to by countrywide responsibilities as President of the Society of Architects. His bouts of illness and 'health cures' resulted in further non-appearances. In the run-up to the 1902 mayoral election he knew that his opponents would bring up the matter, so he held a public meeting to dispel what he claimed were 'false stories' about the reasons for his non-attendance.[14]

However, if he really wanted to be elected Mayor, he made two serious mistakes. Firstly, he lambasted 'John James and Co', as he called those councillors who disagreed with him, citing the many occasions on which he had been right and they had been wrong. His rhetoric delighted his audience, who greeted his speech with 'loud and continuous applause'. They formed a Ratepayers Association, elected Trevail to it and presented a petition to Truro Council, proposing Trevail for Mayor. On the other hand his colleagues on the Council, who had been the butt of his criticisms, were understandably less than pleased.

Then he set off for Paris in the middle of the election period. Not surprisingly, the Council rejected the ratepayers' petition and elected a man who was not even a Councillor, the elderly architect and engineer James Henderson. 'Why,' asked the editor of the *West Briton*, 'is Mr Trevail so popular outside the Council and so unpopular inside?' The answer, to one so well versed in local affairs as the editor, must have been perfectly obvious. For two decades Trevail had never made the slightest attempt to conceal his contempt for what he called the 'narrow-minded, short-sighted spite and jealousy' of many of his fellow councillors. He had made too many enemies, who would take advantage of his absence to unite against him.

When Henderson died suddenly a few months later, Trevail was abroad once more. He could hardly have been expected to know that Henderson was about to die, but he did not return to Truro when he heard the news and the Council elected the Deputy Mayor, Trevail's arch-enemy John James, to the post. In November 1903, Councillors J H Sampson and J J Smith, who had both declined the position of Mayor the previous year, were still unwilling and James was re-elected Mayor. By this time Trevail was rarely seen at council meetings, and when he did appear, in October 1903, instead of dominating the proceedings in his old way he sat apart, a silent and morose spectator. It must have been obvious to all who knew him that he was no longer in the running for the role of Mayor.

Was Trevail a manic-depressive?

Does the evidence we have produced of a relentless series of personal tragedies, professional setbacks and possible political disappointments offer a convincing explanation of Silvanus Trevail's suicide? Or was his self-destruction the final act of a life-long manic-depressive? Undoubtedly he experienced bursts of creative energy, working at fever pitch night and day to bring to a successful conclusion all manner of projects from building the triumphal

Two of Trevail's letter books, each of which covers about 10 months (CRO: AD396).

arches of Truro, defeating a parliamentary railway bill, financing Truro technical schools, unearthing the malpractices of Truro's town clerk, or launching shares in a chain of hotels. He was always a man in a hurry and worked on a short fuse, easily losing his temper with men who were less driven or who stood in the way of his ambitions. He was able to work for long periods without sleep which can also be associated with a manic state, and an almost superhuman energy and vitality were always the hallmarks of a Trevail undertaking. His constant travelling also suggests a hyperactive personality.

Did this behaviour lead to financial recklessness or delusions of grandeur? We may detect financial insouciance in Trevail's dealings, yet they were not spasmodic but persisted throughout his professional career. There can seldom have been a Trevail project that did not cost more than the original estimate. Again we find him on occasions urging his clients to hasten payments of commission, as for example after his lavish spending on entertainment as Mayor of Truro. Perhaps also towards the end of his life he became over-optimistic, for instance in spending money on the Truro Technical Schools before he had received written confirmation of funding for them, or in his extravagant taste in fittings for the Headland Hotel, or his chambers in Westminster, or in assuming he would build Woodside in Dublin for £20,000, when the client only wanted to pay £4,000 (which Trevail pushed up to £5,000). But is this not true of many architects, developers and entrepreneurs? After all, he was only following in the footsteps of a long line of Cornish adventurers. What is more, in the past he had often been proved right while his more cautious and risk-averse colleagues had been wrong.

As for a possible *folie de grandeur*, he always made great play of his associations with the rich and famous. If he was late with plans he might offer the excuse that he was staying with an aristocratic or wealthy family, or even shaking the hand of the President of France or the United States. Yet such behaviour was not uncommon among those who had risen to great heights from modest beginnings. Unlike many other self-made men he did not surround himself with the outward trappings of power and wealth, employ armies of servants, ride in magnificent carriages, acquire an impressive mansion on a country estate, nor a large house with a drive leading up to it. True, he rented expensive chambers in London, but in Cornwall he lived in a rented house with just a cook and maid.

His major extravagances were his trips abroad, when he never stinted himself, staying in the best hotels and dining in the finest restaurants. Yet he left an estate approaching £9,000 at a time when a working man could bring up a family on £50 a year. For an architect in his early fifties, with an expectation of lucrative commissions to come, this seems a comfortable reserve.[15]

While we can find plenty of examples of manic energy throughout thirty years of professional and political activities, there is no evidence in his correspondence to suggest recurrent periods of apathy or deep depression. True, there were times in his later years when his letters to business acquaintances or his family were filled with gloom – 'the old country is going to the dogs'. Yet this was hardly the sign of an irrational state of depression when, in the 1890s, nearly every one of the Cornish metal mines that had once employed a third of the working population had closed down, and hard-working colleagues in the building trade were going bankrupt. He took a fierce pride in his Cornish ancestry and the past and present achievements of his people and it grieved him deeply to see 'Cornwall fast going to pot' as he put it to his sister.

Failing health

Did Trevail harbour an irrational obsession with the state of his health? The rest of his family lived to a ripe old age, but he seemed plagued with ill health and was often laid low during the winter months. This was aggravated by overwork, as when he collapsed after rushing up and down to London on the night train in bad weather to secure further funding for Truro Technical Schools. Yet he would always bounce back again remarkably quickly. After a serious operation in Plymouth early in 1902, he was swiftly on his feet making his presence felt at public meetings. The reason for the operation, however, remains a mystery. In one account he said it was to remove an abscess, in another he claimed it resulted from a fall backwards in his childhood when a lady had removed a chair from under him.

As we saw in Chapter Fifteen, he developed a habit of weighing himself, noting alarming variations in his diaries. Sudden fluctuations of this kind can be symptoms of bi-polar disorder. And while he regularly 'took the waters' at foreign spas to reduce overweight, these trips seemed to end in self-defeating tours of the great continental cities. Trevail was a trencherman of the old school, his life a round of banquets, celebrations and official receptions, all accompanied by the finest food and drink. Even after, alarmed by his growing size, he consulted a Harley Street specialist, the diet that he followed was, to modern eyes, of massive proportions – several meals a day washed down with beer, wines and spirits. Yet once again he was far from alone in these eating habits.

Towards the end of his life, it is true that he sank into a state of apathy, losing interest in politics and even in his architectural work. He told Enys that he hoped to attend George Hicks' funeral 'if I can crawl out at all'. He complained frequently to his sister of complete exhaustion and severe headaches and excused himself from attending a council meeting because he was crippled with neuralgia. When an old acquaintance, with whom he used to trade humorous insults, met him and made a jocular remark, Trevail glared at him and strode off without exchanging a word. In his final days according to his cousin Charles he showed distressing signs of delusions, believing that detectives were searching his home and stealing documents. In this illogical behaviour, he seemed to be following in the footsteps of his father a year earlier, although of course John Trevail was in his eighties while Silvanus was only in his early fifties.

Summing up, it is a difficult task to diagnose a mental condition on the basis of second-hand accounts from the distant past, although this has never stopped historians from attempting it. In Trevail's case there is ample evidence of hyperactive behaviour from his twenties up to his late forties, coupled with extreme irritability and impatience with those who got in his way. Yet this did not lead him to financial ruin or megalomania of the kind associated with famous examples of political leaders or business tycoons. His life seems to have rather more in common with that of the great architect Augustus Pugin, who burnt himself out by the age of forty, intense hyperactivity collapsing into insanity.[16]

During the last year or two of his life we find increasing signs of hypochondria, apathy, financial worries, a morbid obsession with death and paranoia. However, these were not entirely unfounded, except for the paranoia, given the series of bereavements among family and friends, together with personal and business disappointments. What we fail to find in the thousands of documents relating to his business and personal life are examples of acute bi-polar fluctuations. Tregilgas argued that Trevail may have succeeded in repressing or disguising them in earlier life. But since we have no proof that these ever existed, would it not be simpler to conclude that he did not experience them at all? In other words, that he was not a manic-depressive but a man with an uncontrollable and obsessive desire to succeed in everything he undertook until he wore himself out?

A few of the 600 or more bundles of Trevail's plans held at Cornwall Record Office (CRO: AD396).

Unfinished business

As discussed earlier, Trevail left a number of his commissions unfinished. His major project of Bodmin asylum was transferred to a London architect, but the others were completed by his clerk, Alfred John Cornelius, who had been his assistant since 1896. Cornelius offered Laura Rundle £20 for Trevail's office furniture and £100 for the goodwill of the practice, provided that he received the outstanding commissions, which he did. He continued until August 1964 when he fell ill and, three days later, died at the age of eighty-eight.[17] His widow sold the practice to the Truro architect Alec Wells, who found all Trevail's plans and other documents intact in the attic. They are now in the Cornwall Record Office, where they have been catalogued by Hazel Harradence, assisted by other members of the Silvanus Trevail Society. Together with the hundreds of letters, diaries, books and photograph albums belonging to Trevail that are now held by his descendants, they form a unique heritage of Victorian Cornwall in the second half of the nineteenth century.

Trevail's legacy for Cornwall

In August 1906 a stained glass window, inscribed 'To the Glory of God, and in loving memory of Silvanus Trevail, JP, FRIBA ... Erected by his sister Laura Rundle' was dedicated in Luxulyan parish church.[18]

How can we sum up Trevail's achievements? He offers a splendid example of Victorian enlightened self-interest. He worked tirelessly to enhance Cornwall's intellectual infrastructure, reform its public health, improve railway access and promote tourism. What was good for Cornwall was undoubtedly good for Trevail, for he gained commissions for schools, libraries, technical and art colleges, churches and chapels, hospitals, hotels, banks,

Luxulyan Church Memorial window erected by his sister, Laura Rundle.

shops and dwellings of all kinds. One of his greatest contributions to the revival of the Cornish economy, stricken by the collapse of its metalliferous mining industry, was to put the region firmly on the holiday map, and celebrate its unique tourist identity. Had he lived only a few months longer he would have witnessed an event which would have gladdened his heart: the Cornish Riviera Express steaming triumphantly into Penzance, having made the trip from London in record time, together with the publication of the Great Western Railway 'Cornish Riviera' guide, an Edwardian bestseller.

In channelling his abundant energies, tenacity, organisational ability and artistic flair into the design and erection of his buildings he created a lasting testimony to his talents. The functions that many of the buildings served have changed, but their usefulness remains. Schools, churches and chapels have become private houses or apartments, medical centres, art galleries or restaurants. Seaside mansions have been converted into hotels, holiday flats or nursing homes. Interestingly, some of the most impressive renovations have occurred outside Cornwall, such as the fine red brick and stone edifices of Woodside in Dublin and the Passmore Edwards Library in London. Within Cornwall, owners of Trevail houses such as Treventon, Tregaddick and Perranzabuloe vicarage have sympathetically and tastefully restored them to their original splendour.

In one of his last major public speeches, a presidential address to the Society of Architects, Trevail had these words for his audience: 'whatever we build cannot be hidden, and will stand permanently in evidence for or against us, long, long after all those in this hall have passed away and are otherwise forgotten'. It is our hope that this book, together with the much greater heritage of his buildings, will help to preserve the memory of a remarkable man.

In Affectionate Remembrance

OF

SILVANUS TREVAIL,

(Of 80, Lemon Street, Truro),

Who died on Saturday, November 7th, 1903,

AGED 52 YEARS.

Appendix

A list of all buildings associated with the name of Silvanus Trevail, including those incorrectly attributed to him. Listed under categories of churches and chapels; domestic buildings; commercial; hotels; hospitals; public buildings; recreation and schools. Each building is dated, with a short paragraph of description.

Churches and chapels – including tombstones, memorials and bell towers

St Agnes Wesleyan Chapel. Thomas Richards designed the chapel in 1858, but in 1883 Trevail renovated the interior with a new gallery, rostrum, seating and stairs. About 1953 a floor was inserted at gallery level to divide the building into two storeys. Still in use. Listed building.

St Austell Cemetery Chapel. In April 1877 Trevail submitted 3 sets of plans to the St Austell burial board, along with 11 other architects. Trevail was one of the final four, but Henry Lovegrove's design was chosen.

St Austell Congregational Chapel. Erected in 1850 the chapel was renovated by Trevail in 1880 with new seating, a rostrum, organ loft and singing gallery, and alterations to the vestry and schoolroom underneath. A listed building, but demolished in the 1970s.

St Austell, Mount Charles Wesleyan Chapel. A gift of land from Thomas Crowle provided the site for this building in 1873. It was built by J T Smith and S Crocker of St Austell and in use until February 1995. Much loved and cared for by the congregation, it was demolished in 1995.

St Austell Wesleyan Chapel. Now St Johns Church, the old building was completely renovated, including a new facade, windows, ceiling and interior woodwork. The work was spread over several years and finally finished and re-opened in November 1892. Listed building. Still in use.

St Blazey Gate, Leek Seed Chapel. English Heritage has now changed the listing schedule to show F C Jury designed this building, not Trevail.

Bodmin Bible Christian Chapel. In 1877 as well as the basement being divided into smaller rooms and chapel renovations, a little porch was added to the front entrance. The porch is still there, but the building has not been used as a chapel for some time and its future is uncertain.

St Columb Congregational Chapel. Built in 1795 and enlarged three times, Trevail was requested to put in a new floor, seating, rostrum, gallery and stairs in 1876. More work was done in 1889, although it is not certain if this was Trevail's. A youth club later used the building, and then the interior was removed for a commercial enterprise. In 1995 it was converted into dwellings.

Edgcumbe Chapel. Designed with facilities for Sunday school in the basement and built by WJ Winn and Sons from Helston for £670. Services were held in a barn during building work, moving for a few weeks into the Sunday school. The building was fully open by March 1886. Listed building. Still in use.

Feock Wesleyan Chapel. The 1866 building had a very high and heavy roof that was damaging the walls so Trevail was responsible for extensive re-building in 1880. The walls were lowered, the gallery removed and the roof replaced. Still in use.

Fowey Church. A choir vestry added between the west wall and the churchyard in 1894. This entailed cutting an opening through from the church and adding a set of granite steps. The plan shows two roof lights that have since been removed.

Helland Church. Trevail designed a new tower in 1888 and at the same time the congregation raised additional money for a peal of bells. In December 1888 the new tower and peal of bells were officially opened.

Helland Wesleyan Chapel. A new building for 90–100 people set on the very edge of the village with views across the moor, built in 1878. It had a Sunday school, a gig house and stable for the Minister's horse. Still in use.

Kestle Mill Wesleyan Chapel. A new chapel for the parish of Newlyn East, seating 200 people on the main floor with provision for a gallery to be added at a later date. The building opened in October 1888 with a service followed by a public tea. Converted to dwelling.

Lank Free Methodist Chapel. On 25 February 1886 a ceremony was held to lay the cornerstones, followed by a service and public tea. The chapel, costing £400, opened the following September. It closed in the early 1970s and was demolished.

Lostwithiel Congregational Chapel. Built on the site of an older chapel, the memorial stones were laid in September 1878. The building was large enough for 200 people with the Sunday schoolroom, over the vestry, doubling as a gallery when required. It probably closed in the early 1920s and was later converted beyond recognition.

Luxulyan Church bells. As a memorial to his mother the old bells were re-cast and new ones added to make a peal of six. The tower was also strengthened to take them and the official opening was on 14 October 1902 when Trevail asked that 'there should be no narrowness in regard to their use, but they shall be for the inhabitants of Luxulyan on all proper occasions'. In 1904 all the school children in the parish received a dedication booklet containing all the details of the service and a commemoration medallion in the name of his father, John Trevail, who died late in 1902.

Luxulyan Church, chancel screen. WV Gough was responsible for the renovation of the church in 1879 and his plans show a new chancel screen; this was not erected at the time and it is probable that Trevail added it in 1902.

Luxulyan, obelisk in churchyard. Designed for his uncle, Joseph Trevail, who died 5 November 1903. Listed monument.

Luxulyan, sundial in churchyard. The old shaft, dated 1687, received a new dial from Trevail at the time of the renovation to the bell tower. Listed.

Luxulyan, Trevail memorial. A memorial for his parents, erected after the death of his mother Jane Trevail in 1902. The inscriptions now commemorate Jane and John Trevail, Laura Rundle, sister to Silvanus, and Silvanus himself. Listed monument.

Mevagissey Cemetery Chapel. The new cemetery was consecrated in February 1883, the chapel being built soon afterwards. A vestry was added to

Obelisk for Joseph Trevail

the rear at some stage and in 2005 the interior was taken out, the building re-roofed and converted into a workshop.

Mevagissey Congregational Church. One of the largest Trevail designed, it seated 450. The Memorial stones were laid on 4 August 1881 and the building opened 25 January 1883. After amalgamating with the Bible Christian church, the building became known as St Andrew's Church. In 1996 the old Sunday schoolrooms to the rear were pulled down and the church altered to make additional meeting rooms. The upper floor remained a chapel, with the woodwork, windows and organ wonderfully restored, housing for a lift and extra stairs were added and the ground floor divided to meet modern requirements.

Nanpean Church of St George. Services used to be held in the schoolroom for this part of the parish, as the parish church was about three miles away. The building was opened in October 1878 and was the first new church to be built after the restoration of the Cornish bishopric. The bell turret was moved from over the chancel arch to the back of the nave, probably when the organ was installed. Still in use.

Newquay Congregational Chapel. The previous building was too small for the growing population of Newquay and was 'in a back street'. Built by James Julian of Truro for £1,500 the new building opened on 1 August 1888. The pastor, W H Fuller, treated all those involved in the building work to a lunch at the Commercial Hotel where he thanked Silvanus Trevail for the 'beauty of the design of the building'. The building burnt down in 1924.

Padstow Mortuary Chapel. Designed in 1879 for the Padstow board's new cemetery, Trevail was unable to see the building work go ahead, as the new Burials Act did not require a chapel built on the ground.

Par Primitive Methodist Chapel. Sir Colman Rashleigh, Bart, JP, laid the foundation stone on 17 April 1875 and the building opened in August 1876 with a service. The following Monday there was a tea meeting in the afternoon and a public meeting in the evening. Trevail chose to use a pattern of alternate Par bricks in the curved arches over the windows, a similar design to the one he used in the St Blazey Boys School. The local Catholic community later purchased it for use. Demolished 1988.

Penzance St Paul's Church. The church by John Matthews, enlarged by John Trounson, had an enclosed area inside the main door to protect the worshippers from draughts. Trevail was asked to design the little porch on Clarence Street as a memorial to Miss Emily Borlase Bolitho in 1886. The church closed in 2000, its future unknown.

Redruth Wesleyan Chapel. The Trustees agreed, in 1881, to spend over £1,200 on Trevail's renovation of this 1826 building. The work included new iron pillars to support the gallery, making the ground floor all one level, new seating, rostrum, communion rail and gallery fronts. New ventilation was installed and the interior re-painted. Unfortunately the doors that were made to swing in both directions so as not to hamper people entering or leaving tended to blow around in high winds making the chapel draughty. Still in use. Listed building.

Roche Wesleyan Chapel. In 1877 the stone floor was replaced with a raised wooden one, when new pews, rostrum, gallery, organ loft and minister's room were added to this 1835 chapel. The walls were heightened, the roof replaced and new windows added. The Sunday school rooms were added about the same time, although it has not been possible to confirm that these were also by Trevail. Still in use. Listed building.

Rosemelling Chapel, Luxulyan. This was Trevail's first chapel renovation and the building re-opened in March 1872 with new seating and rostrum. Built in the first part of nineteenth century the chapel was in use until the 1950s, then becoming an almost derelict farm store until converted into a dwelling.

Sweetshouse Wesleyan Chapel. The chapel was built for Lanlivery Parish, but out in the countryside, in 1876 for 100 worshippers. There was also provision for the Minister's horse and gig. Left empty for many years, windows broken, pews and flooring removed, slates falling from roof, the building was eventually sold. Poorly converted in 1999. Listed building.

Temple Church. Probably one of the best known of Trevail's buildings, not necessarily for its architect, but more for the history of the Knights Templar. The Bishop of

Left: *Redruth Wesleyan Chapel.* Right: *Roche Wesleyan Chapel and Sunday school.*

Truro opened Trevail's reconstruction on 30 May 1883. The building cost about £450, Trevail did not charge for his work. Listed building.

Temple, building to the south of the church. An outbuilding used as store and made from reused dressed granite. English Heritage has listed the building, crediting it to Trevail. Local people seem to think it was not built until the 1930s.

Truro, Mission Church of St Andrew. It was built by St John's Parish from one of three designs produced by Trevail, who offered buildings priced at £630, £600 or £580, according to the funds available. Mrs Bolitho of Trewidden laid the foundation stone with an inscribed silver trowel on 29 July 1899. The church was partly furnished with generous gifts of an oak pulpit, gas fittings, altar chairs, carpeting and paintings. The site was very small and the vestry was underneath the chancel. It was dedicated on 16 January 1900. Later demolished, the site is now part of a new development.

Truro, St Piran's Chapel. New premises for the Roman Catholics were required and the Rev Father John Grainger purchased the site for a small chapel to be erected in 1884. In 1973 the congregation moved to larger premises. Now used by a pre-school group.

Truro, St Mary's Wesleyan Chapel. Renovation work started in 1884 and was completed for a grand re-opening on 15 March 1885. The contractor, Battershill of Truro, carried out the work in Sambell's 1830 building. The gallery curve was re-aligned, the pillars changed and the floor strengthened. Ceiling decoration was included, as well as new memorial windows all round the building. The seating was replaced, a new rostrum added, Grundy's patent heating apparatus installed and Siemen's patent lights suspended from the ceiling. In the summer of 2000 the downstairs pews were replaced with moveable seating and the foyer enlarged to provide a social area, screened from the chapel by a glass wall. Listed building.

Truro, St Mary's Wesleyan Sunday school. It was announced in 1887 that a new Sunday school was to be built immediately behind the church. Apart from six separate classrooms it contained a ladies working room, committee and prayer meeting room and an assembly hall 63 feet long. Still part of St Mary's Church. Listed building.

Truro, William Street Chapel. Also known as the Lemon Chapel, the lower floor accommodated the Sunday school in several small classrooms, with the chapel on the upper floor. The choir stalls were slightly raised and at the back of the room. Opened October 1887. Later converted for commercial use.

Tywardreath, Trenython Manor Chapel. Bishop Gott of Truro bought the house for his own use in 1891 and the chapel was built some time after that. A small white building with ornamental woodwork at the side of the house, it was still in use when the house was a convalescent home, but became a general store for unwanted items from the house when later used as a hotel. Repaired and renovated by the current owners it is now used for civil wedding ceremonies.

Upton Cross, St Paul's Church. Sampson Trehane of Liskeard was the builder, appointed in November 1885 for a total cost of about £1,250. The design included heating by hot air. The chancel is apsidal, the same as that of Nanpean. The land had been given to the building committee by HRH the Duke of Cornwall. The consecration took place on 2 May 1887. Sensitive renovation work was carried out in 1980.

Upton Cross, St Paul's Sunday school. Designed and built at the same time as the church in matching materials, it consists of one main room with a small porch. Used as a church and village hall.

Domestic buildings – mansions, houses, farms, animal housing

St Allen, Gwarnick farm buildings. The 1879 plans were for a cart and wagon shed and a bullock house. Now part of Tremenwyth, a complex of barns converted to holiday dwellings.

St Allen, Killivose farmhouse. Built on the Prideaux-Brune estate in 1879, it cost £807.15.9d.

St Allen, Tretherras farmhouse. Designed for the Prideaux-Brune estate in 1878, the house was sold to the Carveth family in 1893. Now carefully renovated as a private family home.

St Austell, High Cross Street terrace. St Austell UDC passed designs for a block of four houses of three storeys in September 1901, but later plans of two storey buildings were used. The houses are immediately above the site of the old police station.

St Austell, Moorland Road. Funded by Francis Barratt (later Sir Francis Layland Barratt JP, CC) for local workmen, the houses were erected in seven separate blocks between 1897 and 1900. At a rental of £9 or £12 per year, it was said they were too expensive for many working class families.

St Austell, North Hill conservatory. Designed for J E Veale in 1896 and long since demolished. No photograph of the building has been found.

Top: Upton Cross Sunday school and church rooms.
Bottom: Tretherras farmhouse, St Allen.

St Austell, Sydenham Villa. A rear extension for extra kitchen facilities was added to the house now known as Tremena House. Date unknown.

St Austell, Sylvan Terrace. A row of four houses built in 1896 by a member of the Lovering family. Local tradition says Trevail designed them but no written evidence as yet found.

St Austell, Tregarne Terrace with Tregarne Lodge. A terrace of stone houses built for Francis Barratt in the 1890s. The house at the top of the road was made larger for Barratt himself in 1894, but in 1895 he moved to Torquay. Most are now used for office accommodation.

St Austell, Watering Lane building estate. An

estate of new streets, with building plots, laid out for Edward Coode, date unknown, but still not implemented in 1938. The area has since become a council estate, south of Alexander Road.

Beaworthy, Devon, cottages. A pair of workers' cottages similar to others in style were built to the north of Witherdon house in the 1870s.

Beaworthy, Devon, Witherdon. In 1872 an old farmhouse was developed into a 'Manor' house. Tredenham Hugh Carlyon changed his name to Spry and between 1893 and 1897 Trevail upgraded the house by building new facades and extended it by adding a dining room and kitchen quarters Panelling, fireplaces, new windows and staircase were also added. After Spry's death in 1930 the house suffered when a turkey farmer allowed his stock to roam inside, but was rescued some years later when re-sold. Since 1970 has been a comfortable and much loved family home.

Beaworthy, Devon, Witherdon stables. When the house was renovated in 1893, the new kitchen quarters continued to a wood house that in turn joined the new stable block containing carriage house, harness room and provision for four horses. The coach house is now a garage, but the stables, until very recently, were used for their original purpose.

Blisland, Tregaddick. A holiday home built for Sir Warwick Morshead of Berkshire in 1886 soon after his second marriage. Tregaddick, originally with ten bedrooms, was soon extended to give an extra four. The house remained in the family until 1943, and then became a hotel for a while. It was almost derelict when taken over by the present owners who are lovingly restoring it to a family home once more.

Blisland, Tregaddick stables. Badly treated during the hotel period, the early 1990s conversion to dwellings has removed any trace of the original buildings.

Blisland, Tregaddick Lodge. Built in a style resembling Trevail's, but there are no records.

Bodmin, residence. After several unsuccessful attempts to satisfy J R Collins requirements for a new house in 1894, Trevail finally designed a much smaller house opposite Bodmin General station. It has since been altered and extended on several occasions. Now a social club.

Bodmin, St Gurons. Miss Collins, sister to J R Collins, had many different plans drawn up in 1898 and 1899 for her house – a very large one for a single lady – and then pleaded poverty. Some of the plans are marked 'Design D' and 'Design E' an indication of how many she required. After being used for many years as a dentist's home and surgery the building was carefully converted into small apartments in 2005.

Bodmin, Laninval. For Henry Dennis, a Cornishman, who had the Ruabon terracotta works in North Wales, the building was intended to show off his product to the county. The original house of 1895 was extended in 1903 to provide a billiard room and extra bedrooms and a kitchen that had been previously housed in an old building close by. Later purchased by St Lawrence's Hospital it is now a privately run home for people with special needs.

Bodmin, Lunatic Asylum farm buildings. The asylum committee who had plans drawn up in 1899, suggested a large number of alterations and when they were completed required an estimate of the cost. On being told the cost would be in the region of £3,160, the committee stated they were not prepared to spend more than £2,000 so the idea was dropped.

Bodmin, Lunatic Asylum farm bailiff's residence. These plans suffered in the same way as the farm buildings. When Trevail asked for expenses they would only pay him a percentage of their £2,000 ceiling, not of his estimate. No price limit of £2,000 could be found mentioned in the minutes prior to Trevail presenting the plans.

Camborne, Chapel Street. A house built in the 1880s for A J Tangye, auctioneer and agent. Following re-numbering of Camborne streets it is now numbered 6 instead of 12 as on the plans. A double-fronted house, it contained 5 bedrooms but no bathroom or inside WC. Now offices.

Camborne, Polstrong conservatory. A two-storey aisled conservatory of 1896 for John R Daniel. The house was sold early in the 1900s and over next 90 years received very little upkeep. When the current owners took over there were grave doubts whether the conservatory could be saved. Fortunately much care has gone into its restoration. Listed building.

Carbis Bay building estate. The area between the railway and the road into St Ives was laid out in 1896 for housing. The only road built from this layout is Headland Road.

Carbis Bay, semi-detached houses. Plans are of the same period as the building estate and the block of terraced houses. Presumably Trevail hoping to get the commission for building these villas on the estate. None found.

Carbis Bay, terrace. A terrace of four was planned for landowner William Tyringham of Trevethow in 1896, although only three were erected with the one to the western end being doubled in size. The front of the houses face the bay, with the back elevations facing Headland Road.

St Columb Major, Ashleigh. A new facade to this house was planned with extended rooms and kitchen alterations in 1896 for Miss Martyn. Remains a family home.

Rear view of Carbis Bay terrace.

St Columb Major, Treventon. The house was extended in 1879 for Henry Whitford with a panelled billiard room and a service wing for kitchen accommodation and staff bedrooms. Altered by various owners over the years, it has received careful repairs and alterations turning it into a family home once more.

Dublin, Woodside. The house was designed in 1901 for John Parkes, an iron magnate. Parkes had seen Treloyhan, the house Trevail designed for Edward Hain, and wanted something similar, although a completely new set of plans had to be drawn up. Alfred Cornelius finished the work after Trevail died, completion being August 1904. Trevail wrote on the back of one of Parkes' letters 'My Dublin clients who will be spending something like 20,000 upon this residence.' A more modest house costing just over £5,000 was eventually erected. It is now used by the Irish Pharmaceutical Association and recently renovated.

Falmouth, Trevissome House. The only mention of this building is in *Collectanea Cornubiensis* which states Trevail was responsible for an extension in 1886. No other information found, although a later rear wing could be of that period.

Falmouth, Bosvathick, Constanine. Four sheets of plans by Trevail in 1885 for a large extension to the existing Georgian house. Another layout, by a different architect, was built about ten years later.

Fowey, building land. In 1894 Trevail produced a plan for an estate covering the area where the car park, Fowey Hall and smaller estate have since been built.

Fowey, entrance lodge for Place. A lucky find amongst some unlisted papers, this plan, for C E Treffry, is dated 1882. A neat single storey building on the lower road to Bodinnick Ferry.

Gerrans, Trewince. The house was built in mid eighteenth century, but in 1898 John Thomas, known locally as 'Squire Thomas' wanted an extension containing a billiard room and new kitchen quarters. The new wing also included three bedrooms. The house is now part of a holiday complex and the billiard room used as a dining room. Listed building.

Gerrans, Trewince Cottage. This plan is for a small cottage somewhere on the estate, containing living quarters and a 'tea-room', possibly for entertaining visitors after a carriage drive through the grounds which overlook part of the River Fal. Not found.

Grampound Road, Trenoweth Farmhouse. New home farm house for Robert (later Sir Robert) Harvey's holiday estate. The house has Harvey's initials over the door and the date 1890.

Grampound Road, Trenoweth farm buildings. This complete complex of farm buildings was built by James Julian of Truro at the same time as the farmhouse. The farm buildings purchased from the farm in 1990 have been carefully renovated and converted to provide generous and attractive homes.

Helland, Tredethy. The home of F J Hext, an old house with seventeenth century origins, was extended in 1868. It was further extended by Trevail in 1892 by the addition of a new wing containing a large dining room, additional kitchen quarters and two extra bedrooms. Trevail also put a new facade to the building, added a front porch and renovated the 1868 main hall. Now a country house hotel.

Illogan, Tehidy stables. In June 1894 a large complex of stabling, carriage houses and accommodation for staff was designed. Trevail had acquired plans of stable blocks from around the country to help him with his planning. There were 12 sheets of finished drawings produced, although no specifications or quantities had been drawn up by the time of Trevail's death. A coach house was added to the existing stables in the nineteenth century, similar to Trevail's building, but there is no record of the architect. The whole complex was converted into apartments when no longer required for hospital premises.

St Ives, Draycott Terrace. The terrace was designed in 1894 for the Rouncefield family and used for letting out to holiday visitors. A few retain original windows, one house at least with its pitch pine staircase. Most are now hotels.

St Ives, residence. A house for Captain Harry, mariner and past Mayor of St Ives, was designed in 1893, later known as Morwenstow. The elevation facing the sea is covered with various extensions but the original building can be seen from the road frontage, including a large stained glass window on the stairs. Later a hotel named Chy-an-dour, now to be demolished.

St Ives, Treloyhan. The local shipping magnate, Edward (later Sir Edward) Hain Jnr, JP, CC, had the house built by Thomas Lang & Sons of Liskeard in 1892. It has been said that Trevail also designed the grounds but no evidence has been found and a local historian suggests that it was Edward Hain himself who laid out the gardens. After being used as a hotel, when a large extension was added, a girl's school was evacuated here during WW II and it is now run by the Christian Guild as a conference centre and restaurant.

St Ives, Treloyhan gatehouse. In 1897 the advertisement for tenders to build suggests there were two cottages, as well as the stables. The only cottage found is the gatehouse at the western end of the grounds, similar in design to the stables.

St Ives, Treloyhan stables. By 1896 a need was felt for personal carriage and horses and the stables were built in 1897 on what is now the opposite side of the road into St Ives. The buildings have been converted to holiday accommodation, part of the Tregenna Castle complex.

Ladock, labourer's cottages at Menna. A pair of cottages built in 1878, similar to those erected at Penhale and Witherdon in Devon, consisting of 2 rooms with porch, lobby and pantry on the ground floor and three bedrooms over. The WC was in the yard.

Ladock, Tregear Farmhouse. Tregear was built for the Beauchamp family of Redruth in 1882. The open porch has since been closed in, but very little else has altered. The tenant in 2000 said that all windows were the originals and in good condition. On the opposite side of the road a stone barn of about the same period is in good condition, although its origins are not known.

Lanivet, Churchtown Mill dwelling house. Tenders for the house were requested in March 1886 on behalf of Thomas Grose and John Trevail. The building still stands on the Lanivet to Bodmin road, and is now a private house.

Lapford Wood, Devon, gardener's cottage. The plans show a very elaborate design for a gardener; not only an inside WC but a bathroom upstairs, something that many larger houses were still without in 1902. Alfred Cornelius wrote to Charles Vivian, the landowner, in December 1903 asking if he intended going ahead, but it appears the project was dropped.

Lizard, house and stables. John Roberts, a silk merchant, had the house designed in 1894 after his third marriage. Originally called 'Maenheere' it remained in the family until bequeathed to the National Trust in 1987. It was known locally as the bedstead house because of the ironwork balcony on the rooftop. The house was fully restored by tenants of the Trust.

Lostwithiel, Cowbridge. A wing was added to the side of this building and another at the rear for George Hext in 1894, with new bay windows added to the old front. Currently a nursing home.

Mevagissey, for Dr Monro Grier. A large house was designed in 1892 for the local doctor, overlooking the harbour. Named Polpier, it was built within a year and contained a waiting room and surgery for the patients. The front has been painted and re-painted several times, whilst the rear of the building has several extensions, but not to the same standard. Currently, it needs careful attention and repair.

Michaelstow, Tregenna House. The house was built for William Hocken in 1869 and a succession of inhabitants made alterations. James Muir in 1902 wanted a new glass conservatory-type entrance added but it was never built. A small porch on the left-hand wing could have been built from part of Trevail's main design work.

St Minver, labourer's cottage. The plan was for a single house, designed in 1875 in such a way that another could have been added to one side. It was impossible to find with no indication of where it might be.

Cowbridge, Lostwithiel.

Moretonhampstead, Devon, nurses home. George Wills endowed this in memory of his wife, Lucy, who died in 1898. Problems arose during the planning and building because of objections from Sampson who had a property next door. Alfred Cornelius finally finished the work in 1904. Converted to private apartments.

Newquay, Fistral building estate. A layout for this estate was designed in 1881 and refreshed in 1894. Most of the site is now Newquay Golf Club. Dane Road, Beacon Road and Fistral Road, (later renamed Headland Road), are the only roads to have been built.

Newquay, Porth Veor estate. An estate was laid out on land of William Stephens in 1881. A road called Trevelga Road (now Lusty Glaze) is the only one from the drawings that was built. Trevail designed at least one of the houses eventually built there, Lamorna.

Newquay, Tolcarne estate. The land was the property of Edward Pearce; the building sites were designed in 1883 from the railway line through to where Ulalia Road is now. Tolcarne Road, Edgcumbe Avenue and Edgcumbe Gardens are the only recognisable parts on a map today.

Newquay, Bon Air. This was designed in 1900 for E O Preston from Berkshire, a family home but smaller than Pentowan, and built by Sampson Trehane of Liskeard. A private residence at least until 1939, it later becoming a hotel with many poor unworthy extensions and alterations, being re-named Westward Ho in the early 1920s. Demolished in 2003 to make way for a large block of holiday apartments.

Newquay, Fistral Road terrace. Built in 1896 as Trevail's own investment, this terrace remained as individual dwellings until c1970 when three were converted into a hotel. Now demolished and replaced by a large block of apartments.

Newquay, new road to Fistral Beach. Part of the 1891 improvements was a new road to Fistral Beach, to encourage the new tourist industry.

Newquay, Gover Road improvements. In 1891 Newquay Local Board employed Trevail to look at improvements to the town and widening Gover Road was one that he implemented. The houses used to have front gardens that were taken away and the house on the corner of the main street was removed completely.

Newquay, Lamorna. The house was for John Vivian CC, one of the brothers for whom Trevail designed a store in Camborne, in 1891 on the building estate of William Stephens. It was a house on three floors facing the sea on Trevelga Road, re-named Lusty Glaze in the 1960s. The roofline was altered, additions were made and the whole converted into the Clarendon apartments.

Newquay, Pentowan. This was designed in 1880 for George Hicks overlooking Newquay harbour. A large house with dining and drawing rooms, parlour and study, as well as large kitchen quarters, there were also plans for a billiard room behind the conservatory, but that was never built. There were later additions and then alterations when it became a nursing home. Now lovingly repaired and converted into apartments with further alterations allowing a new wing to be built where the conservatory had been.

Newquay, Porth Veor House. Prior to commissioning Trevail to design buildings sites for his land, William Stephens had him design this house overlooking Porth beach in 1879. Now the Porth Veor Hotel, the building has been lost under piecemeal additions.

Newquay, Tolcarne Road improvements. In 1892 Trevail suggested that retaining walls were built, but it is not known which section was involved.

Newquay, a pair of semi-detached houses. Designed in 1876 for Mr Libby, no trace of the houses has been found. Mr Libby was a builder living on Tolcarne Head.

Newquay, residence. Alfred Sparkes had two different designs for a large home somewhere in Newquay. In 1894 Sparkes was appointed manager of the Newquay branch of the Devon and Cornwall Bank, when he probably lived in the Manager's apartment over the bank. The building designed for him has not been found.

Padstow, Dennis building estate. A scheme for C G Prideaux-Brune of Prideaux Place was planned in 1897, along the river Camel, west of the railway line. The arrangement was that Trevail would be paid commission by the respective builders who took up sites, presumably using his house designs. No buildings shown there in 1908.

Padstow, Pentireglaze estate. A building site for Lord Robartes in 1896, in the area now known as New Polzeath was mooted, although Jenkins, steward to Lord Robartes, did write to Trevail about some alterations to the plan.

Padstow Trevone building estate. Nicholls of Padstow purchased land in 1899 on behalf of a company who intended building good lodging houses. They were also going to build a hotel. None of this happened, although the Sea Spray hotel and Atlantic Terrace were built by someone else between 1899 and 1907, on a road suggested by Trevail.

Padstow, Treator. A house for William M Richards, with drawing, morning and dining rooms and five bedrooms, was built by James Julian of Truro in 1884. Richards later became a JP as well as a County Councillor. In the 1940s the house was bought by the Royal Navy for hospital premises, afterwards becoming a hospital for infectious diseases. Now known as Woodlands Country House, the latest owners have done everything possible to return the rooms to the way they probably once looked.

Padstow, Trevone, a pair of dwellings. Designed about 1899 for Robert Warne, a Trevone builder, the only pair found is difficult to recognise now.

Par, St Mary's Vicarage. The contractor for the Rev Frank Garrett's new house in 1882 was Werry & Bunney of St Blazey. The house, whilst not appearing large from the outside, contained drawing and dining rooms, a study and three bedrooms. The work was completed for £392.13s. No longer required as a vicarage, it has become a private house.

Penzance, Heamoor. Poltair Terrace for A C Jenkins in 1896 was a terrace of eight houses, many still unchanged in their appearance.

Perranporth, Droskyn. In 1885 a visitor to Perranporth drew attention to the encroachment on The Droskyn, and the house built on the site of the old fish cellars. This house, known as Droskyn Castle, in 1894 was the home of T H Pill who had Trevail design additional rooms under a mansard roof with access from one of the towers. The work was never carried out.

Perranzabuloe Vicarage. In 1884 Trevail started designing a vicarage, but with the time needed for the Ecclesiastical Commissioners to make alterations and approve specifications and costs, it was not until 1888 that the building went up. The vicar's study at the rear of the house, had access to a waiting room for parishioners, who entered through a back door. Unused and almost derelict in mid 1990s, the current owners have put a lot of time, thought and care into retrieving an unusual home. Listed building.

Pool, Wheal Agar cottages. This was another scheme of Trevail's, to provide homes for workers, on land provided by Lord Robartes in 1892. On the eastern side of Trevithick Road, twenty-five homes with 3 rooms downstairs, and 3 bedrooms, were built.

St Stephens, Penhale cottages. Farm workers cottages in 1881 at Penhale Farm were planned for landowner E B Beauchamp. The cottages are similar to those designed for Beaworthy in Devon and Menna, Ladock.

St Stephens, Penhale Farm. These were additional farm buildings for the occupier, John Smith, of a cow house and turnip house. Old materials were to be re-used and the cost was estimated at £48.15s. The buildings form part of a rectangular yard. Undated but probably the same time as other work, 1881.

St Stephens, Terras Farm. A farmhouse extension planned in 1881 for a new kitchen and scullery area. Not built.

St Stephens, Terras farm buildings. These buildings were for the occupier Robert

Hicks in 1881. The buildings do not appear to have been erected here, but whilst looking at Penhale Farm, the same design of building was found. So although Robert Hicks never had his new building, John Smith got two new ones.

Totnes, Devon, Dundridge. This was the holiday home of Robert Harvey, a close friend of Trevail, where friends were invited for several weeks at a time. In 1898 Harvey's billiard room was renovated with new woodwork, fireplace and ceiling cornice. A staircase was added to give access to the first floor, removing the necessity for the players to enter the main part of the house.

Trebarwith building site. Trebarwith Estate was the property of the Earl of Wharncliffe and in 1895 laid out for 31 dwelling houses. Most of the site is still unused, being to the east of the road running down to Trebarwith Strand and on a very steep incline. The plan was produced about the time Trevail was trying to persuade several landowners, including Wharncliffe, to invest in King Arthur's Castle Hotel, but there was little money available.

Trebarwith bridge and road. Tenders to build these were requested in advertisements dated February 1896; Trevail wrote to Wharncliffe's solicitors that he wished the job could be a larger one, so that it could be the means of taking some of the unemployed now being driven into the workhouse. The road serves one house on the slope above the road.

Trebarwith farmhouse. Close to the village, this building was suggested to the Trevail Society as being a Trevail design. No evidence yet found.

Trebarwith Strand houses. A pair of houses on the left approaching the sea was suggested to the Trevail Society as being Trevail's design. No evidence yet found.

Tregony Almshouses. The old houses dated from 1696, but were in a ruinous condition when Trevail was asked by the Boscawen Charity to draw up plans for their renovation in 1894. They were described as a long-standing eyesore. Three dwellings were on each floor, four with separate living room and bedroom, the remaining two being a combined living and bedroom. They are still used as dwellings, although altered. Listed building.

Tregony, Trewarthenick House. Plans were made for Sir Lewis Molesworth about 1900 to put in a hot water system. The plan shows pipes and sinks on first and second floors, as well as in the kitchen and butler's pantry. The system would have been taken out when the house was converted into apartments, if not before.

Tregony, Trewarthenick stables. Trevail's plans in 1900 for Sir Lewis Molesworth were for a major renovation, including a new carriage house, and extensions over the stables to provide accommodation for stable staff. The tender received from Trehane the builder was for £1,450 and Molesworth wrote it was more than he thought and the work did not go ahead.

Truro, Agar Road. H G Pool had alterations made about 1902 to his house, known as 'Fernleigh'. The single storey scullery at the rear of the house had a first floor built over it to provide a bedroom, the small existing bedroom being turned into a bathroom.

Truro, Castle Hill. A small cottage for T Farr in 1893 next to the passageway to Pydar Street, thought to have been demolished when the cattle market site was used for the crown court building.

Truro, St John's Vicarage. Four Truro architects were invited to send in plans, including Trevail. The design of W Swift, also of Lemon Street, was chosen in 1887.

Truro, Lambesso piggeries. William Hocking came to Lambesso sometime during the early 1900s and required a pig house containing six pens and a boiling house. There is a similar building quite close to the house and built during the right period, but was used as stables. Piggeries not thought to have been built.

Truro, Lemon Mews. In 1890 a stable block was designed for Walter Hitchens containing two loose boxes, six stalls and a harness room. The plans received permission from the council, so no doubt went ahead, but it is not possible to identify them now due to building work for the market.

Truro, Lemon Street carriage entrance. A decorated archway through to the rear of the properties and although undated this plan is thought to have been produced at the same time as the stable block. It can be seen at 73 Lemon Street and the entrance to the market.

Truro, 80–81 Lemon Street. Trevail first rented the pair of houses in the early 1880s, living in one, with Bullen as tenant in the other. Bullen vacated his in 1901 and Trevail undertook to cut doorways through the party wall at ground and first floor levels to make one large house. He then re-arranged the rooms to provide better living and working accommodation. There were new ceilings for the breakfast and bedroom, a fireplace for the dining room and panelling for the walls. He also purchased new furniture, although the sideboard design by Cohen with his papers in the CRO is not one he used. In July 1902 he entertained members of the Devon and Exeter Architectural Society to lunch in his newly arranged premises. His sister Laura removed the dining room fireplace and the furniture from the building after his death, including the sideboard that Trevail designed himself. Listed building.

Truro, St Piran's Presbytery. A tall, narrow house, the presbytery was built next to the small, neat church in 1884. At the rear was a covered passageway into the church. There were seven bedrooms in all, one probably for servants. Now converted to letting rooms.

Truro, 9 Princes Street. A square columned porch with steps, walling and railings were added to this house in 1893. Princes House was built c1740 for William Lemon and from 1885 was the home of Samuel Polkinhorne an agricultural merchant. Listed building.

Truro, railwaymen's dwellings. Trevail spoke many times on the need for housing for workers, and after many years Lord Robartes provided a piece of land in 1892 to build a terrace for railway workers. The houses at 16–19 Harrison Terrace were designed with a parlour, living room and scullery with three bedrooms.

Truro, residence. G H Chilcott wanted an imposing residence, without having to pay very much money for it. Having changed his mind over the site, he decided on one near the top of Mitchell Hill although it had 'a bad approach'. Trevail produced a full set of plans in 1900 for a large house that had a frontage of nearly 100 feet, including stables and coach-house. In the end Chilcott decided to drop the idea and find a house either in Truro or Falmouth.

Truro, Sylvania. This was the name Trevail gave to a house design he produced as a letter heading. The house resembled that designed for G H Chilcott, but it is believed the two were not connected.

Truro, Trevaylia. Two letterheads were produced under this name. One showed the house built for John Parkes in Dublin, the other was the house built for Edward Hain, but reversed. It is possible Trevail was thinking of a house for himself and trying out various designs to see which suited.

Tunbridge Wells, Rusthall Beacon. A chimneypiece consisting of fire surround and grate was designed, the date unknown. Being minor internal works these were not investigated.

Tywardreath, Trenython entrance lodge. The Rev John Gott, Bishop of Truro, bought the big house for his residence for about £11,000 in 1891. The new lodge had an open porch with living and dining rooms, kitchen, scullery and three bedrooms. The outside was plastered, with decorative woodwork to the first floor. Over the years several alterations have changed its appearance considerably. Now separate premises to Trenython, the current owners have made an effort to bring back some of the Victorian features.

Commercial buildings – shops, warehouses, banks.

St Agnes, Devon and Cornwall Bank. Built about 1900 and by 1908 suffered badly from dry rot. Now used as parish rooms.

St Austell, Coode, Shilson & Co. Now universally known as the 'Red Bank', these premises built in red brick and terracotta caused a great deal of interest in the town in 1898. The re-building on this corner allowed the streets to be widened and make room for a footpath. Not only are the walls curved, but the windows and glazing were also designed that way. Listed building.

St Austell, Devon and Cornwall Bank. Minor work included new windows on the side of the building and internal alterations, undated. The windows can still be seen on the corner of High Cross and Cross Lane.

St Austell, Hawkes & Co. George Hawkes premises were next to the new Liberal Club building and the adjoining wall had to be taken down and rebuilt in 1889. At the same time a new front was added and a new roof structure. This has since been altered, the original roofline showing on the side of the Thin End restaurant.

St Austell, Mr Hodge's shop. Henry Hodge, a seedsman, florist and nurseryman, opened his new shop at 22, Fore Street in March 1889. It was considered 'very artistic'. Living accommodation was on three floors over the shop. The ground floor has been altered several times but the upper floors remain almost untouched.

Door to Bodmin Post Office.

St Austell, Market Place shop. Very small premises on the corner of Market Hill were rebuilt in 1898. The ground floor was a barber's shop; a staircase from Market Hill gave access to a hairdresser's on the first floor, with stairs to the second floor store-room. Now part of Tregonissey House.

St Austell, Veale & Co Ltd. Electrical works in Menacuddle Street were extended to provide new workshops, rest rooms, offices and stores in 1898. Mostly demolished, a small section remains as office accommodation.

Bodmin, post office and shops. In March 1884 a new post office and three shops, each with living accommodation, were opened in Honey Street. The builder was James Godfrey of Liskeard, whose workmen had a narrow escape when one of the new chimneys fell down, taking with it several rafters. Now all retail premises.

Bude, post office and shops. A terrace of three premises each with living accommodation was built for J T Perry in 1902. The post office, now a bank, was to be on the corner of Villa Road; the shop at the opposite end of the terrace had to be wedge-shaped to fit the site. They still retain many original features.

Camborne, Fiddick & Michell. An imposing building built on a curved site on Commercial Street in 1893, the building included premises for the Devon and Cornwall Bank, the pillars of which can still be seen. Unfortunately one section of first floor windows has been poorly treated.

Camborne, Vivian Bros. Carefully worked out plans in 1897 enabled the drapery business to continue running on part of the site, whilst the new, large and elaborate building was erected. Vivian's then moved into the finished part of the new building so the old one could be knocked down, making room for the second stage. Said to be unsafe it was pulled down less than a hundred years later.

St Columb, Barclays Bank. This 1872 listed building has been credited to Silvanus Trevail, but we do not believe it was his work. Unfortunately we cannot find out who did design it.

St Columb, Cornish Bank. The first set of plans in 1891 were for a three-storey building, containing seven bedrooms, but a more modest two storeys were erected on the site previously occupied by Charles Bennett, a butcher. The manager's quarters on

Left: *Fiddick and Michell premises, Camborne.*
Right: *Cornish Bank, St Columb.*

the first floor were entered by the door on the left; the banking hall was to the right. Now occupied by Lloyds TSB. Listed building.

Falmouth, Devon and Cornwall Bank. Opened in 1898 in Church Street, this two-storey building is in Plymouth limestone with granite dressings. The manager's room near the back of the building was to have a glass roof. On the 1st floor the drawing room looked out over the river Fal. Now a restaurant.

Fowey, Devon and Cornwall Bank. Planning work started in April 1901 but was not passed by St Austell RDC until June 1903. Trevail blamed this on the bank authorities who dillied and dallied so long that the Cornish Bank took the best site. The yellow terracotta for the building came from the Ruabon works in Wales. Cornelius finished supervising the work and received his final payment in January 1905, although the bank was in operation by 1904. Now occupied by Lloyds TSB. Listed building.

Fowey, quayside store. The undated plan shows a three-storey building, next to the Customs House, at the riverside with quay space to one side. Not built.

Helston, Cornish Bank. A magnificent four-storey building designed for this site was later cut back to two plus basement. Built in 1891 by Winn & Son of Helston. Problems arose when Martha Cotton, owner of the building on the corner of Meneage and Wendron streets complained about the loss of light. In the High Court she was awarded only £50 for damages that were considered to be greatly exaggerated, but the Bank incurred heavy costs. Now used by Lloyds TSB.

St Ives, Devon and Cornwall Bank. An older building that had been used by Robert Harris, draper, was altered at ground floor level, with a new granite front, bank vault and banking hall. The bank announced in July 1894 that business would be carried on whilst alterations were in progress. Now used by Lloyds TSB.

Newquay, Cornish Bank. The Cornish Bank purchased a house on the Central Square site in 1890 and in 1894 alterations were made. Rooms were changed, making living accommodation on the upper floor whilst the banking hall had a new granite front added. The building was demolished in 1913.

Newquay, Devon and Cornwall Bank. On the corner of Bank Street and Beachfield Avenue a large building was erected in 1900; it had manager's accommodation to the rear as well as over the banking hall. The contractor was John Coliver but unfortunately a lot of his decorative work has been lost under render and paint. Madam Hawke changed the small windows for the larger ones in 1910 when she took over the premises for her knitting factory. Now retail premises.

Penzance, Devon and Cornwall Bank. The bank was in Chapel Street when in the late 1880s Trevail designed an extra storey to give more space in the manager's accommodation and to put a WC on the ground floor for the staff. It was decided instead to build new premises in Market Place, which James Hicks designed in 1893. Now a shop.

Polruan, piers. In 1874 Trevail wrote to a local paper complaining there was nowhere safe to land from the ferry at Polruan. He had already drawn up plans to extend the piers at Hocken's yard but a certain gentleman was prevented from doing so for a trivial reason according to Trevail. At some stage circumstances must have changed as the pier extensions went ahead, although the ferry now stops further along the waterfront.

Truro, Boscawen Bridge store. Trevail and Samuel Polkinhorne wanted to extend the site for this building about one foot (30cm) on to the riverbed. The Town Council said it could not be done and the two sides continued to be at loggerheads for some while. Polkinhorne threatened to take his business out of the town, but later built a warehouse in Princes Street. Alfred Cornelius designed the store that eventually went up at Boscawen Bridge in 1907 but was later demolished. Haven House now occupies the site.

Truro, Burton's. The site on King Street was only 24 feet wide, but extended through to the Leats giving a length of 115 feet. A shop was designed in 1890 on three floors with a separate storage area and a yard at the back. Trevail may have entrusted some of the work to an assistant as he has written comments on the plans, such as 'This cabbage must be revised or omitted' and 'This pudding shaped shaft cannot possibly be allowed'. A hard taskmaster, but he insisted on perfection.

Truro, Burton's. Burtons had a china gallery in the old assembly rooms building in High Cross and a furnishing warehouse in the building next door and plans were in hand to open up the wall between the two buildings and remove some internal walls. No date was given. Both buildings have now been altered considerably, so impossible to find Trevail's work.

Truro, Cathedral Lane and Boscawen Street. Currently premises for Samuels, this building, faced with white brick, has been incorrectly credited to Trevail, but Alfred Cornelius designed it in 1904. Listed building.

Truro, Devon and Cornwall Bank. Henry Rice built the first bank in 1872 in Boscawen Street and in 1891 Trevail designed his larger and more impressive building next door. Walls were knocked through to join them together. Shuttering was put up round the building whilst work was in progress and space sold on it for advertising. Now used by Lloyds TSB. Listed building.

Truro, Exchange Building. An Exchange building was set up in Boscawen Street some time after 1881, at Reed's premises, when Trevail added the new front to the building and did some internal alterations to form a coffee tavern. Later demolished.

Truro, Gill & Son. Plans for factory premises on Market Quay were drawn up prior to 1903, but are not the same as those seen in many photographs of the area. It is possible that Gills continued using the older premises.

Truro, 107 Kenwyn Street. Although originally attributed to Trevail, English Heritage has now agreed to change their list entry. Leonard Winn designed the building.

Truro, King Street shop. Undated plans drawn up for Aubrey W Buckingham show floor layouts but no elevations, so it is impossible to find.

Truro, J H Martin & Son. New stores and stabling at Lemon Quay for the corn, seed, coal and manure merchant. Bray, Clare and Farley did the work in 1885. It was demolished in 2001 for Marks & Spencer's.

Truro, 15 Nicholas Street. Although originally attributed to Trevail, English Heritage has now changed their list entry. James Hicks designed the building.

Truro, Oscar Blackford. Blackford's were using the 'Great House' in Princes Street for their printing works and required extra space. In 1903 Trevail lifted the roof by

Nankivell & Co, River Street, Truro.

building on to the existing walls and then inserted skylights. Alfred Cornelius finished the work during 1904. Listed building.

Truro, Polkinhorne's warehouse. This was erected in Princes Street in 1888 after the earlier clash with the Town Council. At this time a warehouse was not a store place, but a shop where goods were also made on the premises. Trevail seems to have attempted to dwarf the older Mansion and Princes houses on either side, by bringing his building line much closer to the road. Now known as the 'Wearhouse'. Listed building.

Truro, Post Office and Exchange. First proposed as a joint venture in 1880, plans were drawn up for a building next to the Market House. The post office authorities were slow to respond so eighteen months later the scheme was abandoned.

Truro, Post Office. Lord Robartes eventually entered into negotiations with the authorities and commissioned Trevail to design the building in High Cross on his land five years after the first scheme was discussed. Henry Tippett built the premises, and Bevan and Sons of Falmouth and Penzance undertook the fitting out and furnishing. It was open by December 1886 and demolished less than ninety years later.

Truro, Prince's Dining Rooms. Some very impressive alterations were made to an existing building in 1893 for C E Tregonning, a confectioner and caterer, who offered refreshments. The premises next door were taken over and a grand mahogany staircase led through a pair of swing doors to a dining room on the first floor. Alfred Cornelius made further alterations for a smoking room and sitting room. The bakery business of Treleavens was there in later years but the building was demolished in the 1960s.

Truro, Public Benefit Boot & Shoe Co. On the corner of King Street and Boscawen Street, after allowing for the frontage to be moved back about 12 feet, a large ornate building on three floors was erected, in 1901, for this national company. In 1920 The London Joint City and Midland Bank altered the ground floor of the building to form banking premises, but the red brick and terracotta work remained until the 1960s. At this time Midland Bank bought the premises next door and built an extension, changing Trevail's building to match the bland 1960s extension. Now used by HSBC.

Truro, River Street. A red brick building was built in 1891 for the wine and spirit merchant Nankivell & Co. The shop front and granite wagon entrance was in River Street, but the stabling and stores reached as far as the Leats, almost opposite the back of Burton's. A narrow tramway ran from the wagon entrance round to the storage area, so that casks could be moved on small trucks. In 1913 Alfred Cornelius altered the shop front for Redruth Brewery Co Ltd who had taken over the business. The wagon entrance has been converted into a shop. The stabling, now reached from the Leats, is separate retail premises.

Truro, West End Stores. Incorrectly credited to Trevail, this red brick and terracotta building was enlarged and partly re-built by Alfred Cornelius in 1908. Listed building.

Hotels.

Bude, Globe Hotel. In 1903 Walter Hicks, proprietor of St Austell Brewery, commissioned this building which included eight bedrooms on the second floor. The ground floor contained the bar, tap room, parlour and billiard room, whilst the first floor had kitchen quarters, dining room and sitting room. Alfred Cornelius finished the building in 1905. The upper rooms are now private accommodation.

Exeter, Great Western Hotel. Trevail's 1899 plans for a prestigious corner site close to St David's Station were never used. The hotel of the same name on that site has developed from the buildings that Trevail intended to demolish.

Falmouth, Falmouth Hotel. In 1890 Trevail added a large building, which had a flat roof, to the landward side of the existing hotel. This has since been connected to the main building and now has a hipped roof. He also drew up plans for a four-storey portico and entrance, but only the ground floor section has been implemented. Listed building.

Falmouth, Pendennis Hotel. Trevail had hoped the Cornish Hotel Co Ltd would finance this building in 1892, which he intended to call the 'Gyllyngdune'. He also drew up the same plans in the name of the Tourist Hotel Co Ltd, but eventually the Falmouth Hotel Co, already having one hotel on Cliff Road, bought the site. Trevail's plans were to be used, so another set, with the same design, were produced in the name of the Falmouth Hotel Co Ltd, some with the name 'Gyllyngdune', and others with 'Pendennis', which was the name eventually used when it opened in 1893. Although with similar facilities to all Trevail's other hotels, this was known as a boarding house and used to close during the winter months. Now known as the Royal Duchy Hotel.

Guernsey, St Peter Port, Grand Hotel. Plans were drawn up and a prospectus announcing the formation of a company to acquire land was prepared. Nothing came of the idea, and although there is no date on the papers, it is thought to have been about 1899, but the project never went ahead.

Housel Bay Hotel. Built almost entirely in local stone and granite in 1894 on land belonging to Lord Robartes, who built a road to it, it has had some extensions without blocking out the original building. Arthur Carkeek was the contractor and furnishings were by Graves & Sons of Devonport. Water came from a spring and was stored in a tank which held 12,000 gallons.

Isles of Scilly, Tregarthen's Hotel. In 1895 the daughters of the late Captain and Mrs Frank Tregarthen were running a small hotel, the site of which had attracted attention for a new building. It was intended to remove some private dwellings to make more space, but none of the plans were followed through. The hotel of that name today has continued to develop and expand from the original building.

St Ives, Carbis Bay Hotel. John Colliver of Truro started work in July 1894 and the hotel was ready to open twelve months later. During the first winter the bridge to the hotel and beach was swept away after a storm, but was quickly replaced. Alfred Cornelius extended the building about 1910 and since then there have been other additions which have greatly altered the appearance.

St Mawes, Ship and Castle Hotel. For Walter Hicks of St Austell, the plans were drawn up in 1899 and included stables in the back yard. Hicks appears to have spent nearly £800 for the land and by the end of 1900 had spent a further £6,600 on the building, including a bill of £750 to Maple & Co for furnishing. Alterations to the entrances and extensions to ground and first floor facing the harbour have since been made.

Newquay, Atlantic Hotel. Built by the Cornish Hotels Co Ltd, of which Trevail was the Secretary, the Atlantic Hotel opened in 1892. Trevail even worked out the placing of furniture in the rooms as plans and watercolour sketches. Alterations to the roofline and various extensions have greatly changed the look of the building.

Newquay, Great Western Hotel. The 1879 building by Trevail looked like a large country house with pitched roofs, gable ends and attic windows. The first extension on the seaward side bore no resemblance to the original and subsequent alterations in 1931 mean there is nothing to be seen of Trevail's building.

Newquay, Headland Hotel. A lack of communication with local people caused them to riot over a building that was never intended to be on the land given to the town. This, together with planning problems caused by Newquay council, delayed completion until July 1900 by which time a large rival hotel, the Victoria, where construction had started later, was already open. The contractor for the Headland was Arthur Carkeek of Redruth with the terracotta coming from Ruabon, North Wales. James Shoolbred & Co of London supplied most of the furniture. Listed building.

Tintagel, King Arthur's Castle Hotel. The idea of building near ancient remains was instrumental in the formation of the National Trust, whose first purchase was the nearby Barras Head. Trevail never intended using Barras Head for his hotel the planning for which started in 1896. Lessons learned from other hotels were incorporated in this, with comments on the plans such as: 'this will hold too much wind'. With lifts, electric light in all rooms, running fresh water as well as cold and hot sea water baths, the building had all the modern comforts that could be supplied. The hotel contained over 60 bedrooms, some of which were specifically allocated for accompanying servants. Opened summer 1899. Listed building.

Tintagel, King Arthur's Castle Hotel stables. Soon after the opening of the hotel in 1899 a post boy was reported complaining that after taking travellers to the hotel, accommodation for the horses had to be found at other hotels in the village. Within a few weeks plans were drawn up for a carriage house and stabling a short distance from the hotel. Now converted into flats, it bears no resemblance to its origins.

Tintagel, King Arthur's Castle Hotel engine house. The engine was first housed within the hotel, but was either too noisy or not big enough, so this detached house, complete with caretaker's accommodation was built in December 1899. The original building had design elements associated with the hotel, but now extended and converted into a dwelling, these have been lost.

Trevone Bay, hotel. It was first announced in 1882 that sites would be available for good lodging houses and two hotels were going to be erected, but not until 1899 were plans produced. A new road would be built through almost to the cliff edge, with a hotel near the end. The plans were never developed.

Truro, The Red Lion Hotel. The best-known elevation was the one on Boscawen Street, altered by Trevail in 1889, when he added two extra floors to the seventeenth century inn. In 1893 he altered the St Mary's Street elevation by building over the stable block and adding a large pitched-roof dining hall, with a gable end almost entirely in glass. In 1967 a runaway lorry damaged the ground and first floor on one side of the main doorway in Boscawen Street. A decision was made to demolish the entire building.

Truro, The Royal Hotel. In 1898 plans were drawn up to include the living accommodation above the two shops to the right of the main doorway into the hotel. At the same time a rear extension for a billiard room and two floors of bedrooms above was planned. Only the ground floor of this extension was built.

Public buildings – libraries, municipal rooms.

St Austell Public Rooms. Opened in July 1896 by Sir Charles Sawle the ceremony was followed by a public luncheon and grand concert. The building contained a drill hall, storeroom, kitchen, and boardroom for the local council on the ground floor, as well as storage for the town's fire engine. Above was a large hall with stage and balcony, meeting rooms and offices. Now used for retail premises.

St Austell Union, board room. The room used at the workhouse by the newly formed District Council was not big enough for their needs and in January 1895 a plan for a new entrance, cloakroom and other facilities was drawn up. The Council considered Trevail's plans were too expensive and after discussion and reluctance on the part of some members it was decided to accept his offer of new accommodation in the Public Rooms, which were under construction.

Bodmin Free Library. Bodmin Town Council took nine months to decide where to site the library offered to them by John Passmore Edwards. They also asked him to provide a hospital, which he declined. Lord Robartes sold them the site and in January 1896 Passmore Edwards chose Trevail to design the building. It opened in May 1897, but two months later there were still no books in the lending library. In 1898 the classrooms for the art school were let. Listed Building.

Bodmin Public Rooms. Trevail was first asked in 1879 by Bodmin Town Council to prepare plans for a new guildhall and was consulted again in 1888 and 1889. His plans in 1889 were for a building costing £4,000 with another £1,000 for furniture and fittings but when asked he agreed to reduce his costs by £500. In 1890 promoters of the Bodmin Public Hall Company decided to advertise for plans of a building costing £2,300 and received twelve sets. Trevail said that having already produced three sets of plans over the past twelve years he would not take part in a promiscuous scramble. In 1892 the building of Ralling and Tonar of Exeter cost £3,500.

Camborne Public Rooms. The contractor for the building in Trevenson Road was

James Julian of Truro, appointed in June 1890. There was a large meeting hall with a gallery on three sides and a stage, together with dressing rooms, meeting room, billiard and reading rooms and a kitchen. The building opened in July 1891 but Hickes, a County Surveyor, put a large number of objections forward when the directors applied for a licence to perform stage plays. None of his arguments were reasonable and the licence was obtained. It has since been used for workshops, museum, snooker club and retail premises.

Camborne Assembly Rooms. A small first floor extension over the town hall and Magistrates room was planned in 1893, giving a meeting room with small platform and matching the original exterior in all details. There had been considerable alarm raised in the newspapers that space was being taken from the Market House, but this does not appear to have happened. Further alterations were made to the Market House in 1911.

Camborne Free Library. In November 1893 Passmore Edwards offered to build a library for £2,000 and in April 1894 laid the foundation stone for a building opposite the Public Rooms. Symons from Blackwater was the contractor and when he informed the Local Board there was not enough of Passmore Edwards' money to pay for installing lighting and heating equipment, some members were not in favour of using ratepayers money to make up the difference, or to pay for stocking the library. The building opened in May 1895, but some rooms were at first used for municipal offices.

East Ham, London, Passmore Edwards Public Library. Passmore Edwards laid the foundation stone in October 1898, but the contractor James Jerram of Forest Gate had trouble with his supplies. First of all the Bath stone was not supplied quickly enough to keep his men on the site and then East Ham council was not satisfied with the quality of the roofing timbers. Also in 1899 Trevail was ill and unable to deal with the problems. The building was ready for opening in September of that year, when Herbert Gladstone MP performed the opening ceremony. The Superintendent Registrar for the London borough of Newham now uses this magnificently restored building. Listed building.

Hayle Institute. Passmore Edwards offered to erect an Institute in memory of his father in May 1893. A working committee agreed a scheme considered suitable for the town and Passmore Edwards appointed Trevail to draw up the plans. The site was given by Harvey & Co Ltd, engineers, but was ground made up from foundry and factory waste. This meant more care had to be put into the foundations, making them deeper and wider than normal. Plans also included provision for a covered way leading to a gymnasium and skittle alley closer to the river, but this was never developed. Opened by Mrs Passmore Edwards in April 1896. Listed building.

St Ives Passmore Edwards Free Library. James Hicks prepared the sets of plans for various sites in 1895, but in November of the same year Passmore Edwards asked Trevail to send in plans. Then Hicks died unexpectedly and by March 1896 it had been decided that the plans of John Symons of Blackwater would be used.

Ladies and Gents Convenience. A design for the British Sanitary Works in May 1898 of a neat little building with small turret, possibly for a clock, was made. It is not known if the company used the design.

Launceston Library. Launceston council had difficulty in making up their mind which site to use for Passmore Edwards' gift. The larger site at Northgate was chosen and the foundation stone laid in September 1898. The building opened April 1900 and later that year it was suggested that more rooms should be added but these were not built. Converted into flats.

Moretonhampstead, Devon, Bowring Library. A gift to the town in 1901 from Thomas Benjamin Bowring, whose family had developed the wool trade there. Harley Goss built it in yellow terracotta from Ruabon and it contained science and art class-rooms on the first floor. Listed building.

Newton Abbot Public Library. John Passmore Edwards presented the library to the town and laid the foundation stone in October 1902. Built in yellow terracotta from Ruabon by Harry Goss, later finished by Mark Willis, Alfred Cornelius supervised the completion of the work following Trevail's death. The library was designed in con-junction with the Science, Art and Technical Schools next door, which were funded by Devon County Council. Viscount Ebrington, Lord Lieutenant of Devon opened the library in August 1904. Listed building.

Truro Free Library. Truro was a joint benefactor of the Ferris bequest with Falmouth, Redruth and Camborne and Passmore Edwards offered to build each town a library on equal terms in 1894. The foundation stone was laid in May 1895, the contractors Clemens and Battershill, together with James Julian who was responsible for the inter-nal fittings, completed the building ready for an opening ceremony in April 1896. The library now extends into the Technical Schools next door, the planning for which start-ed in May 1896. Listed building.

Tywardreath, reservoir. Built in 1873 to supply water to houses in Par Green and at Par. It fell into disrepair and was demolished more than fifty years ago.

Hospitals.

Acton, London, Passmore Edwards Hospital. Trevail produced plans in 1898, but those of Charles Bell were chosen.

Cornwall Lunatic Asylum, Foster block. A new 250–bed structure designed in 1899, completely independent of the existing buildings, with its own bakery, kitchens, and workshops, but not opened until July 1906. After Trevail's death in 1903 Alfred Cornelius applied to continue the work, but the committee chose John Kirkland from London. The building was closed for several years, although the NHS is now convert-ing part of one wing for training purposes and office accommodation.

Cornwall Lunatic Asylum, isolation hospital. Built in 1897 to serve the inmates of the asylum, it was a self-contained unit. The contractor was Sampson Trehane of Liskeard. It was first used late in 1899 for two nurses who had scarlet fever. Later known as Harrison Clinic, it now stands empty and boarded up, its future uncertain.

Cornwall Lunatic Asylum, Long Building. Designed by Norman and Hine of Plymouth in 1870, it was later known as the Kendal building. Trevail added extra stair-cases about 1898. The building was gutted by fire in 2001 and demolished.

Cornwall Lunatic Asylum, medical superintendent's house extensions. The house was built in 1838 to George Whitwick's design. In 1898 Trevail was asked to pro-

Top: *The Passmore Edwards Hospital, East Ham (Family papers).*
Bottom: *Fowey Workingmen's Club.*

vide an extension over the ground floor scullery to provide a closet and bathroom. He also added a flat-roofed porch to the front entrance. Later known as Townsend House, it has been converted to a pair of houses. Listed building.

East Ham, London, The Passmore Edwards Hospital. John Passmore Edwards offered £4,000 to build a hospital and Trevail was commissioned to design the building. It consisted of 20 beds in wards for men, women and children and included dispensary, kitchen and mortuary. It opened in 1901 and is now part of Newham Community Health Care Trust.

Truro Wesleyan College, isolation hospital. The building erected was much smaller than that originally designed in 1893. It is now converted to the caretaker's cottage.

Recreation.

St Austell Liberal Club. Francis Barratt CC had the building erected at his expense in 1890. A shop was placed each side of the entrance to the club, and an arched wagon entrance included to allow access to Hawkes warehouse at the rear. The club premises on the first floor consisted of reading and smoking rooms, separated by a moveable screen so a large room was available should the need arise, a library and a kitchen. Above this was an office and a billiard room large enough for two tables. Under the floor of the billiard room several inches of sand were placed to provide sound insulation so the noise from the snooker players did not reach the rooms below. Shortly before his death in 1933 Barratt transferred the lease to St Austell Urban District Council. It was a privately owned restaurant for many years and is soon to be converted into apartments.

Fowey Workingmen's Club. The club was formed in 1868, but it was not until 1877 that Trevail drew up plans for a new building on the Town Quay. It contained a library, reading and bagatelle rooms and a large hall for meetings and entertainment. Now used by the Royal British Legion.

Fowey Masonic Lodge. Trevail drew a preliminary plan of the ground floor, but it was announced in 1880 that the plans of A S Clunes would be used.

Newquay Masonic Hall. This was erected in 1880, at the time on open ground, in local rubble stone. Part of the end wall remains in Beach Road.

Newquay Recreation Ground. It was part of the Newquay Town improvements Trevail was asked to present to the Urban District Council in 1892. The recreation ground was about 5 acres of land given by C E Treffry and Trevail planned for seats, shelters, tennis courts and a flagstaff. In March 1903 Trevail said not a penny appeared to be spent on roads, footways or fences, no lamps or public lighting.

Truro, Cornwall Fisheries Exhibition. The exhibition was to last for three weeks during the summer of 1893, and for this Trevail's temporary layout consisted of four large wooden buildings to be used as galleries with other buildings for offices and a luncheon room, with an open bandstand and a large turreted entrance. The open spaces were planted and had gravel walks. The Green was afterwards returned to its original condition.

Truro Public Baths. The need for public baths in Truro was under discussion from 1885 and at the beginning of 1890 it was announced that Trevail was one of the directors of the company formed. The YMCA building in St Mary's Street was to be adapted, the work being carried out by Matthew & James Clemens and T Battershill. Bradford & Co of London was responsible for the engineering. The building opened in December 1890, although during the winter the swimming bath was covered over and the space used for meetings. The company went into liquidation and the building was demolished.

Truro, Triumphal Arches. In 1880 these temporary arches were erected for the visit of the Prince of Wales to Truro for the service of consecration at Truro Cathedral. The arches in wood and stone were erected by Paul and Smith of St Austell and Olver of Falmouth on Boscawen Bridge, Lemon Bridge, in Lemon Street, River Street and at the railway station. Each was to a different design and theme. The ceremony took place on 21 May 1880, but nothing was discussed about the removal of the arches until one blew down two weeks later. They were then all removed.

Truro, Consecration Arch. In 1887 the Price of Wales returned to Truro for the consecration of the parts of the Cathedral that had been completed at that time. A triple arch at High Cross was decorated with scarlet cloth, flags and bunting and a work shed was decorated as a reception room for the Prince, all to Trevail's designs, at a cost of £54. 5s. 6d.

Truro, Royal Institution of Cornwall. The Institution in 1887 was housed in Union Place and Trevail suggested that the town could celebrate Queen Victoria's Jubilee by erecting an extension fronting onto Pydar Street that would form technical schools and an art gallery for the town. The scheme was dropped.

Schools – elementary, grammar, technical and art colleges.

St Austell, Carclaze Board School. It opened 15 April 1879 and was only half the size it is now, with the Master's house on the right hand end. The school used to have a bell tower and the playground sloped down to road level. The Clerk to the School Board drew up plans for the extension in 1883. Still in use.

St Austell, Carthew Infants School. The school was built in 1877 by John Dawe and John Paul. In 1967 it was being used as a furniture store but was empty in 1980. Sold November 1981 for conversion to a dwelling.

St Austell, Central Schools. Opened 1873 this is one of the few schools that mentioned Trevail by name on the plaque. Later extended on several occasions and used as a secondary school, a technical college and a centre for adult education. Demolished 1998. The inscription panel now preserved on a block of flats on the site.

St Austell, Mount Charles Board School. This was opened 2 December 1872 and often claimed as the first Board school to be erected in Cornwall, but that distinction went to Carnkie school which opened three months earlier. Clerk to the board, H Syd Hancock extended the building and added very tall windows extending into the roof. Mount Charles Band made their headquarters here for a short while and then in 2004 it was converted into dwellings.

Biscovey Board School. Trevail added a new wing onto William Kitt's National school in 1877, and it was used until a new school was built in 1952. Now an art gallery.

St Blazey Board School for Boys. Opened 5 May 1875 as just a single room 58 feet by 18 feet. The girls' school was in a separate building in Church Street. The boys' school was demolished 1995 to make way for a youth club which had the school plaque re-erected on an inside wall.

Bodmin Science and Art School. Opened in 1897 on the first floor of the Free Library, maintained by the Technical Instruction Committee of Cornwall County Council. See under Bodmin Free library.

Boscastle Board School. Trevail wrote to the school board in April 1875 asking to prepare plans and again in August 1877 when they accepted his offer. Opened on 14 July 1879. Still in use.

Brassacott School, North Petherwin. Work started in 1876 but was not finished until 1879. It was big enough for nearly 300 children with a master's house at one end. Still in use. Listed building.

Camborne School of Mines. The first building was erected in 1883 and in 1894 Trevail was commissioned to design a large extension on the corner of Fore Street and Market Place. A proposed extension of 1901, also by Trevail, did not take place.

Delabole Board School.

Demolished to make way for a Tesco store.

Chacewater Board School. Originally a National school, the first extension in 1861 was by William White, the second by James Hicks in 1878 and in 1896 Trevail added another classroom and a cloakroom. Still in use. Listed building.

Chyvelah Board School. A small school, costing £639, which opened on 23 May 1898 with 49 pupils, but was demolished to make room for a road widening scheme.

St Columb Major Central School. A building costing on average £5 per child, opened in 1876. This design helped Trevail win the silver medal of the Royal Cornwall Polytechnic at the annual exhibition in August 1874. Later extended. Still in use.

St Columb Minor, Fair Park Board School. Formally opened on 18 June 1877, but school did not start for another week as there were no desks ready. Closed in 1982 and later converted for light industrial units.

Coombe Board School. Opened 30 September 1878, the school consisted of only one room 24 feet 6inches x 18 feet. (7.5m x 5.5m). Now converted to dwelling.

St Day Board School. The school was built for 400 children, but on the first day, 13 May 1878, only 27 boys attended. The builders were Board & Gard from Helston. First extended in early 1900s. Still in use.

Delabole Board School. There was already a small Board School in the village, but Trevail's building was opened on 7 June 1879. When the girls school mistress started on 4 August, she found there was no furniture and had to work that way with over 70 children for a couple of weeks. A tall bell turret was designed, but only the base remains. Still in use. Listed building.

Dobwalls Board School. The school was situated next to the cemetery on the main road, but has since been demolished. Five architects submitted plans in 1879 but Trevail's design was not used.

Downend National School. The main building was built in 1850 and Trevail added a new wing to the rear in 1878. Now known as St Winnow CP School. Listed building.

Fowey Board School. Trevail's design work for infants, girls and boys schools, together with a master's house started in 1875, the building opened 3 May 1878. Trevail extended it with two rear wings in December 1894. It was used as a school building until late 1980s and converted into apartments in 1995.

Fowey Infants School. Plans dated May 1894 and thought to have been another solution to the overcrowding in the Board school, with a covered playground in the basement and space for a fire engine, were drawn up but not used.

Fowey Board School for Boys. The extension to the Board School was obviously not a satisfactory answer to the overcrowding, so this building was designed in 1896 and erected next door for 230 boys. It was used as a school building until the late 1980s and converted in 1995 to a family home.

Fowey Grammar School. Erected in 1879, a new building for an old established school and easily visible from many points along the river. Later extended in a similar style it was demolished in 1999 to make way for modern housing.

Gorran Board school. The first Board School opened on 23 April 1877, but Trevail's new school building was not ready until 5 January 1880. Made famous by Anne Treneer's book 'Schoolhouse in the Wind'. It was destroyed by fire in 1967.

Top: High Street Board School.
Bottom: St Just Board School.

High Street Board School. John Curra's building partner absconded during the building of this school, so matters were delayed a little. Trevail's first building opened on 26 March 1878 and in 1891 he added a new wing. It became Lanjeth CP School in 1911 and closed in December 1963. Now converted into a family home.

Indian Queens Board School. Schooling first started in an old building in January 1877 and in January 1879 the School Inspector said no more children could be admitted until the new building was ready. The new building for 150 children opened in April 1879. Built by Borlase of Zelah it also had a master's house and cost £1,500. Closed 1980. Now used as units for light industry. Listed building.

St Ives Board School. Trevail was asked to submit plans to the Royal Commission, with a view to exhibition in the fine art section of the Paris Exhibition. The plans were not those eventually used by the School Board, but very similar. One of Trevail's largest schools, it opened 17 January 1881 and closed in 1984. Villagers fought hard to prevent the building from being demolished and, with a sympathetic extension, it now houses the medical centre.

St Just Board School. Built for 79 children in two rooms, the building probably opened in 1894. Now used as retail premises.

Lanivet Board School. Trevail was asked to

design a new building in July 1878, but by March 1879 the School Board felt that as the population in the district had decreased, there was no need for a new building. The village eventually had a new school in 1906.

Lanner Board school. The Gwennap School Board had Trevail working on this building at the same time as their school for St Day. Lanner School opened 15 July 1878, but moved to new premises in September 1980. The old building was subsequently demolished.

Launceston Technical and Art Schools. Opened 1900 as part of the Free Library building, it was maintained by the Technical Instruction Committee of Cornwall County Council. See under Launceston Free Library.

Lockengate Board School. Built in 1879 for infants to save them travelling into Luxulyan village. It closed in 1931, but re-opened to take evacuee children during WW II. Later converted into dwellings.

Luxulyan Parochial School. By avoiding setting up a school board the village did not have to pay rates for the new building as the money was raised by donations. This was Trevail's first commission of his architectural career. The new school opened on 25 March 1872, the children coming from at least two other schools around the parish. B C Andrew of St Austell altered the entrance porches in 1905. It was used as a school until April 1968 and has since been converted into a dwelling.

St Mawes Board School. The Board was concerned about the cost of building this and the St Just School and had Trevail re-do the plans after receiving tenders which they felt were too high. They could not decide if a master's house was necessary at St Mawes and had two sets of plans to consider. A new Board was elected and made the decision to go ahead, including a master's house. Work began in 1890 and Trevail received his final payment in November 1895. Still in use.

St Mawgan in Pydar Board School. William Butterfield designed the National School in 1863, but by 1876 space was needed for nearly 100 extra

Top: *Lockengate Board School, Luxulyan parish.*
Centre: *St Mawes Board School.*
Bottom: *St Merryn Board School.*

children. Trevail's extension, matching but larger than the original, was finished by June 1877. Still in use. Listed building.

St Merryn Board School. Built in 1876 with two classrooms to hold about 100 children. For such a small school it also had a master's house attached. Some rear sections of the building have been painted and rendered and a modern extension in the playground recently completed. Listed building.

Mevagissey Board School. John Weeks Hosking from Saltash built this in 1876 for about £2,000 including the master's house. Not an easy site to work with as the building had to go in steps up a sloping site. It opened in October 1877 with 276 children. Infants were to be charged 1 penny a week, children 6–9 years two pence and older children 3 pence per week. The building was later extended but a new school was built further up the road in the late 1980s and the old building sold. Converted into small flats in 1997.

St Mewan Board School. The St Mewan Inn on the corner of the main road was to be repaired as accommodation for the teacher and a new school built next door. The school cost £1,250 and was opened 6 April 1874 with 140 children. It cost the ratepayers an extra 5 pence in the pound per quarter on their rates. Still in use.

Moretonhampstead Technical and Art Schools. Classrooms were included in the library endowed by Thomas Bowring in 1901. Local groups now use these rooms. See Moretonhampstead Library entry.

Nanpean Board School. There was a very old National school in Nanpean for which Trevail built an extra two classrooms. However in 1898 the whole building was demolished and a new one designed by Sampson Hill built in its place, which is still in use.

Nanstallon Board School. It opened in July 1878 on land given to the parish by Thomas and Ann Grose. The village's WW I memorial is on the wall of the school, above which is the school's inscription stone, cut by Joseph Polsue, a stone mason and author of the *Parochial History of Cornwall*. Still in use.

Newquay Crantock Street Girls School. The boys already had a school on the site when Trevail was commissioned to draw up plans for the new girls' and infants' school in 1877. Additional children were refused admission for twelve months because of overcrowding but the new building was ready on 10 January 1878. The old building was then refurbished as additional space for the boys. Demolished in 1973.

Newton Abbot Science, Technical and Art Schools. Opened in August 1904 by Lord Clifford, being completed by Cornelius after Trevail's death. The building was joined to, but separate from, the Free Library. Devon County Council funded the schools. The ground floor is now part of the library but the upper floors are still used for education purposes. Listed building.

Padstow Board School. The first Board School in Padstow opened in July 1873 in the old National School and the Board asked Trevail to draw up plans for a new building soon afterwards. These drawings were among those that won a silver medal for Trevail at the Polytechnic Exhibition at Falmouth. The school opened 31 January 1876 and closed in 1987. Converted into apartments.

St Paul Board School. Trevail's plans are dated April 1878, but in July of that year it was announced that James Hicks was the architect.

Pentewan Board School. St Austell Board was the authority for this area and approved the plans 31 March 1872. Exactly twelve months later the school opened. H Syd Hancock, Clerk to the Board, later extended the building towards the village and put in two tall windows with dormers, similar to those he put in the Mount Charles building. Exactly 66 years after opening, the building closed and the villagers started using it as a community hall. Unfortunately for them it had to revert to the Tremayne estate and now houses a restaurant.

Penzance School of Art. Five sets of plans were considered for this building, the £5 prize and the contract going to Trevail. The foundation stone was laid in February 1880 and the building ready for opening in March 1881. In 1892 Henry White doubled the size of the building, to make space for a library. He also changed the roofline and added balustrading and terracotta details. Trevail's building is still used for art classes.

Perranwell Board School. The contractor, John Blight, had finished his work by the end of October 1878, less than twelve months after his tender was accepted. It opened on 13 January 1879 and 60 children were enrolled, increasing within two weeks to 116. There have been extensions to the building since then, but in a similar style. Still in use.

Plymouth Oxford Street Board School. It was built for girls and infants and had separate accommodation for 'babies', opening in 1880. Although surviving the blitz, the buildings were pulled down as part of the town centre redevelopment in the 1950s.

Polperro Board School. This was the responsibility of the Talland and Lansallos United District School Board who appointed Trevail in May 1876. The contract went to James Godfrey of Liskeard for £1,550. The school opened 2 September 1878, closed in 1966 and the building is now the village hall and community centre.

Polruan Board School. The building had two rooms, opened in 1878, and was used for boys who had left the infants' school. It was hit by a stray bomb during WW II and had to be demolished.

Port Isaac Board School. Special efforts were made with this building to ensure that it could withstand the fierce winds blowing in off the sea. There were also difficulties in the restricted size of the site and Richards was paid £25 for part of his garden to be added to the school grounds. The building opened April 1877 and closed in 1977. It was then converted into a hotel and still contains the honours board of pupils gaining scholarships. Listed building.

Redruth, Trewirgie Board School. There were four sets of architect's plans presented in 1884 and Trevail insisted that the discarded ones should also be sent to the Education Department for a decision as he felt that his met the requirements of the Department better than those chosen. Trevail's design not used.

School of Art. The plans are dated 1890, but there is no indication of where the building was to be. 'Nasmyth' is written on one plan and as this was the name of Trevail's assistant in the 1890s it could have been part of his portfolio. Building not found.

School Board offices. Designed in a similar style to that of the School of Art above, so possibly some more of Nasmyth's work. Building not found.

Sharplands School. Built about 1881 for 80 children, the school was converted into a pair of semi-detached dwellings in the early 1960s.

Shortlanesend Board School. The Kenwyn School Board received five sets of plans in 1875 and chose those of James Hicks. Trevail's design was not used.

St Stephen's Churchtown Board School. Originally a National School with two rooms, it was enlarged by Trevail in 1876, more than doubling the space available. In 1888 Paul of St Austell then added another classroom, taking the building right up to the roadside. A new school was built in 1984 and the old building now houses offices and light industry.

St Teath Board School. Trevail designed and built this at the same time as Delabole school, both coming under the St Teath, Michaelstow and Lanteglos by Camelford United District Board. John Oliver from Bodmin was the builder of this school for 166 children. It opened in December 1878. Both schools now show truncated remains of a bell tower. Still in use. Listed building.

'Tre-Pol-Pen'. A name used by Trevail when the competition to provide designs for a building required the name of the architect not to be disclosed. One set of plans matches those he did for Truro College and the second set is for a board school, but does not match any of the schools with which he was known to have been associated, although similar to his later St Ives School. Trevail did not win the Truro College competition.

Trevarrack Board School. The Uny Lelant Board held discussions with St Ives about the possibility of a joint venture, but it was decided not to go ahead with the scheme. Trevail designed a building for 215 children, with a master's house, which opened in May 1880. It was said that when finished it would 'present a model of strength'. Now converted into an hotel.

Trevarrack Board School.

Treverbyn Board School. Another school built by St Austell Board, the size of which was clearly not sufficient for the area. John Paul and Henry Ede completed the original building for £1,400 in 1878, but H Syd Hancock added another classroom, extended the infants room and another classroom and altered the porch in 1896. He also added another bedroom onto the Master's house. Hancock's work was faulty and caused many problems for the school until they moved into a new building erected in 1999. The Master's house has been demolished and the school likely to become apartments.

Trewidland Board School. Plans were submitted to Liskeard school board in 1879, at the same time as those for Dobwalls. Unfortunately they suffered the same fate, Trevail's design was not chosen.

Truro British School. Now known as Bosvigo School, it opened in January 1898 and was intended for 450 children. On the ground floor were two rooms for infants and one for 'babies', the older boys and girls having their rooms upstairs. Generously there were cloakrooms and lavatories on both floors. Extensively repaired and modernised in 2004 it is still in use.

Truro, Central Technical Schools for Cornwall. This, the largest building of its kind in Cornwall, was erected in the middle of Truro. Partly funded by John Passmore Edwards, Trevail secured additional finance from the Department of Education, London; Drapers' Institute, London; Cornwall County Council; Truro City Council and others. The designs were exhibited at the Royal Academy's Exhibition in London in 1897. Lord Mount Edgcumbe, unlocking the door with a gold key presented to him by Silvanus Trevail, opened the building 24 October 1899. It is now part of Truro library.

Truro Wesleyan College. A large number of architects entered the competition in 1881. Trevail's plans were exhibited at the Paris, Sydney and Melbourne Exhibitions, but the design of Elliott Elwell of West Bromwich was chosen for the school. See also Isolation hospital entry under 'Hospitals'.

Truro Wesleyan Day School. Originally the Sunday school building, it was adapted in 1893 for teaching 300 children, by adding a first floor to the full-height building and internal partitions. Alfred Cornelius did further work to the building at the end of 1903, after Trevail's death, and in 1908 Sampson Hill put heating in the upstairs class-room as none had been provided. It closed in 1911 and is now used as offices.

Upton Cross Board School. Another competition between architects saw Trevail chosen in 1875 to build this school. Silvanus Trevail is recorded on the school inscrip-tion panel, along with the builders Perkins and Earl who came from Callington. Upton Cross has one of the very few surviving bell towers, recently completely overhauled. An open fronted shelter was provided to give the children some shelter in the play-ground. Both the shelter and the school are still in use.

Wadebridge Board School for Boys. The School Board were extremely careful with ratepayers' money over this building, refusing to sanction a bell tower and bell and vot-ing against a water closet in the master's house. They did change their minds over the second item. The building opened in October 1878, two extra classrooms were added at the back in later years and then in 1991 a new school was built. Converted into dwellings 1995.

Wadebridge Board School for Girls. In 1875 plans were made to treble the size of the existing building, the girls and infants already there being moved to the old Independent Chapel during construction work. They were able to move back in January 1877. Later additions were made and in 1991 the children were moved into the new premises with those from the boys' building. Converted into dwellings 1998.

Washaway Infants School. It was felt that Wadebridge was too far for the local infants to travel to school, so this little building was erected for them. On 10th January 1881 when it opened there were 12 children, but it was later found that a large number of older children were attending so they did not have to go into Wadebridge. When first built it measured 25 feet by 16 feet. Now private house.

St Wenn National School. Jacob Barry designed the school in 1855, but with so many more children needing education, Trevail was asked to provide plans for a class-room extension at the northern end, against the roadside. When the end of the old building was taken away to join the two together in January 1875, it was so cold that many children stayed away. It took another six months for work to be finished. Still in use.

Notes

One: An age of adventurers

1 His date of birth, as displayed on his memorial window in Luxulyan Church, and as celebrated by his family, was the 31 of October, but on his Birth Certificate the date is recorded as the 11th of November. We have been unable to find any reason for this discrepancy.
2 C T Trevail, *The Life and Reminiscences of CT Trevail*, Luxulyan, 1926, 2nd ed., 1927.
3 Silvanus Trevail, 'President's Address', Society of Architects, 1902, p. 5.
4 Hazel Harradence, 'Searching for the Family Tree', STSN, 1996.
5 *WB* 1 January 1903.
6 These are retained in the Trevail family's possession.
7 Trevail, 1927, pp. 12–15.
8 Charles later became Clerk and then Chairman of the Luxulyan School Board, Justice of the Peace for Cornwall, assessor of taxes, member of the Bodmin School Guardians, Rural District Councillor and first Chairman of Luxulyan Parish Council in December 1894. Trevail, 1927, pp. 19, 20, 27, 84; Luxulyan Parish Minute Book.
9 Trevail, 1927, pp. 18–19.
10 *WB* 9 October 1884, 10 November 1885, 4 February 1886; James Whetter, 'Silvanus Trevail, Architect', *An Baner Kernewek*, 1993.
11 *WB* 4 March 1869.
12 Silvanus Trevail, *Address Book*, c 1902.
13 Peter Laws, STSN, 2002.
14 George Vaughan Ellis, RIBA, who inherited the architectural practice of Rice, has done much to revive interest in Rice's work. See Ronald Perry, 'Henry Rice, Liskeard architect and public health reformer', *STSN*, 2003, p. 5.
15 Andreus Augustin, *Meet You in Paddington*, London, 2002, 35–43.
16 Trevail, 1902, p. 11.
17 Reginald Turnor, *Nineteenth Century Architecture in Britain*, London, 1950, p. 83. Scott's assistant around this time was the Liskeard-born Richard Coad, but there is no evidence that he and Trevail ever met in London.
18 Later Silvanus would have come across Cornish buildings in a similar fashion such as Penlee House in Penzance, erected in 1865 at a cost of £1,000 by the wealthy local merchant John Branwell.
19 J B Lewis, *A Richly Yielding Piece of Ground*, St Austell, 1997.
20 Ronald Perry, 'Cornwall's Mining Collapse Revisited', *Cornish History Network*, 2001.
21 For further discussion, see Ronald Perry, 'The Making of Modern Cornwall: A Geo-economic Perspective', in Philip Payton (ed.), *Cornish Studies Ten*, Exeter, 2002, pp. 166–189.
22 Silvanus Trevail, *Luxulyan Parish Church Dedication of Bells*, Truro, 1902.

Two: 'Mr Trevail's landmarks'

1 CRO, AD396/664 27 June 1876.
2 *WB* 2 January 1873.
3 Family papers.
4 *WB* 11 June 1872.
5 Peter Laws, STSN, 2002.
6 *WB* 26 December 1872.
7 The others were at St Teath, St Merryn, Fair Park at St Columb Minor, Nanstallon and additions to Wadebridge Girls School, Biscovey and Nanpean.
8 The others were High Street, Treverbyn and an extension at St Stephens Churchtown.
9 The others were Wadebridge Boys, Polruan, Perranwell, Carclaze, Carthew and Coombe.
10 The others were Boscastle, Indian Queens, Lockengate, Washaway, Trevarrack and Sharplands, with additions at Downend.
11 CRO, AD396/665 letter of 13 January 1896 to Captain Harry.

12 Anne Treneer, *Schoolhouse in the Wind*, 1944, repr. London, 1982, p. 12. As a pupil teacher, she later did teaching practice at Treverbyn School.
13 CRO, SR/GOR/1/I.
14 R S Best, *Clay Country Remembered*, Redruth, 1986, pp. 68–9.
15 *WB* 27 August 1874.
16 CRO, SRB/PAD.
17 *WB* 9 December 1875.
18 *WB* 24 December 1874.
19 *WB* 27 August 1874, 17 June 1875; *British Architect* 25 February 1876.
20 *WB* 18 October 1877, family papers 14 October 1877.
21 *WB* 20 January 1881.
22 The Palace was burned to the ground in 1882.
23 *WB* 23 December 1880.
24 CRO, SRP12–13; CRO, SRB/KEN.
25 Nikolaus Pevsner, *The Buildings of England: Cornwall*, Penguin, 1970, p. 218.
26 Added in 1886. The church is no longer used.
27 *WB* 26 September 1871, 7 April 1873. It held many plaques and stained glass windows commemorating local families, but was later disfigured by a rear extension, which served as one reason for demolishing it in 1995.
28 St Columb was stripped of its contents some years after it closed in the late 1900s; Lostwithiel was converted into housing in early 1920s.
29 The last-named since demolished. Part of the site forms the British Legion Garden of Remembrance. Lank Chapel demolished late 1970s.
30 *WB* 24 August 1876.
31 *WB* 4 May 1885.
32 *Kelly's Directory*, 1897. In 1988 the building was demolished.
33 An illustration in *The Architect*, 3 April 1880, has a bell turret over the chancel arch and a photograph of the early 1900s confirms this. Today, however, the turret is at the opposite end of the nave.
34 CRO, DC/AUSF/25; the lodge is on the corner of what is now Alexandra Road.
35 CRO, DC/PAD/1.
36 From around 2000, this property was carefully and extensively restored by its new owners. See Ann Perry, *STSN*, 2003 and Felicity Penneycard, *STSN*, 2006.
37 CRO, PB/7/309 letter to John Coode 9 December 1879.
38 Peter Laws, in P A S Pool, *History of Penzance*, Penzance, 1974, attributes the terracotta work to Trevail. This was later one of his favourite materials, but on this occasion it was White who introduced it.
39 *WB* 24 December 1877, 11 April, 1 August, 14 October 1878, 21 April 1879. The hotel was reported to contain 40 bedrooms, but doubts were expressed whether a building of this size could be constructed for the small announced cost of £2,000.

40 *The Architect*, 18 December 1880.
41 Now partly demolished.
42 CRO, GRA84; Helen Doe, *Jane Slade of Polruan*, Truro, 2002, p. 40; we are indebted to Helen Doe for this anecdote.

Three: Competition, income and travel

1 George Vaughan Ellis, 'Richard Coad, Architect, 1825–1900', *JCALH*, 50, 2005, pp. 36–52.
2 Ronald Perry and Sharron Schwartz, 'James Hicks, Architect of Regeneration in Victorian Redruth', *JRIC*, 2001, pp. 64–77.
3 WDM, 21 March 1877.
4 'County Surveyors and Private Practices', *Architects' Magazine*, II, 14, 1901, p. 23.
5 Silvanus Trevail, 'President's Address', Society of Architects, London, 1902, p. 7.
6 The Council was changed to an Architects' Registration Board in 1997. We are indebted to Alec Wells, FRIBA, for this information.
7 CRO, AD396/664 4 September 1875.
8 CRO, AD396/664 letter of 4 September 1875 to F W Webb, 27 Market Place, Reading.
9 CRO, AD396/664 letter of 4 September 1875 to Sargeant, a Liskeard builder.
10 CRO, SRB/END/1.
11 *WB* 10 April 1876.
12 CTT, 1902, p. 12.
13 CRO, SRB/AUS.
14 CRO, SRB/MEV/2.
15 CRO, SRB/BREO/1.
16 *WB* 18 December 1879.
17 CRO, SRB/GWE/1.
18 CRO, SRB/BOS.
19 CRO, SRB/MEV/2.
20 CRO, SRB/NOP.
21 CRO, SRB/LIS/1.
22 *WB* 30 December 1880.
23 *WB* 22 March 1877.
24 Most information comes from school board minutes, but in a few cases we have assessed the cost of a building by comparing it with other projects of similar size for which we have figures.
25 Newspaper reports are the main source here, and again gaps are filled by estimates based on comparison with the known costs of similar buildings.
26 The Great Western Hotel, for instance, was estimated by a newspaper to cost £2,000, but this seems a low figure for a hotel of this size. On the other hand he probably never received payment for the seaside estates he surveyed, since he hoped to make his money from commissions for houses built there.
27 For example, prizes of £5 and £10 from St Austell School Board in 1871 and 1872.
28 From December 1871 to February 1880, a variety of addresses appeared on his plans and drawings

and also in references to him in the *West Briton*, *The Architect* and *The London Architect*. The most prevalent was Tywardreath (his parish); the second most common was Par Station, a postal district at the time. But combinations of these two addresses were used, sometimes with the addition of Carne or St Blazey. On at least one occasion his address was given as Carne, St Blazey, Par Station, Tywardreath, which suggests that all these addresses referred to the same place. However, we now know definitely that, when he left his parents' house, he resided at Hill House, opposite the church at Tywardreath, before moving to Truro.

29 Roderick Floud and Donald McCloskey, *The Economic History of Britain*, 2001, II, p.8.
30 WB 30 June 1873.
31 Family papers 16 July, 2 August 1876, 22 June 1877.
32 Family papers 29 July 1874.
33 *WB* 15 November 1877 to 3 January 1878.
34 Family papers 14 October 1877.
35 *WB* 18 February, 4 and 11 March 1878.
36 *WB* 17 June 1880.
37 We are indebted to David Anderton for this information.

Four: Triumphal arches, harbours of refuge and politics

1 *RCG* 7 February 1895.
2 For a fuller discussion of these localities, see Ronald Perry, 'The Making of Modern Cornwall', in Philip Payton (ed.), *Cornish Studies Ten*, 2002.
3 WB 3 March 1881.
4 The Bodmin Town Arms Hotel was unprofitable. *WB* 3 March 1881.
5 *WB* 20 September 1877.
6 CRO, *A Hundred Years Ago*, Truro Cathedral, 1980.
7 Silvanus Trevail, 'President's Address', Society of Architects, 1902, p. 11.
8 Viv Acton, *History of Truro I*, Truro, 1999, p. 208.
9 *WB* 18 July 1878. The Council decided to advertise for more plans.
10 Ann Perry, 'Myths and Triumphal Arches', *STSN*, 2001.
11 John Julian, William Tippett, Bray and Buzza were the carpenters, T Solomon carried out all the decorative work and the heraldic signs were drawn by Fouracre and Watson of Stonehouse, *WB*, 20 May 1880; CRO, BT/T/77. The cost ranged from £42 for the Railway Station Arch to £60 for the one at the top of Lemon Street, plus from £20 to £40 per arch for decorations and flags. Family papers 2 May 1880.
12 A lithograph of another arch, depicting a Bishop's mitre, to be sited near the Cathedral appears in *Creation of a Cathedral* by Barham Fisher, n.d., as if this structure was built in 1880, but this was not the case. Trevail built an arch at High Cross in 1887 for the consecration of the Cathedral, but nothing has been found to suggest the style used.
13 Family papers 2 May 1880.
14 Family papers 2 May 1880. Prints of 20 Cornish corporate seals as used in the arches are contained in Truro Cathedral Muniments, CRO, TCM 173–5.
15 *WB* 28 October 1880.
16 *WB* 20 January 1881, 3 and 10 February 1881.
17 *WB* 12 and 19 May 1881.
18 Family papers 29 July 1881 to 25 January 1882.
19 *WB* 8 June 1882.
20 *WB* 17 November 1884.
21 Edwin Jaggard, *Cornwall Politics in the Age of Reform*, Royal Historical Society, 1999.
22 *WB* 11 September 1882; 2, 5 and 30 October 1882; 6 November 1882; 11 December 1882, 17 March 1884.
23 Bert Biscoe, *Long Evenings in the Reading Room: Silvanus Trevail and the Cornwall Library Suggestions Book*, Truro, 1999.
24 Boase, Truro, 1890, p. 1074.
25 *WB* 9 July 1891.
26 *WB* 9 October 1884.
27 *WB* 19 November 1885.
28 Pauline Howard, 'Harbours of Refuge', *STSN*, 2007.
29 *WB* 12 May 1884.
30 *WB* 10 and 17 July 1884.
31 *WB* 22 May 1884.
32 *WB* 12 June 1881.
33 WB 23 June 1884.
34 S Trevail, *Harbours of Refuge*, Truro, 1884.
35 *WB* 13 November, 11 December 1884, 23 November 1885.
36 *WB* 9 and 15 February, 28 June, 5 July 1883, 8 May, 3 and 7 July, 2 October 1884.
37 *WB* 9 April, 21 May 5, 19 and 22 October, 23 November 1885, 10 May, 19 July, 30 September 1886.
38 *WB* 23 November 1885, 10 May 1886. The exchange was demolished in the twentieth century.
39 *WB* 30 December 1886; CRO, DCCRK 888/20. It was demolished in 1974 to make way for an incongruous modern intrusion.
40 *WB* 5 June 1882.
41 Built by James Julian of Truro.
42 *WB* 2 January and 9 November 1882, 4 January 1883 and 3 March 1884. The builder was James Godfrey of Liskeard, supervised by John Dennis of Bodmin.
43 *WB* 8 August 1881, 20 January 1883. It was beautifully restored in 1995–7 as a joint ecumenical project with the members of the Bible Christian Chapel.
44 CRO, P171/2/19 specification of October 1880; *WB* 8 June 1882. Situated close to the old Biscovey School, much of the building's character has been lost by the removal of its bay window, recessed porch and wooden window frames.

45   *WB* 28 May, 28 June 1883.
46   CTT, 1902, p. 7.

Five: Trevail 'gets his knife' into some powerful men

1   Edwin Jaggard, *Cornwall Politics in the Age of Reform*, Royal Historical Society, 1999; Bernard Deacon, 'Conybeare for ever', in Terry Knight (ed.), *Old Redruth*, Redruth, 1992, pp. 37–43.
2   CRO, WH/1/5843/2 plan of 1881.
3   Ironically, after Trevail's death, his successor Alfred Cornelius negotiated the sale of some of these plots.
4   *WB* 26 October 1882.
5   *WB* 17 and 24 September 1885.
6   *WB* 8 October 1885.
7   *WB* 24 July 1884.
8   *WB* 14 December 1882. He protested at the increased rate assessment for his property quoting the rates for several similar properties elsewhere in Cornwall. *WB* 18 September 1884.
9   *WB* 10 December 1885.
10 Family papers 18 October 1881.
11 *WB* 4 and 15 February, 8 March, 5 and 12 April, 24 June 1886.
12 *WB* 4 and 18 June 1885, 4 November 1886.
13 WB 2 January, 5 May and 29 December 1890, CRO, DCCRK 888/79. The Truro Baths Company was wound up in 1914. HL Douch, *The Book of Truro*, 1977.
14 *WB* 28 February 1884, 20 May 1886.
15 *WB* 12 January 1885. He was later (1891) to join forces with two farmers and merchants from Hayle, Samuel Hosken and John Henry Trevithick, to form HTP Ltd., the largest firm of agricultural merchants in the west, with branches in Devon and Cornwall.
16 *WB* 19 and 30 March, 16 April 1885, 3 May, 30 September 1886, 13 August 1888.
17 The Boscawen Bridge warehouse, however, was not built until 1907, after Trevail's death, when it was designed by his successor Alfred Cornelius. It does not appear to have been used by Polkinhorne or HTP, but by Nancarrow and later Penrose. It was demolished around the 1960s.
18 *WB* 1 and 4 November 1886.
19 Boase, Truro, 1890, p. 1075.
20 *WB* 11 November 1886.
21 W Thornhill, *The Growth and Reform of English Local Government*, London, 1917, pp. 197–9.
22 Trevail's vendetta with the Chief Clerk is discussed at greater length in Ronald Perry, 'Skulduggery in the Council Chamber', *JCALH*, 2006.
23 Only in a town of 50,000 to 100,000 population would a salary of £500 to £1,000 be paid and these were full-time posts. Truro was only around 10,000. J Redlich and F W Hurst, *Local Government in England*, London, 1903, pp. 321–3.

24 The average annual income of clerical and professional workers in Britain was then about £70 a year, while many manual workers earned under £50. Roderick Floud and Deidre McCloskey, *The Economic History of Britain*, Cambridge, 1999, II, p. 8.
25 The site in question was on the corner of King Street and Nicholas Street, where a bank (now Lloyds TSB) designed by James Hicks, the Redruth architect, still stands. CRO, B/TRU/94/10/1.
26 *WB* 7, 14, and 21 June, 7 October 1888. Later in his career Trevail himself was apparently not averse to secret commissions. According to his successor Cornelius, he received a 'secret commission' of five per cent on all purchases of terracotta from his friend Henry Dennis of Bodmin, owner of the Ruabon works in North Wales. CRO, AD396/667 letter from A J Cornelius of 20 February 1904. Does this help to explain Trevail's lavish use of the material on buildings such as the Headland Hotel, Newquay?
27 *WB* 31 March, 3, 7 and 28 April 1890, 7 September 1891.
28 CRO, AD396/665, letter from Trevail to Roskilly of 16 January 1896. Only £188 had been paid into the Cornish Bank to meet overdue calls for £382.

Six: The 'Chancellor of the Exchequer' meets a setback

1   Bert Biscoe, *Long Evenings in the Reading Room*, Truro, 1999, entry of March 1885.
2   *WB* 7 September 1885.
3   *WB* 24 December 1885.
4   *The Architect*, 24 July 1885. Some of the stonework was rendered over and the windows in the presbytery are thought to have been replaced. Unusually for the twentieth century, it proved to be too small for its congregation, who moved to a larger building in 1972. June Palmer (ed.) *Edwardian Truro*, Truro, 1994; WJ Burley, *City of Truro*, Truro, 1977.
5   *WB* 18 June, 3 August 1885.
6   *WB* 16 March 1885, 28 November 1887. M Clemens, mason, and Battershill secured the contract for the chapel but not for the school, which went to William Tippett, carpenter and John Farley, mason, for £2,244, plus the cost of fittings.
7   CRO, DCCRK 888/50 (Carrick sanitary committee) letters of 26 February, 12 March 1887. The old building was used as a workingman's club (*WB* 10 and 28 March, 16 October 1887). The new Chapel closed about 1962 and was later converted for commercial and social uses (Truro Buildings Group).
8   *WB* 15 May 1882.
9   *WB* 11 October 1888.
10 *WB* 22 March 1888, 8 December 1890, 17

December 1891, 7 November 1892.

11 *WB* 14 October 1886; CRO, MR/F 456.

12 *WB* 12 November 1885.

13 The elaborate west elevation, illustrated in *The Builder*, was simplified to reduce the cost from £1,500 to under £1,000; *WB* 22 December 1887, 16 August 1888; Emily Furse, *A Story of a Hundred Years*, Newquay, 1967; Archives of the Newquay Old Cornwall Society. The building was destroyed by fire in 1924.

14 *WB* 26 July, 25 Oct 1888.

15 His father, Sir Frederick Treise Morshead was JP for Cornwall as well as Berkshire and the first Baronet, his grandfather, held the office of Lord Warden of the Stannaries.

16 The house remained in the family's hands until 1943, when it was sold, becoming a hotel and then remaining unoccupied until the 1990s when it was purchased and carefully renovated as a family home.

17 *WB* 30 September 1886.

18 CRO, TF/855.

19 *WB* 13 November 1884.

20 CRO, X491/59 of 29 December 1887.

21 *WB* 17 March, 18 April 1887.

22 *WB* 30 June 1887. The house was acquired in the 1990s by a structural engineer and his wife, an architect turned sculptor, who painstakingly restored it with sensitivity and professional understanding. See Helen Michael-Trust, *STSN*, 2003.

23 Silvanus Trevail, 'President's Address', Society of Architects, London, 1902, p. 5.

24 *WB* 8, 19, 22 March, 5 April 1888.

25 *WB* 4 April 1889.

26 *WB* 9 August 1888.

27 *WB* 19 April 1888.

28 For instance at St Columb. *WB* 12 March 1888.

29 *WB* 17 October 1889.

30 *RCG* 7 November 1889.

31 *WB* 7 February 1889.

Seven: Grand plans for tourism

1 *WB* 4 July 1872, 28 July 1892.

2 The deficit for the first half of 1880 was £2,808, *WB* 24 February 1881.

3 *WB* 24 August, 23, 26 October, 2 November 1882.

4 *WB* 26 October, 9 November 1882 .

5 CRO, WH/1/5843/2.

6 CRO, DC/RES 733–4, DC/NEWQ 218.

7 The Quaker families still held control and, as discussed later, added the Pendennis Hotel (later Royal Duchy) and in 1909 the Bay Hotel (designed by Alfred Cornelius).

8 *WB* 15 November 1883.

9 *WB* 12 June 1884.

10 CRO, DC/NEWQ/40, 41.

11 *WB* 2 September 1889, 30 October 1890.

12 *WB* 2 July 1894, 20 July 1899.

13 *WB* 30 June 1881.

14 See Memorandum and Articles of Association in CRO, AD396/79 and *WB* 11 December 1890.

15 *RI* 9 August 1889.

16 *SAS* 23 October 1891.

17 The wealthy Thomas Lang of Liskeard rebuilt Lanhydrock House after its fire, built the St Ives and Lizard branch railway lines and constructed the Porthminster Hotel for Edward Hain at St Ives and the Victoria Hotel at Newquay for Michael Williams. These were designed by designed by other architects.

18 These subscriptions were obviously important to Trevail, for he recorded them in a special ledger that he wrote in his own hand; family papers.

19 *WB* 8, 22 January, 12 February 1891.

20 *WB* 2 July 1891.

21 *SAS* 6 March 1891.

22 *WB* 14, 18 January 1886.

23 Lang was also to become a shareholder, possibly a move on Trevail's part to avoid paying cash. *WB* 2 April 1891.

24 *RI* 9 August 1889.

25 CRO, DC/NEWQ/40, 41; *WB* 2 April, 8 June 1891, 4 February, 28 July 1892.

26 CRO, AD396/663/17. Unlike some of his other hotels, where local springs provided water, Trevail depended on the town water supply. Sewage however, drained into the sea, approved by Newquay Board. CRO, DC/NEWQ/41.

27 CRO, AD396/663; *RCG* 30 March 1893.

Eight: County Councillor, educational and health crusader

1 W Thornhill, *The Growth and Reform of English Local Government*, London, 1971, pp. 3–4.

2 For short biographies of the Councillors and Aldermen, see *WB* 4 April 1889, 'Cornwall County Council: Illustrated Special Edition'.

3 *WB* 4 April 1889, 13, 20 February, 13 November, 11 December 1890.

4 Silvanus Trevail, 'President's Address', Society of Architects, 1902, p. 5.

5 *WB* 7 March 1889, 13 March 1890.

6 A L Dennis, *Cornwall County Council*, Truro, 1989, p. 7.

7 The Act for the Distribution and Application of Certain Duties of Customs and Excise allocated £300,000 for Police Superannuation and just over a million for technical education.

8 CRO, CC1/1/3 County Council Minutes; WB 26 January, 5 February 1891. Similar controversies occurred in many parts of Britain. See Walter E Houghton, *The Victorian Frame of Mind*, Yale, 1985; Michael Sanderson, *Education, economic change and society in England*, Cambridge, 1995.

9 *WB* 5 February 1891.

10 *WB* 29 January 1891.

11 *WB* 19 February 1891.

12 *WB* 9 March, 30 April, 21 May, 11 June, 6 July 1891.

13 *WB* 6, 27 August, 3, 10 September, 1, 19, 29 October, 12, 19 November, 28 December 1891, 28 July 1892; *RCG* 18 February 1892.

14 *SAS* 19 February, 4 March 1892.

15 CRO, CC1/1/3, pp. 321, 470.

16 Alan Bennett, *Cornwall Through the Nineteenth Century*, Titchfield, 1987, pp. 10–16; Charles Barham, *On the Sanitary State of Truro*, HMSO, 1840, pp. 3–4.

17 *RI* 3 May 1889.

18 *WB* 7, 21 July, 8 September, 8 December 1887.

19 *WB* 5 July, 20 September, 18 October 1888, 28 July 1892. In 1888 Trevail sent out copies of a booklet he had entitled 'The Main Drainage Problem' to 'such residents of this City as I think will interest themselves in the subject' CRO, BT680/35, October 1888.

20 CRO, CC1/1/3 page 271; *WB* 18 September, 6, 13 November 1890, 14, 18, 21 May, 15 October 1891.

21 CRO, CC1/1/3 pp 470,472; WB 12 November 1891. Cornwall County Council 'Red Book 1892–4'.

22 *RCG* 18 February 1892, 31 August, 12 October 1893, 25 January 1894; *WB* 11 August, 20 October 1892, 14 September, 29 March 1894.

23 *WB* 11 August, 15 September 1892, 12 January 1893; *RCG* 14 September 1893.

Nine: Railway hero, fisheries, housing the rich and poor

1 *RCG* 5 January, 16, 23 February; *WB* 16, 23 February, 9 March 1893.

2 *WB* 16 March 1893.

3 *WB* 17 August; RCG 17 August, 23, 30 November 1893.

4 *RCG* 26 April 1894.

5 *WB* 12 April; *RCG* 26 April 1894.

6 *RCG* 3, 24, 31 May 1894; *WB* 3, 10 May 1894.

7 *WB*, RCG 7 June 1894; 'Testimonial Fund', Cornish Bank, Truro, June-July 1894.

8 According to the Cornish Bank 'Testimonial Fund', 242 subscribers donated over £320. In later reminiscences these figures swelled to 'upwards of 400' subscribers and 500 guineas. *Architects' Magazine*, II, 13, 1901, p. 4.

9 *RCG*, WB 7 February 1895.

10 *WB* 19 November 1891.

11 *WB* 15, 26 October 1891, 18 May, 10 July 1893; *RCG* 7 April 1892, 25 May, 22 June 1893.

12 *WB* 20 July, 10, 17 August 1893; Pauline Howard, 'Fings are still what they used to be', *STSN*, 2002.

13 *Architects' Magazine*, II, 13, 1902, p. 16.

14 *SAS* 20 January 1893; *WB* 12 January 1893.

15 A Harris, *Cumberland Iron*, Truro, 1970.

16 *WB* 4 March 1889. Under the floor of the billiard room was a sand tray, either for fire prevention purposes or to deaden the sound of clicking billiard balls; Andy Ward, private communication, 1998. Hawke's roofline has since been altered, leaving its mark on the wall of the Liberal Club.

17 *SAS* 11, 16, 17, 18 and 25 July 1890.

18 CRO, CCC/1/3, p. 376; AD11/76/6. The premises have since been used as workshops, a museum, snooker club and retail premises.

19 CRO, AD396/665 of 24 December 1895, 21 March 1896. Barratt only sold Tregarne House a year before he died in 1933.

20 *WB* 12 June 1890. Julian's business was opposite Trevail's house in Lemon Street and this expedited matters.

21 The farm buildings have been sympathetically converted into a complex of private dwellings.

22 The building is listed.

23 *WB* 15 October 1891.

24 In the 20th century the gatehouse was extended and the interior modernised.

25 *WB* 7 May 1891.

26 *RCG* 21 January 1892.

27 *WB* 1, 12 November 1888.

28 *WB* 15 January 1891, 25 February, 10 March, 12 May 1892.

29 CRO, AD396, notes in Trevail's hand on presentation of plans to Truro Council Improvement Committee, 25 February 1892; *WB* 25 February 1892.

30 *WB* 16 February 1893.

31 *WB* 15 February 1894.

32 *WB* 13 July 1893. The address of the houses is now Trevithick Road, Illogan Highway, Pool, and the sea view has been lost.

33 *WB* 16 August 1894; Peter Gilson, *Upper Fal in Old Photographs*, Falmouth, 1994.

34 CRO, AD396/671 from 19 August 1895 to 3 April 1900, and numerous plans between these dates.

35 A large detached house by Trevail at the end of South Street was demolished for road widening in 1923. A very similar detached house along Moorland Road was not designed by Trevail but by Frederick C Jury, the St Austell architect, in 1913. CRO, DCRES/1249/61.

36 *WB* 29 November 1886.

37 CRO, AD396/670, correspondence from 25 February to 9 November 1897.

38 With a new roof and interior renovation, it is now used by the country club as a setting for civil weddings.

39 The School Board decided to insure both the St Just and St Mawes Schools in 1894; CRO, SRB/JUR/1.

Ten: Resurrecting the tourist plan

1 *WB* 2 September 1889, 30 October 1890. Only the ground floor of the entrance was actually built. The annex was joined to the main building by a service tunnel, and it is possible that the cellars of the extension housed machinery producing

electricity or hot water for the hotel.

2   *WB* 4 February 1892, 9 February, 19, 26 June 1893
    22 February 1894; *RCG* 29 June 1893. It still exists
    as the Four-Star Duchy Hotel, whereas the
    Falmouth Hotel now has Three Stars. Trevail and
    his successor Cornelius were later involved in
    other developments on the Gyllyngdune Estate,
    see CRO, DCCRK/26B/39/1 for correspondence
    from 1896 to 1906 re sale, purchase, leasing etc.

3   The Wicketts had interests in several Lizard
    hotels, as well as inns along the length and breadth
    of Cornwall.

4   *WB* 23, 26 January, 14 December 1893, 7 June
    1894, 26 December 1895. The licence seems to
    have been issued before the Housel Bay Annual
    Report for 1898. RCG 12 January 1899.

5   *WB* 29 March 1894. In 1987 Maenheere was
    bequeathed to the National Trust and carefully
    restored by the leaseholder, an architect.

6   *RI* 9 September 1892.

7   *RCG* 21 June 1894; WB 28 June 1894; SIWS 25
    March 1893; Co 2 June 1994.

8   *WB* 11 January 1892. Treloyhan featured in *The
    Architect* 1 January 1892, and Trevail may have laid
    out the gardens, although we have found no plans
    for them, and it is possible that Hain designed
    them himself. After some changes of ownership,
    Treloyhan is a restaurant and conference centre.

9   CRO, AD396/667 June to July 1904, Cornelius
    asked for payment for copies of plans sent to Hain.
    The stables were later acquired by the Tregenna
    Castle Hotel and converted to holiday lets.

10 Later, with many additions, it became the Chy-an-
    Dour Hotel, now waiting for demolition.

11 Most became guesthouses.

12 Sanson and Lang were later architect and
    contractor for the Victoria Hotel, Newquay.

13 Wendy Smaridge, 'Carbis Bay after the mines
    closed'; *St Ives Trust Archives News*, 2004, pp. 8–9.

14 *RCG* 21 June, 19, 26 July 1894; *WB* 28 May, 28
    June, 5, 26 July 1894; *SIWS* 23 June 1894.

15 *RCG* 17 September 1896; *WB* 19 September
    1895, 28 July 1898, *Black's Guide to Cornwall*, 1898.
    Some years later, important Carbis Bay Hotel
    documents, including the shareholders'
    addresses, were lost and Trevail resigned as
    Secretary, becoming a Director, and appointed a
    new manager.

16 Trevail's Headland Hotel was the only building
    erected on this site. The original scheme was to be
    developed by 'The Properties Development
    Company' of London.

17 This was not the Vivian with whom Trevail had
    quarrelled over access to Stephen's land, but a
    merchant with offices in London, for whom
    Trevail later designed a magnificent shop in
    Camborne. The builder was John Colliver, who
    also constructed the Carbis Bay Hotel and other
    Trevail ventures. CRO, AD396, contract dated 11
    September 1891, signed by William Stephen, John
    Vivian and John Colliver. Trevelga Road was

renamed Lusty Glaze Road in the 1960s. Trevail
later designed additions to the house and, with
many alterations since, it is now known as
Clarendon Apartments.

18 *WB* 17 September 1885, 18 August 1892.

19 CRO, AD396/665 of 13, 17, 20 January, 20
    October 1896.

20 *WB* 15 April, 23 May 1889, 25 May 1893, 31 May,
    14 June 1894; *RCG* 14 June 1894; Nikolaus
    Pevsner, *Cornwall*, Penguin, 1951, p. 232.

21 *RCG* 26 July 1894.

22 *The Hotel*, quoted in *WB* 25 January 1894.

Eleven: A crowded Mayoral year

1   This had occurred elsewhere, Trevail pointed out,
    for instance in Plymouth, Devonport,
    Okehampton and Barnstable. *WB* 15 November
    1894.

2   *RCG* 8 November 1894.

3   *WB* 5 November 1894. See also *Parish, District and
    Town Council Gazette* 26 October 1895.

4   *WB* 15 November 1894.

5   *RCG* and *WB* 15 November 1894.

6   *RCG* 15 November 1894.

7   *WB* 26 November 1891, 10 March, 13 October
    1892, 16 February, 11 May 1893, 15 February, 15
    March 1894; *RCG* 14 July 1892, 14 September
    1893; *RCG* and *WB* 11 February, 12 May 1892.

8   *WB* 13 December 1894, 10, 24 January, 7 March,
    25 April, 6, 13 June, 12 September 1895; *RCG* 28
    February, 7 March 1895.

9   *WB* 15 November 1894.

10 *RCG* 23, 30 May 1895.

11 Details of many of his activities are contained in
    the 'Mayor's Scrapbook' kept by his sister Laura
    and still in the possession of the family.

12 *RCG* 24 October 1895.

13 *Parish, District and Town Council Gazette*, 26
    October 1895.

14 *WB* 14 November 1895.

15 CRO, AD396/665 letter of 30 October 1896 to W
    Stevens of Native Guano Company (see Chapter
    Twelve for the connection). Passmore Edwards
    had written to Heard, urging the latter to be
    mayor, and Trevail also proposed Heard but he
    refused to stand. CRO, AD396/665 7 November
    1896.

16 CRO, AD396/665 17 January 1896.

17 CRO, AD396/665 13 January 1896.

18 *WB* 15, 29 August, 12 September, 24 October
    1895.

19 *WB* 11 July, 15 August 1895.

20 Trevail designed a further extension in 1901 to
    include a lecture room, library, smoking, card and
    billiard rooms and a caretaker's residence but this
    was not built. In the 1980s the School of Mines
    building was demolished to make way for a
    supermarket.

21 *WB* 28 February 1895. Now known as Tremena
    House.

22 CRO, AD396/665 June, October 1896; *WB* 24 November 1892, 20 March, 31 May, 11 October, 8 November 1894, 31 January, 30 May, 9 December 1895, 3 August 1896. Originally Sir Charles Sawle had offered a plot for £1,000, but the company financing it, with a capital of £5,000, decided to take over a new lease on land rented by Sawle to Walter Hicks the brewer. The hall was used for a variety of purposes over the years: skating rink, boxing matches, operas, dances and as a magistrates' court. Now a shop, the roof timbers and balconies have been exposed again and can be seen on the upper floor.

23 I D Spreadbury, *The Church of St Fimbarras*, Fowey, 1986. Trevail's plans show roof lights that have since been removed.

24 CRO, SHM 980/1, signing of a deed of indemnity.

25 Still used as a school, it is a listed building.

Twelve: Trevail in the world of commerce, banks and shops

1 CRO, AD396/665 3 August, 2 December 1896.

2 CRO, AD396/665 October, November 1896.

3 Ronald Perry and Sharron Schwartz, 'James Hicks, Architect of Regeneration in Victorian Redruth', *JRIC*, 2001, pp. 64–77.

4 CRO, AD396/665, correspondence from January to March 1896 with Alfred Lanyon, Arthur Carkeek, Edward Hain, John Vivian, Thomas Bedford Bolitho and Polkinhorne.

5 Family papers 13 July 1881.

6 CRO, AD396/665, correspondence of February to October 1896 with Native Guano Company, also Glynn Mills and the Bank of England.

7 Family papers 26 March 1902.

8 Peter Herring and Nigel Thomas, *The Archaeology of Kit Hill*, Truro, 1990, p. 20.

9 The use of felspar, found in the granite, to make glass was in its infancy and little used for this purpose until the 1914 War. W R Jones, *Minerals in Industry*, Middlesex, 1943, repr. 1995, p.47.

10 CRO, AD396/665, correspondence from August to October 1896.

11 John Jose, Director and later Chairman of Trevail's Cornish Hotels Company, was an important shareholder. *WB* 7 February 1881.

12 *WB* 26 March 1874.

13 *WB* 22 May, 4 September 1890, 12 November 1891. It is now Lloyds TSB.

14 *WB* 13 November 1890. Trevail designed extensions to his home, Treventon, in St Columb.

15 CRO, AD396, plans of 24 September 1891; *WB* 24 September 1891.

16 Ann Perry, 'Visit to St Columb Major', *STSN*, 2003.

17 *WB* 15 August 1889.

18 *WB* 16 July 1891.

19 Pauline Howard, 'In the Lizard Area', *STSN*, 1999.

20 Silvanus Trevail, 'Presidential Address', Society of Architects Journal, 1902, p. 9.

21 CRO, DC/NEWQ/41. In 1902 the Cornish Bank had been taken over by the much larger Capital and Counties Bank, and in 1913 it was demolished to make way for a new building.

22 *WB* 8 November 1894.

23 The council contributed £35 for shelving their documents.

24 CRO, AD396/665 and AD396/670 June 1896 to April 1899.

25 CRO, AD396/665 from September 1896 to January 1897.

26 CRO, AD396/665, letter of 6 October 1896.

27 Hazel Harradence, 'St Austell in June', *STSN*, 1999.

28 CRO, AD396/670 20 April 1898.

29 CRO, AD396/665 and AD396/670, correspondence from June 1896 to November 1900.

30 CRO, AD396/670 6 December 1897.

31 CRO, AD396/670 correspondence between Trevail and Pridham, Paige and Glasson, September 1897 to February 1899.

32 CRO, AD396/671 from September 1899 to August 1900; AD396/673, from October 1900 to March 1901. In 1910 the important local dress designer and clothing manufacturer Madame Hawke acquired the building and installed the large semicircular windows on the north and east sides.

33 CRO, AD396/667 and AD396/670 March 1899 to September 1904.

34 Family papers 27 June 1903.

35 CRO, AD396/672 from April to May 1901; AD396/663 June 1903; AD396/667 from February 1904 to January 1905. This bank is now a listed building.

36 Charles G Harper, *From Paddington to Penzance*, London, 1893.

37 Ward Lock, *Guide to Devon and Cornwall*, London, 1903.

38 Hawke's building has been greatly altered, but its original higher roofline shows on the east side of the Liberal Club, for many years a restaurant. Hodge's ground floor is also changed, but its upper floors remained untouched.

39 The business went into voluntary liquidation in 1899, was taken over by St Austell and District Lighting and Power Company and most buildings were later demolished. *WB* 6 March 1899; CG 30 December 1904.

40 *WB* 23 August, 20 September, 4, 18 October 1888.

41 *WB* 7 December 1893.

42 The firm was later called Nankivell, Laverton and Co. The original front is illustrated in *WB* 30 November 1891. In 1913 Cornelius altered the frontage for the Redruth Brewery Company. The granite arched entrance is now a separate shop.

43 Now all shops.

44 CRO, AD396/666 May 1903. Although the upper storeys still look the same, the two shops have lost

the columned and granite entrances, having been made into one. A bank now in the place of the post office has retained the granite front.

45 *WB* 8 November 1894. Unfortunately one section of the first floor windows has been poorly treated.

46 Trevail designed 'Lamorna' at Newquay for one of the brothers. See Chapter Ten.

47 CRO, AD396/670 from February 1897 to May 1901 between the Vivian Brothers, Trevail, Colliver and other suppliers. A century later, the building was declared unsafe and pulled down to make way for a medical centre.

48 A building, not by Trevail, with PBBC on it stands in the Greenmarket at the top of Market Jew Street, Penzance.

49 CRO, AD396/673 from January 1900 to January 1901; AD396/672 from March 1901 to December 1901; AD396/663 March 1903. In 1920 the London Joint City and Midland Bank acquired the ground floor and in the 1960s the Bank bought the premises next door and built a new extension, obliterating Trevail's design to match the bland extension .

50 CRO, DCCRK 888/ 258; AD396/667 from December 1903 to September 1904.

51 The original lettering on the windows remains. It is now a wine bar.

Thirteen: Passmore Edwards and Silvanus Trevail

1 *WB* 29 May, 8 July, 24 August, 21 September 1893, 7 May 1896. The sailors' rest room, gymnasium and skittle alley were not built. The Institute is a listed building.

2 *WB* 23 April, 11, 18 May, 4, 11 June, 13 July 1885, 7 January, 4 February, 11 March 1886. Penzance already possessed what became known as the Morrab Library, founded in 1818, which moved to Morrab House in 1889. Penwith History Group, Treasures of the Morrab Library, Penzance, 2005.

3 *WB* 18 August 1892.

4 *The Building News* 13 April 1894; *WB* 5 March, 12 April, 6, 16 August, 22 October 1894, 14 January, 30 May, 13, 20 June 1895; Ann Perry, 'Summer Walk in Camborne', *STSN*, 2005.

5 *WB* 27 May 1895; RCG 10 September 1896.

6 *WB* 17 June, 12 December 1895; CRO, AD396/665 of 13, 14, 17, 18 January, 3 February 1896.

7 *WB* 24 May, 15 October 1896; CRO, AD396/665 of 21 March, 17 November 1896. The library is a listed building.

8 CRO, AD396/670 of 27 November 1897; newspaper cutting, undated, untitled in Trevail file CRO, AD396/670.

9 John Allen, *The History of the Borough of Liskeard*, Marazion, 1967, p.156. The foundation stone was laid in 1896, see RCG 30 April 1896.

10 CRO, AD396/665 of 23 January 1897.

11 *WB* 20 July, 17 August 1895, 15 February 1896; *SIT* 23 November 1895.

12 CRO, AD 396/665 of 13 January 1896.

13 *WB* 30 October 1895, 30 January 1896; CRO, AD396/665 from 18 January to 19 August 1896.

14 *RCG* 30 April 1896.

15 CRO, AD396/665 of 15 March 1896; *WB* 27 May 1897.

16 CRO, AD396/665, 670 and 673 from 11 July 1896 to May 1901. The library is a listed building.

17 CRO, AD396/663 of March 1897, AD396/670 of January 1897 to February 1898.

18 CRO, AD396/670 of 6 February 1898.

19 CRO, AD396/670 copy of letter from Passmore Edwards of 26 July 1898 in the Mayor's handwriting, sent to Trevail.

20 CRO, AD396/670 from August 1898 to April 1900.

21 CRO, AD396/673 from April to November 1900; CDP 28 April 1900. Later the Council Surveyor drew up plans for a two-storey extension that was never built. The library has been converted into flats.

22 On the construction and administration of these schools see the voluminous correspondence in CRO, AD396/663, 667, 670 and 673 from April 1898 to November 1901.

23 CRO, AD396/665 letter of 21 March 1896 to William Polkinghorne of Liskeard.

24 *WB* 14 April 1898; RCG 16 June 1898, 10 August 1899.

25 *WB* 3, 17 May 1900, 7 February 1901.

26 Alex Koch, *Academy Architecture and Architectural Review*, 1897, 11, pp. 28, 30.

27 *WB* 26, 30 October 1899, 7 March 1901.

28 *LWN* 11 January 1902.

29 CRO, AD396/671 from January to August 1900; AD396/672 April to December 1901; AD396/673 January 1900 to March 1901.

30 *Kelly's Directory*, 1906.

31 CRO, AD396/ 671 January to September 1900, AD396/673 January 1900 to March 1901, AD396/672 March to December 1901. The library is now a listed building.

32 CRO, AD396/667 from December 1903 to February 1905. Now converted into apartments, the nurses' home still bears the inscription 'In Memory of Lucy Wills, 1898'.

33 For details of the construction of the library see CRO, AD396/670 from March 1898 to March 1899, AD396/663 of October 1899, AD396/671 of October 1899 to January 1900; *WB* 7 November 1898; *RCG* 10 November 1898. The library has been beautifully renovated, with additions in the style of the original building and is used by the superintendent registrar of the borough of Newham for colourful multicultural weddings.

34 Trevail had produced plans for a hospital for Passmore Edwards at West Acton in London in 1898, but those of Charles Bell were chosen.

35 *East Ham and Stratford Express* 28 July 1900.

36 For details of the construction of the hospital see
    CRO, AD396/671 from November 1899 to
    September 1900, AD396/673 from July 1900 to
    March 1901, AD396/672 from February to
    December 1901. The hospital was extended in
    1914 and again in 1928, but most of the original
    front elevation is still to be seen.
37 CRO, AD396/666 of November to December
    1901, AD396/667 of February 1904 to January
    1905; Roger Jones, *A Book of Newton Abbot*,
    Bradford on Avon, 1986. The library and technical
    schools are listed buildings.
38 These portraits hang in Bodelwyddan Castle,
    North Wales.
39 CRO, AD396/665 of 13 March 1896.
40 *WB* 10 May 1894.
41 CRO, AD396/670 letter from Passmore Edwards
    of 26 July 1898 to the Mayor of Launceston
42 *RCG* 10 February 1898.

Fourteen: Seaside problems and Newquay riots

1   CRO, AD396/665 21 December 1895; *RI* 15
    March 1895.
2   CRO, AD396/665 7, 11, 13 February, 20 July, 5, 7,
    8 August 1896.
3   His salary was £72.50 a year plus £5 postage and
    other expenses. CRO, AD396/665 9 September,
    16 October 1896.
4   CRO, AD396/665 letter of 8 October 1896 to John
    Thomas and 21 October 1896 to Cook.
5   *RCG* 31 December 1896. The hotel is a listed
    building.
6   For further discussion of this issue, see Ronald
    Perry, 'Silvanus Trevail and the Development of
    Modern Tourism in Cornwall', *JRIC*, 1999, pp.
    33–42.
7   CRO, AD396/665 of 29 September, 6 October
    1896, Howard Fox of Falmouth collected
    contributions for the National Trust. *WB* 5
    October 1896.
8   CRO, AD396/665 8 October 1896.
9   CRO, AD396/665 letter to Robert Harvey 16
    September 1896.
10 CRO, AD396/665 9 August, 1, 6, 26, 28, 29
    September 1896.
11 The stables have been converted into flats that
    bear no resemblance to the original. The features
    of the engine house originally matched those of
    the hotel, but were lost after conversion to a
    dwelling. The hotel is a listed building.
12 For details of the construction and finance of the
    Headland Hotel see CRO, AD396/665 from
    October 1896 to January 1897; AD396/663 from
    February 1897 to June 1898; *WB* 25 June 1896, 15,
    18 March, 1, 12 April 1897; *SAS* 19 July 1900.
13 CRO, AD396/665 17 November 1896.
14 *WB* 22 April, 28 June, 1, 8, 12. 26 July 1897.
15 Family papers 5 September 1897.

16 *SAS* 21 October 1897; *WB* 16 September 1897.
17 CRO, AD396/663 9 October 1897; SAS 7, 14
    October 1897; *WB* 20 September, 7 October, 20
    December 1897.
18 CRO, AD396/663 2 February 1898; *WB* 17
    February 1898.
19 *WB* 22 July, 7, 11 October 1897; *RCG* 5 August
    1897.
20 CRO, AD396/666 3 April 1901.
21 *SAS* 5, 12 March 1903.
22 CRO, AD396/665 February to March 1896. The
    hotel has continued and extended, using the old
    buildings.
23 Family papers 17 May 1899; CRO, AD396/671
    and 673 June 1898.
24 CRO, AD396/672 25 March 1901; AD396/666 17
    April 1901; AD396/663 30 September 1902.
25 CRO, AD396/665 letter of 16 September 1896 to
    Robert Harvey. See letters of same date to George
    Hicks and to J Boyd Harvey for list of subscribers.
26 CRO, AD396/671 from April 1899 to August
    1900; AD396/673 from September to November
    1900; AD396/672 from November to December
    1901. Entrances have since been altered and
    extensions made to ground and first floors.
27 CRO, AD396/663 from January to March 1903;
    AD396/667 from December 1903 to February
    1905. The upper rooms have been converted to
    private accommodation.
28 According to A G Jenkin, Tyringham's solicitor,
    four smaller houses were preferred, the estimate
    for which was £1,400. CRO, AD396/665 February
    and March 1896. Tyringham, owner of Trevethow,
    overlooking the Hayle estuary, was the son of
    James Praed, MP for Birmingham, but dropped
    the Cornish name.
29 CRO, AD396/665 from March to October 1896;
    AD396/670 from January 1897 to February 1898.
    Three of the four houses were later converted into
    the Fairway Hotel and all have now been
    demolished
30 CRO, AD396/665 10 October 1896.
31 CRO, AD396/665 from February to September
    1896 including advertisements in *CDP*, *WB*,
    WMN and *RCG* for building the bridge and road;
    AD396/670 August and October 1897. Trevail
    wrote to Venning of Devonport that the
    'conditions' were 'quite good enough for a
    £10,000 job'. A farmhouse and pair of dwellings
    elsewhere in Trebarwith have been suggested as
    Trevail designs, but we have found no evidence to
    support this.
32 CRO, AD396/670 September, October 1897.
33 CRO, AD396/670 October to December 1897;
    WB 16 April 1903. In 1904 Cornelius wrote to
    Bathurst the solicitor informing him of Trevail's
    arrangement that a commission would be paid by
    any builder who developed the sites, but the 1908
    Ordinance Survey map shows no sign of building.
    By 1938 Trevebyn Road and Egerton Road were
    shown as about one third of their present length.

34 Again we have no record of any development.
35 Apparently Tredwen pulled out of the scheme. CRO, AD396/671 from October to December 1899; CG 1 July 1904. A pair of dwellings for Robert Warne, a local builder, can be attributed to Trevail, but the Sea Spray Hotel and Atlantic Terrace, constructed about this time, were the work of others, although the road on which they are situated was suggested in Trevail's plans.
36 CRO, AD396/670 22 March 1897.
37 CRO, AD396/673 from September 1900 to July 1901; AD396/672 from April to November 1901. With many additions it became the Westward Ho Hotel, demolished in 2003 and replaced with a much larger block of apartments.
38 WB 12 September 1895.
39 CRO, AD396/666 8 November 1901. For further discussion of this topic, see Ronald Perry and Hazel Harradence, 'What caused the Cornish Hotel Boom of the 1890s?' JCALH, 48, 2004, pp. 32–6.
40 WB 16 February 1899.
41 WB 16 March 1899.
42 WB 12 March 1903. It burnt down in 1905 and was not rebuilt until 1909.
43 WB 26 March 1903.
44 CRO, AD396/666 4 March 1901; WB 17 September 1903.
45 CRO, AD396/666 letter of 20 March 1901.
46 WB 17 September 1903.
47 CRO, AD396/666 of 28 August 1901.
48 The London Gazette 12 June 1903; WB 17 December 1903.

Fifteen: Public and private health problems

1 WB 29 August 1895.
2 WB 28 March, 11, 25 April, 6 June, 15, 29 August 1895.
3 CRO, AD396/665 of 14 January 1896 from Trevail to Baldwin Latham and 14 January, 30 October 1896 to Santo Crimp; WB 16 July, 13, 27 August, 10 September; RCG 17 September 1896.
4 RCG 28 February, 26 December 1895; CRO, AD396/665 of 13, 14, 18 January, 21 March 1896.
5 RCG 7 February 1895, 17 September 1896.
6 This was the figure he gave in his President's Address to the Society of Architects, Architects' Magazine 1901, p. 5.
7 Although the commission was 3 per cent, not 5 per cent as in private practice.
8 CRO, AD396/665 of 1 September 1896, 21, 23 January 1897.
9 For details of schemes see WB 16 September 1897; RCG 17 September 1897, 14, 21 December 1899, 13 February 1902.
10 RCG 5 August 1897.
11 SAS 17 January, 16 May 1890, 7 October 1897.
12 For plans etc for the farm, bailiff's house and

Isolation Hospital of July 1900 see CRO, HCI/1/6/99. For correspondence relating to the asylum see CRO, AD396/663 from March 1898 to July 1901; AD396/666 from June to November 1901; AD396/667 from December 1903 to May 1904.
13 Family papers 27 February 1900.
14 Cornwall County Asylum, Proposed Extensions. To Builders and Contractors, notice from Robert Edyvean, 25 May 1901.
15 WB 8, 26 August 1901. The figure quoted by the West Briton would appear to be an underestimate, if Trevail was receiving a 3 per cent commission.
16 Private communication from Matthew Saunders, Secretary of the Ancient Monuments Society. Of the buildings designed or extended by Trevail, the Kendal Building was gutted by fire in 2001 and demolished, the medical superintendent's House, known as Townsend House, was converted to a pair of private homes and is a listed building. The isolation hospital is closed, its future uncertain, The Foster Block is now owned by Community First, Cornwall. See Hazel Harradence, JCALH 2000, 39, p 2–12.
17 Building News, 13 November 1903.
18 CRO, AD396/667 from December 1903 to March 1904.
19 Later known as Michaelstowe House, then Michaelstowe Manor, holiday chalets were built around it. The owners since 2000 have been returning the house to its former state.
20 Carefully restored, after neglect in the twentieth century, it is a listed building.
2 It is not known if the conservatory was built as no trace of it remains. CRO, DCRES/1249/168.
22 Still in use, it is a listed building.
23 CRO, SRB/KEN/1.
24 CRO, AD396/670 from April to December 1897.
25 CRO, AD396/670 April to September 1897; building certificates of May 1897. Spry kept a polo field, horses and hounds and lived there until his death in the 1930s. Later a turkey farmer kept ducks and geese in the house, but it has since been restored by new owners.
26 CRO, SRB/KEN/1; CRO, AD396/ 670 October to December 1897.
27 CRO, SR/KEN/1 and SR/KEN/2/1; CRO, AD396/670 from November 1897 to June 1901. The building was later demolished for road widening.
28 Their solicitor William Coode informed Trevail that Mrs Thomas was delighted that negotiations had fallen through, since she always thought the house too inaccessible. For discussions on alterations see CRO, AD396/665 from August to December 1896; AD396/670 from October to July 1899. Trevail seemed very friendly with the Thomas family. E C Thomas invited him to dine at his home in Kensington Palace Gardens. John Thomas' son, Arthur L Thomas, corresponded with Trevail from 9 New Street Worcester.

29 *WB* 6 June 1898. Now part of Tregonissey House, the new building had a ground floor barber, a second storey hairdresser and a storeroom on the third floor.

30 CRO, AD396/670 October 1897 to April 1899. After extensive repairs in 2004, it continues in use.

31 CRO, AD396/671 from September 1899 to February 1900. Later demolished, its site was then part of a car park, now under further development.

32 *RCG* 30 September 1897.

33 From 1926 onwards the house was used by St Lawrence's hospital as part of the asylum, and for years ran a flourishing poultry farm employing twelve patients. In 1986 it was sold as a private hospital.

34 Her cousin was an influential man, tireless in the promotion of the industrial regeneration of Cornwall.

35 CRO, AD396/670 from September 1897 to March 1899; AD396/671 from November 1899 to October 1900. At one time a dentists', it was carefully restored and converted into apartments in early 2005. See Ann Perry, 'A Visit to Collins Country', *STSN*, 2002.

36 CRO, AD396/667 December 1903.

37 CRO, AD396/671 from December 1899 to August 1900.

38 Family papers 8 September 1901.

39 CRO, AD396/672 from June to December 1901; AD396/666 October 1901; AD396/667 June and July 1904.

40 Notes of the various tenders were found in Trevail's address book.

41 Family papers 9, 11, 16 September 1902.

42 In 1927 the house had been renamed The Palace and was occupied by Archbishop Gregg. It appears to have been acquired in 1952 or 1953 by the Pharmaceutical Society of Ireland and became the School of Pharmacy of Dublin University circa 1980 but around 2000 reverted to the Society. We are indebted to Ann Martha Rowan of the Irish Architectural Archive for this information. The exterior has now been beautifully restored.

43 *WB* 10 December 1896; *RCG* 17 December 1896.

44 Family papers 22 June 1897.

45 Family papers 1, 9, 19, 20, 24, 27 August, 2, 11 September, 1 October 1898. Trevail's surveyor's journal contained notes of his weight.

46 Family papers 9 August, 11 September 1899; *WB* 23 February, 3, 16 March 1899.

47 CRO, AD396/663 September 1899.

48 Family papers 20, 23 October 1900.

49 *WB* 26 September 1901.

Sixteen: Presidential glories and personal tragedies

1 Alex Koch, *Academy Architecture and Architectural Review*, 1897, 11, pp. 28, 30.

2 CRO, AD396/671 of 20 January 1900.

3 *RCG* and *WB* 5 December 1901.

4 Address of 19th Annual Dinner of the Society of Architects, 21 May 1903.

5 *Architects Magazine* II, 14, 1901, p.32.

6 *Architects Magazine* II, 14, 1901, pp. 34–6, II, 15, 1902, p. 51, 3, 32, 1903, p. 163; *RCG* 5 December 1901.

7 Society of Architects, Presidential Address, 1902, pp. 6–11; *Architects Magazine* II, 15, 1902, p. 62; 3, 32, 1903, pp. 180–1.

8 *Architects Magazine* II, 13, 1901, p. 7.

9 *WB* 22 May 1902.

10 *WB* 8 May 1902; *Building News* 13 November 1903.

11 The illustrated address remains in the possession of the family.

12 Family papers 27 March 1902.

13 Family papers 11 November 1902.

14 CRO, AD396/666 of 21 March 1901.

15 Family papers 30 March 1902.

16 A design from the catalogue of B Cohen and Son, described in Edwardian Truro, edited by June Palmer, 1993, p. 85, as being a sideboard for the dining room, was in fact a dressing table in the bedroom. The sideboard that Trevail used was one of his own designs.

17 *WB* 24 July 1902; Postcards to family from 11, 17 August and 2 to 21 September 1902.

18 *WB* 27 November 1902; *SAS* 18 December 1902, 1 January 1903.

19 Family papers 8, 11 November, 2, 12, 15, 16 December 1902.

20 *SAS* 1 January 1903. Silvanus gave 50 guineas (£52.50) to the hospital committee in recognition of their care for his father, and they made him a Vice President.

21 *WB* 29 January 1903.

22 Family papers 26 January 1903; *RCG* 29 January 1903; *WB* 29 January, 12 February 1903.

23 CRO, EN/2251 letter of 29 January 1903.

24 Family papers 1, 14 February 1903.

25 *WB* 26 February 1903.

26 *WB* 5, 12 March 1903.

27 *WB* 12, 19 March 1903.

28 *WB* 19 March 1903.

29 Family papers 16 April 1903.

30 Family papers 1898.

31 *WB* 16 April 1903. Trudgeon narrowly lost the by-election.

32 Family papers 6 April 1903.

33 *WB* 30 April 1903.

34 Family papers 27 March 1902.

35 *WB* 16 April 1903.

36 *RCG* 16 April 1903.

37 *WB* 16 April 1903.

38 *WB* 7 May 1903.

39 *Architects Magazine*, 3, 32, 1903, p. 168; *WB* and *RCG* 21 May 1903.

40 *Architects Magazine*, 3, 32, 1903, p. 164; *WB* 28 May 1903.

41 *RCG* 16 July 1903.
42 *WB* 9, 12 November 1903.
43 *WB* 12 November 1903.
44 CRO, AD396/666 30 October 1903.
45 *WB* 10 December 1903.
46 *WB* 9, 12 November 1903.

Seventeen: What drove Trevail to self-destruction?

1 *SAS* 12 November 1903.
2 *WB* 12 November 1903.
3 *WB* 10 December 1903; Sheila Bird, *Cornish Tales of Mystery and Murder*, Newbury, 2002; Michael Holgate, *Murder and Mystery on the Great Western Railway*, Devon, 2006.
4 James Whetter, 'What drove Trevail to destruction?', *ABK*, 1997, 87, pp. 12–17, and 'Mystery of train suicide', *WMN* 14 January 1997; Henry Tregilgas, 'What drove Trevail to Destruction', *ABK*, 1998, 91, pp. 15–16.
5 Family papers 27 June 1903.
6 *RCG* 16 October 1902
7 For further discussion of this topic, see Ronald Perry and Hazel Harradence, 'What caused the Cornish Hotel Boom of the 1890s?' *JCALH*, 48, 2004, pp. 32–6.
8 Family papers 27, 30 June 1903.
9 *The London Gazette*, 12 June 1903, 18 March 1904.
10 *WB* 19 July 1900.
11 *WB* 9 November 1903.
12 *RCG* 9 September 1901.
13 Family papers 9 August 1898.
14 *WB* 13 November 1902.
15 Silvanus Trevail left his entire estate to his sister Laura, with a gross value of £6,908, later increased in the probate register to £8,739. A newspaper reported a dispute between two prospective beneficiaries, one claiming inheritance from a will made six months earlier, the other from a second will dated two to three months later. The first beneficiary was said to be claiming that the later will was made when Trevail was 'not in his right mind'. (*CE* 11 December 1903) Neither person was named in the newspaper account, and Trevail family papers offer no reference to a dispute, although they contain a draft will in favour of his father, written in Trevail's own hand and dated the 5th of June 1901. After his father's death, Silvanus had to make a new will, which he did on the 3 August 1903, naming his sister. Possibly this gave rise to the newspaper story, for no other close relation existed who would seem to have a legitimate claim on the estate.
16 Rosemary Hill, *God's Architect*, London, 2007.
17 CRO, AD396/667 correspondence from December 1903 to February 1905. For a discussion of his work, see Hazel Harradence, 'Alfred John Cornelius' *JCALH*, 52, Autumn 2006, pp. 28–33.
18 *CG* 4 August 1906..0

Index

Truro Councillors (TC); Truro Aldermen (TA); County Councillors (CC); County Aldermen (CA); Privy Councillor (PC); Deputy Lieutenant (DL); Doctor of Civil Law (DCL).

ABC Railway Guide: 143

Adams, Professor J C: 130

Adams, M B (architect): 124

Adams, D: 153

St Agnes: Devon and Cornwall Bank 118; school 32; Wesleyan Chapel 51, 64

St Allen: Killivose and Tretherras farmhouses 28; Gwarnick farm buildings 28

Amalgamated Society of Railway Servants: 94

Ancient Lights Laws: 166

Andrews, Ambrose (builder): 117, 118.

Architect, The: 23, 25, 28, 38

Architects Association of Ireland: 31

Architects, Society of: 52, 62, 153, 154, 164, 165, 167, 169, 171, 179, 184; banquet 173

Architectural Association: 23, 165

Athemeum, The: 140

St Aubyn, J Piers (architect): 30, 91

St Austell: 30, 41; Burngullow 113; Carclaze School 30; Cemetery Chapel 27; Central School, West Hill 21, 30, 34; china clay industry 19, 41, 81, 113, 127; Coode-Shilson 'Red Bank' 115–116, 160; Congregational Church 27, 51, 65; County Finance Meeting 109; Devon and Cornwall Bank 117; Free Library (proposed) 127; Hawkes premises 91, 120; Higman versus Lee Court Case 162; Hodge's shop 120; Ledrah House 15; Liberal Club 91–92, 120; Market Hill shop 159; Moorland Road houses 96, 109, 156, 159, 178; Mount Charles School 21; Mount Charles Wesleyan Chapel 26; North Hill Conservatory for Veale 156; possible centre for County Council 80; Public Rooms 110; School Board 21, 25, 32, 38; Sydenham Villa 110; Tregarne House and Terrace 92, 109; Veale and Co Works 120; Watering Estate 93; Wesleyan Chapel (St John's Church) 25, 65, 97; workhouse (proposed extension) 110

Ball, James: 94

Barham, Dr Charles: 83

Barings Bank: 75

Barratt, Francis (CA, JP, later Sir Francis Layland-Barratt): 76, 90–92, 96, 97, 109, 141, 143, 149, 159

Bartlett: 149

Basset, Sir Francis: 123

Basset, G C: 125

Barry, Sir Charles (architect): 17

Bath Stone Co: 129

Battershill, Thomas (builder): 64, 119, 127

Beauchamp Beauchamp, Edmund (JP): 50

Beaworthy, Devon: Witherdon House 93, 157; workers cottages 28

Bedford, G: 136

Bell, R: 94

Bennet, Richard Gully (DL, CA, JP): 142

Bertini: 150

Best, R S: 23

Biscovey School: 25, 33

Blackford, Oscar: 123, 178

Blake, W E (builder): 123

St Blazey: lectures in 40: school 21, 23, 33

Blenkinsop, Alfred (TA): 81, 111, 133

Blisland: school by Snell 29; Tregaddick Lodge 66, 184

Boase, Edward (St Ives Town Clerk): 100

Bodmin: 174; asylum, building of Foster block 153–6, 176, 178, 182; asylum extension by Hine 29; asylum farm buildings 154; Bible Christian Chapel 27, 51; Cathedral (possible site) 41, County Council (possible centre) 80, Free Library and Science and Art School 128, 129, 137, 176, Gas Co. 160; St Guron's 160, GWR 88; Guildhall 68; Laninval 115, 159; lectures 47; St Nicholas House 109, 111, 160; Post Office and shops 50; public health 85; Public Rooms (proposed) 27, 68; Tregenna, Michaelstowe 156

Boer War: 150, 164, 177

Bolitho: company 138; family 90; Mrs 159; Thomas Bedford (JP, MP) 76, 87, 128, 131, 140

Bond, Frank (High Sheriff of Berkshire): 168

Boscastle: 142, School Board 36; Wellington Hotel 138

Boscawen family: 96

Boscoppa School by Hancock: 30

Bowring, Thomas (later Sir Thomas) Benjamin and Library: 133, 134, 173

Branwell, John: 76

Brassacott (Brazacott) School: 21, 37

St Breock and Egloshayle United School Board: see Wadebridge

Bristol: 170; Temple Meads Station 16

Bristol Cornish Association: 167

British Architect, The: 24

Brown, Rev J R (Helland): 51, 65–6

Brunel, Isambard Kingdom: 16, 17, 72

Buck, Henry: (TC) 60, 69, 81, 85, 86, 88, 89, 95, 104, 105–7, 109, 120, 126, 149, 152, 153

Buckingham, Anthony A: 123

Bude: UM Church by Harbottle 29; chapel by Hine 29; Globe Hotel 120, 145, 178; post office and shops 120

Builder, The: 27, 166

Building News: 125, 166, 167

Bullen, William (TA): 105

Bullmore, G C (Newquay councillor): 143

Burt, William (Launceston Councillor and builder): 129, 130, 157

Burton, Edward: 120

Caldwell, Oliver (architect): 30

Callington School by Rice 29

Calstock School by Snell 29

Camborne: Chapel Street House 28; Cornish Bank 115; Devon & Cornwall Bank 115; Dolcoath Mine 113; Ferris Bequest 125; Fiddick and Michel 115, 120; Free Library 107, 125, 128, 137; Parliamentary Election 53–5; Polstrong Conservatory 156; Public Rooms 92; School of Mines 109; Vivian Bros shop 120–21

Camelford NCR: 88

Carbis Bay: see St Ives

Carclaze School addition by Hancock: 30

Carkeek, Arthur (Redruth Councillor & builder, later Sir Arthur Chairman CCC): 76, 90, 99, 140, 143, 151, 175, 176

Carlyon, E Lawrence (Coroner): 132

Carlyon family: 129

Carlyon, Major: 51

Carlyon, T Hugh (later Spry): 93, 157

Carnegie, Andrew: 125

Carus-Wilson, Edward Shippard (JP): 47, 48

Celtic cross designs: 28, 168

Chacewater: National (later Board) School: 25, 111, 157

Chamberlain, Joseph (President Board of Trade): 48

Charlestown School by Hancock: 30

Chilcott, Gilbert Hele (TC): 160, 161

Chirgwin, Thomas (JP, TA, CC): 69, 76, 83, 85, 89, 104, 105

Clarence, Duke of: 90

Clark, Dr James: 132 133

Clay Workers, Institute of: 167

Clemens, A C (architect): 67

Clemens, Albert (surveyor): 61

Clemens, M (builder): 127

Clifden, Viscount: 173

Clinton, Lord (DL, JP, Devon County Alderman):112

Clunes A S (architect): 67, 74

Coad, Richard (architect): 29

Cock, F Hearle (Truro Town Clerk): 57–61

Collins, Digby (DL, JP, CA): 82, 90, 131, 132

Collins, Rev E V (of Blisland): 160

Collins, John Basset: 168

Collins, JH: 45

Collins, JR: 109, 111, 160

Collins, Miss M S: 160

Collins, RC: 78

Colliver, John (builder): 114, 115, 118, 121, 133, 159

St Columb Major: Ashleigh 157; Cathedral (possible site) 42; Congregational Church 27; Cornish Bank 114; school 21, 24; public health 153, 154; Treventon 27, 184

Contagious Diseases (Animals) Act: 85

Conybeare, Charles Augustus Vansittart (Liberal candidate): 53–5, 92, 113, 141, 164

Coode, Edward: 93

Coode, family: 129

Coode, William (County Treasurer): 27, 93

Coode and Shilson: 17, 115, 116, 123, 158

Cook (Trevail's assistant): 45, 139

Cornelius, Alfred John (Trevail's assistant & successor): 72, 116, 118, 119, 123, 134, 137, 145, 156, 160, 162, 172, 174, 175, 182

Cornish Hotels Company: 75, 98–102, 104, 138

Cornish Riviera Express, GWR Guide: 183

Cornwall County Council: newly formed 69; funds from 131

Cornwall, Duchy of: 57, 88, 144

Cornwall Railway: 75

Courtney, Leonard Henry (later Lord): 47, 128

Crimp, Santo (engineer): 152

Daniel, John R: 156

Daubuz, John Claude (JP, CC): 76, 90, 138

St Day School: 21, 32, 35, 38

Davidstow Church by Hine 29

Delabole: 21; Church by Hine 29: school 21, 23, 38

Dennis, Henry: 100, 113, 115, 116, 159, 160

Devon County Council: 136

Devon and Exeter Architectural Society: 169

Dickens, Charles: 166

Dingle, John William Darley (CA): 153

Dobell, Robert (Truro Councillor, later Town Clerk, CC): 131, 173

Dobwalls school (proposed): 27, 38

Dorien-Smith, T: 144

Dorrington, Theophilus Lutey (TA, CC): 61, 152

Downend School: see Lostwithiel

Drake, Dr H H (schoolmaster): 15, 16

Drew, Sir Thomas 162

Dublin, Woodside: 161–62, 170, 178, 180, 184

Dunstan, W H: 117

Durning-Lawrence, Sir Edwin: see Lawrence

East Cornwall Mineral Railway: 113

Ebrington, Viscount (DL, JP, Vice Chairman Devon CC): 137

Ecclesiastical Commissioners: 68

Edgcumbe Wesleyan Chapel, Wendron: 65

Edvean, Robert Phillips (Deputy Coroner) 129, 174, 175, 176

Education Act 1870: 19

St Endellion: see Port Isaac

Ennor, John Jun (Newquay Councillor & builder): 30, 143

Ennor, John, Snr (builder): 30, 147

Enys, Francis Gilbert (JP, DL, Sheriff): 42

Enys, John Davies (CC): 126, 131, 172, 181,

Exeter: 170; Great Western Hotel (proposed) 144, 145, 177; Rougemont Hotel 145

Falmouth: 72, 75, 95; Chamber of Commerce 88; Devon and Cornwall Bank 117; Docks 88; hotel and company 45, 73–4, 88, 98–9, 138, 150, 160; Ferris Bequest 125; Free Library Technical and Art Schools 125; GWR 88; Pendennis Castle 170; Pendennis Hotel 88, 98–99; public health 85; railway service 41

Falmouth, Lord: 53, 56, 89, 160

Faull, William (St Ives Alderman): 137

Feminism: Cornwall Library 47; Parliamentary Election 53

Feock Wesleyan Church: 27

Ferris, Octavius: 125, 137

Fiddick and Michel: 115, 120

Fish Trade Association: 88

Forbes, Stanhope: 90

Foster, Sir Walter (MP): 173

Fowey: Church vestry 51, 111; Devon and Cornwall Bank 118–19, 176, 178;

entrance lodge for Treffry 67; St Fimbarras Church 111; Grammar School 21; Hotel 150; lectures in 40; Masonic Hall 67; railway 21, 74; schools 25, 38, 97; Workingmen's Club 28

Fowey Consols Mine: 18

Fowke, Francis (engineer): 17

Fox, Howard: 45, 90

France, President of: 112, 180

Fradd, Martin: 141

Free Libraries Acts: 125

Fuller, Rev W H (of Newquay): 65

Garling, Henry (architect): 16, 17

Gatley, Charles: 75, 76, 98, 141

General Railway Workers Union: 94

Gerrans: Trewince 157–9

Gill, N and Sons: 123

Gladstone, Rt Hon Herbert (MP): 56, 135

Goss, Harry (builder): 134, 136

Gott, Rt Rev John, Bishop of Cornwall: 94, 97, 107

Gough, Hugh Romien FRIBA: 62

Gould, J F (architect): 29

Graham, Rev George (of Par): 27

Grampound Road, Trenowth estate: 92

Graves-Sawle, Sir Charles: see Sawle

Great Western Railway: 87–9, 94, 100, 101, 109, 141, 144, 145, 176, 183; gift of books 137; Newquay Junction Bill 88, 89; sale of land for Newquay improvement 73; subscription to Newquay Waterworks 71; takes over Cornwall Railway 75

Grier, Dr Monro: 103, 109

Grylls, W M (JP, CC): 45

Guernsey Grand Hotel (proposed): 144, 145, 177

Gwennap School Board: 32

Gwarnick farm buildings: 28

Gwinear Road Railway Station: 74

Hain, Edward (later Sir Edward) (JP, MP, St Ives Councillor & Mayor): 82, 88, 90, 100, 101, 128, 161, 173

Hancock, H Syd (Board Clerk): 25, 30

Harbottle, Edward H (Devon County Surveyor, architect): 29

Harbours of Refuge: 47–9

Hardwick, P C (architect): 17

Harris, Josiah 48

Harris, Walter H 145

Harry, Captain Thomas Row (St Ives Councillor & Mayor): 101, 128

Harvey family (of Hayle): 141

Harvey, Robert (later Sir Robert): 89, 92, 134, 138, 140, 151, 172, 173, 174

Hawke, George: 91

Hawkins Estate: 75

Hayle: Institute 124–5; public health 85; technical education centre 82

Headley (Manager, King Arthur's Castle Hotel): 151

Heard, Edward Goodridge (TA & Mayor, CA): 49, 58, 68, 69, 76, 80, 83, 86, 90, 105, 106, 108, 173

Hearn, John (TA): 105, 107

Helland: Tredethy house 93; Parish Church tower 51, 66; Wesleyan Church 27

Helston: 166; Cornish Bank 115; Great Western railway link 74

Hender, Thomas B (Launceston Councillor): 129

Henderson, James (Truro Mayor & architect): 42, 45, 48, 161, 173, 179

Hendy, James 92

Henley on Thames: Red Lion Hotel 145

Hext, Francis John (JP, CA): 93

Hext, George: 93

Hickes, Thomas James (County Surveyor): 92

Hicks, George: 28, 48, 71, 76, 78, 138–41, 164, 171, 176, 181

Hicks, James (architect): 25, 29, 41, 42, 49, 74, 111, 112, 114, 127

Hicks, Walter (brewer): 121, 145

Hine, James (architect): 29

Hobbah, John (schoolmaster): 14

Hocking, Joseph: 140

Holman Bros of Hayle: 90

Hoskins, John (builder): 36, 37

Housel Bay: see Lizard.

Housing of the Working Classes Act 1890: 95

Houston, E M (Trevail's assistant): 32

Hoyte, William: 76

Hoxley Samuel (MP): 46

Hussey family: 123

Illogan: School Board 21; cottages 96

Imperialism: 47, 54

Indian Queens School: 25

Infectious Diseases (Notification) Act: 154

Insurance companies: 112, 141

International Exhibitions: 25, 40, 69, 164

St Ives: Captain Harry's house 101; Carbis Bay Hotel 100–102, 104, 146, 151; Carbis Bay building estate 145; Devon and Cornwall Bank 117; Draycott Terrace 101; Free Library 127, 137; Great Western Railway 21, 74, 101; Hotel sites 75; Porthminster Hotel 100, 101, 102, 143; Stennack School 21, 22, 25, 38, 128; Technical education centre 82; Tregenna Castle Hotel 74, 100;

Treloyhan Manor 100–101, 161

Jacob, John Towler (TC): 57, 120

James, John (JP, TC): 60, 76, 104, 108, 126, 173, 179

James, Dr W Dale: 153

Jenkin, Alfred Hamilton (Solicitor): 97, 144, 156

Jenkin, Pearse (agent): 94, 95

Jenkyn Charles (St Ives Alderman): 137

Jennings, Amos (JP, TA): 105

Jerram, James W (builder): 135

Johns, William James (TA, Truro Mayor): 108,

Jose, John (JP, CA): 75, 76, 78, 90, 138

Julian, James (builder): 65, 67, 90, 93

Julian, John Nankivell (builder): 38

Kendall, Rev R Sinclair (of Luxulyan): 167

Kimberly, Lord: 98

Kinsale, Lord (CC): 83

Kirkland, John (architect): 156

Kit Hill Quarry: 113

Kittow, John (JP, Launceston Councillor & Mayor): 129, 130

Knight, T L (East Ham Council): 135

Ladock: Tregear farmhouse 50

Lake, T H: 88

Lang, Thomas (builder): 76, 78, 101, 143

Lanhydrock House improvements by Scott and Coad: 29

Lanivet: mill house 50, 65; proposed school 27

Lank Free Methodist Chapel: 27, 65

Lanner School: 21, 32, 35, 38

Lapford, Devon: cottage (proposed) 160, 170

Latham, Baldwin (engineer): 152

Lanyon, Alfred (CC): 76, 83

Lanyon, John: 90, 174

Launceston: Free Library 128, 129, 137; GWR 88; historic centre 80; Post Office by Hine 29; public health 85, 153; school by Peter 29; technical education 133

Laverton, Arthur (TC): 120

Lawrence, Edwin (later Sir Edwin Durning-Lawrence) (MP): 89, 127, 131

Laws, Peter 117

Lee, H Austin, CB, (Ambassador): 144

Lelant School by Wise: 29

Lennard, Thomas J: 123

Lethbridge, W H (builder): 118

St Levan, Lord: 173

Lewannick School by Hine: 29

Lewcock (architect): 27

Linkinhorne: Church 65; Upton Cross School 21, 32; Sunday school 65; Sharplands School 22

Liskeard: Chapel by Rice 29; Church by Coad 29; County Court case 35; Free Library 127; public health 153; school and Chapel by Skentlebury 29; school by Wise 29; School Board 38

Liverpool: Lord Mayor 109

Lizard: 74, 75; Coverack Headland Hotel 150; Housel Bay Hotel 99, 102; Maenheere 99, 100; Poldhu Hotel 74; Polurrian House 74

Local Government Act 1888: 79

London: 17, 174, 176; Albert Hall 17; Baring's Bank failure 75; Bridge Street office 165; buildings (proposed) 177; Chancery Division High Court 115; Cornish Association 167; Crystal Palace 17; Department of Education 23, 32–36, 67, 131, 158; demolition 17; East Ham Hospital 132–6; East Ham

Public Library, Plashet Grove 135, 184, Great Western Royal Hotel 17; Home Dept 154; Honourable Drapers Co. 131; Harley Street 81; Lombard Street 18; Lunacy Commission 154; Master Builders Association 172; Paddington Station 16; Palace Chambers, Westminster 165, 172, 180; Public Works Loan Commissioners 20, 33, 34; Sherborne Street office 165; South Kensington Science Museum 90

London and South Western Railway: 87, 88, 109, 145

Looe: school and Town Hall by Gould 29; school and chapel near Looe by Skentlebury 29

Lostwithiel: Congregational Church 27; Cowbridge house 93; Downend School 25; farmers' dinner 82

Lovegrove, (architect): 27

Luxmore: 93

Luxulyan: 145, 168; birthplace of Trevail 13; Carne Farm 13, 39; Church Bells 167, 168, 176, 177; Church window 183; dynamite explosion 39; funeral 175; Higher Menadue and Lower Menadue Farms 13; medallion 171; Rosemelling Wesleyan Chapel 14, 26; School Building Committee 19, 20, 174; sundial 168; Vicar 39

MacKenzie, Harman: 141

MacLeod, M L: 147

Martyn, Miss: 157

Masonic membership: 40

Masterman, Mrs: 175, 176,

St Mawes: school 97; Ship and Castle Hotel 145; Steamship and Ferry Company 75

St Mawgan-in-Pydar School: 21, 25

McArthur, William Alexander (MP): 65, 89, 92

McKinnon, T (London CC): 135

Mead, Major John (JP & Falmouth Council): 75, 76, 78, 98, 138, 141

Meeres, Rev C R (of Perranzabuloe): 68

Melbourne, International Exhibition: 25

Menna: workers' cottages 28

St Merryn School: 25

St Mewan School: 21, 23, 32

Mevagissey: school 21, 34, 36; Congregational Chapel 51; Gorran School 21, 22; Mercantile Association 167; Polpier 103

Midland Cornish Association: 153

Molesworth, Sir William: 129

Morley, Earl of (PC, DL, JP, Chairman Devon CC): 136

Mount Edgcumbe, Earl of (PC, DCL, Chairman CCC): 49, 76, 79, 83, 89, 90, 133, 142

Moyle, W H and Mitchell (builders): 157, 158

Moretonhampstead: Bowring Library 133–4; Nurses Home 134, 178

Morshead, Sarah Elizabeth Wilmot: 66

Morshead, Sir Warwick Charles: 66, 172

Muir, James: 156

Mullion: Poldhu Hotel 74; Polurrian House 74

National Trust: 140

Nankivell: 120

Nanpean: Mission Church of St George the Martyr 27, 65; school 25

Newquay: 70, 75; Atlantic Hotel 75–7, 99, 102, 104, 139, 141, 142, 177; Bon Air (Preston's Bungalow) 149; Commercial Hotel 73, 115; Congregational Church 65; Cornish Bank 115; Cornwall Minerals Railway 70; Council and Local Board 71, 73, 78, 143, 145, 172; Crantock Road Infants & Girls School 21; Devon and Cornwall Bank 118; Fistral Bay Estate 72, 102; Fistral Terrace (now Headland Road) 145; Glendorgal 54; Great Western Hotel 28, 47, 71, 73, 76; Great Western Railway 21, 71, 73, 76; Headland Hotel 17, 140–143, 150–51, 160, 176, 178, 180; Lamorna 103; Masonic Hall 28; Mercantile Association 78, 143; Newquay Junction Railway Bill 88; 'Newquay Riots' 141, 176; Pentowan 28, 48, 71; Porth 28; Porth Veor Estate 54, 72;   Quay House 149; regatta 141; road widening 57; Tolcarne Estate 72; Towan Blistra Estate 71; tourism 149, 172; Victoria Hotel Company 143, 150; waterworks 48, 71

Newton Abbot: 170, 174; Free Library 136–7, 176, 178; Technical School 136–7, 176, 178

Native Guano Company: 113

Nicholls, John Michael (St Ives Mayor & Councillor): 100

North Cornwall Railway: 87–89, 109, 143, 149

North Petherwin School Board: see Brassacott.

Northey: 54

Norway, Arthur: 140

Oliver, E J (Borough Surveyor, Bodmin): 129

Oliver, J Cardell (Newquay Councillor): 143

Oliver, John (builder): 37

Oxford University Certificates: 16

Paige, J Square (Devon & Cornwall Bank): 117, 118

Padstow: 86; Board School 23, 24, 25; Cemetery Chapel 27; North Cornwall Railway and Prideaux-Brune 45,147; Prideaux Place 28, 149; Woodlands, Treator 50

Par: Consols Mine 18; Cornwall Minerals Railway 70; St Mary's Vicarage 51; Primitive Methodist Chapel 27

Parker, Henry Theodore (Newton Abbot Councillor): 136

Parkes, John: 134, 161, 170

Parkhouse, Rev W (of Perranzabuloe): 68

Parkyn and Peters (clay merchants): 113˙

Parkyn, Major Edwin (JP): 81

Passmore Edwards, H: 173

Passmore Edwards, John: 107, 124–137

Passmore Edwards, Mrs 125

Paul, Robert Macleane (TC): 58

Paxton, Joseph (architect): 17

Payne, William & John: 101, 102

Pearce, Edward: 72, 73

Pearce, James: 78

Pearson, John Loughborough (architect): 42,

Pemberton, Joseph (builder): 162

Pendarves, W Cole: 90

Pentewan school: 21, 34, 38

Penzance: Art School 28; Church by Trounson 30; Devon and Cornwall Bank (proposed) 114; Free Library by White 30; GWR 88; Poltair Terrace, Heamoor 156; St Paul's Church porch 25, 30, 51; public health 85; Queen's Hotel 72; technical education centre 82

Perranporth: Droskyn Castle 103; lodgings 74

Perranzabuloe Vicarage: 67, 68, 184

Perry, J T: 120

Peter, Claude Hurst (Launceston Town Clerk): 129

Peter, Otho Bathurst (architect): 29

Petherwin, South: Church by Hine 29

Pethick Bros (builders): 155

Pevsner, Nikolaus: 25, 104

Pill, Thomas Henry: 103

St Pinnock School by Hine: 29

Plagiarism: 30, 31

Plymouth: 170, 181; Devon and Cornwall Bank Head Office 113; Devonport 113; lectures 47; Oxford Street School 21, 24, 25

Polkinhorne, Samuel James (TC): 57, 58

Polperro: 96; school 21, 32, 35

Polruan shipyard: 28

Porth and Porth Veor: see Newquay

Port Isaac: Polzeath Estate 147; public health 85; school 21, 25, 32, 38

Preston, Edward Oxenford: 141, 150, 173

Prideaux-Brune, Charles: 28, 89, 173

Prideaux-Brune, Hon Mrs: 149

Pridham, A H (Devon & Cornwall Bank): 117, 119

Proktor, William (JP, Launceston Councillor & builder): 129, 130, 158

Public Health Acts: 61, 82, 85

Publicity: 31

Pugin, Augustus (architect): 182

Quiller-Couch, Arthur Thomas (JP, later Sir Arthur CA): 175

Rashleigh, Lady 20; Sir Colman: 27

Rashleigh, Evelyn William (JP, CA): 90, 132

Ray, Frederick Robert (CC): 154

Red Bank: see Coode & Shilson

Reed, Sir Charles (MP): 22, 128

Redruth: Bacon Factory 87; Brewery Company 99, 145; Clinton Estate 112; Ferris Bequest 125; Free Library 128; Illogan Board School 21; Illogan cottages 96; lectures 47, 56; Parliamentary election 53–5; Trewirgie School 67; Wesleyan Chapel 51, 63; Workhouse by Scott 29

Rice, Henry (architect): 16, 29, 113

Rice, Hugh, (TC): 80, 88, 111

Richards, William Martyn: 50

Robartes, Lord (CA): 45, 49, 53, 76, 83, 88, 89, 95, 96, 99, 101, 107, 128, 140

Roberts, Edward (TC): 57, 95, 105, 106, 108, 152

Robins, N: 117

Robson, E R (architect): 159

Roche Wesleyan Chapel; 27, 64

Rochester: RIBA visit 174

Rogers, Joseph (TC, Mayor of Truro, CC): 88, 104, 108, 109, 111, 132, 152

Rowe, William (Falmouth Councillor): 75, 76, 98

Rows, Richard Gundry (JP, CA), 79, 82, 87, 88, 99, 131, 133

Rowse, A L: 116

Royal Academy: 133

Royal Institute of British Architects: 17, 25, 91, 165, 167, 173

Royal Institution of Cornwall: 40, 42, 45, 68, 81, 169, 174

Ruabon Terracotta and Brick Works: 100, 141, 145, 159

Rundle, Laura: see Trevail

Rundle, Richard: 14

Rutter family: 46

Sampson, J H (TC): 61, 179

Sanson, John (architect): 101, 143

Savage, W H (builder): 135, 136

Sawle, Sir Charles Brune Graves (JP, DL, Sheriff): 110

Scott, Sir George Gilbert (architect): 17, 29

Scientific American, The: 66

Scilly, Isles of: Tregarthen Hotel project (proposed) 144, 177

Sharplands School: 22

Shilson and Coode: see Coode and Shilson

Shilson, D H: 90

Shilson, family 90

Shortlanesend: proposed school 27

Skentlebury, A E (architect): 29, 38

Smith, George John (DL, JP, CA, later Sir George): 48, 90

Smith, J J (TC): 179

Smith, Thomas (builder): 30, 114

Snell, Henry John (architect): 29, 74

Spry: see Carlyon

Stennack School: see St Ives

Stephens Estate: 28, 103

Stephens, Richard: 76

Stephens, William: 28

St Stephen in Brannel: school 32, 38; farms at Terras and Penhale 50

Stokes, Henry Sewell (of Truro): 83, 123

Strauss, Bernard 141

Sweetshouse Wesleyan Chapel: 27

Swift, W (architect): 67

Sykes, Godfrey (artist): 17

Sydney, International Exhibition: 25

Symons, John and Son (builders): 125, 127, 128

Talland and Lansallos United School Board: 35

Tangye, A J: 28

Tangye: family 46; company 112

Tangye, Richard (later Sir Richard): 45, 54, 65, 71

St Teath School: 25, 38

Technical Instruction Act 1889: 80

Temple Church: 51, 66

Tennyson, Lord: 137, 139

Thomas, James (CCC): 82

Thomas, John: 140, 158

Tintagel: 142; King Arthur's Castle Hotel 111, 120, 138–9, 146, 151, 159, 171, 178

Tourist's Hotel Company Limited of Cornwall: 99

Town Planning: 166

Travel: America & Canada 45–6, 55, 166; Britain & Ireland 45, 162, 166, 170; India 41; Scandinavia 149, 163; Paris 40; 69, 163, 164, 179; other European 40, 112, 163, 166, 172, 173

Trebarwith: bridge 111, 147; estate 147

Tredwen: 149

Treffry, Charles E: 71, 76

Treffry, Joseph Austen: 13

Tregarthen, Capt and Mrs Frank: 144

Tregilgas, Henry: 175, 182

Tregony Almshouses: 96

Tregonning, C E: 120

Trehane, Samson (builder): 129

Tremayne, Colonel Arthur (JP, CC): 79, 80, 89, 90, 131, 153, 155, 163

Tremayne, John (CC, MP, Sheriff): 88

Treneer, Anne: 22

Trenouth and Powers (builders): 37

Trenowth: see Grampound Road.

Tresidder, W H (borough surveyor): 125

Tretherras farmhouse: 27

Trethewey, William (CA): 75, 76, 78, 138

Trevail, Charles (paternal grandfather): 13,

Trevail, Charles T (cousin): 14, 16, 171, 174, 182

Trevail, Jane (mother): 13, 167, 168, 171, 176

Trevail, John (father): 13, 16, 39, 168, 169, 171, 172, 176, 182

Trevail, John & William (brothers of Silvanus): 14

Trevail, John (great uncle): 14

Trevail, Joseph (uncle): 19, 174, 176

Trevail, Laura (sister): 14, 142, 171, 176, 182, 183

Trevail, Silvanus: Family background and childhood 13–14; village school and St Austell academy 14–16; architectural training in London 16–18; first professional commission 19–20; member of Architectural Association, prizes, awards, quality of design 23–5; unfulfilled projects, competition from architects and plagiarists 29–31; problems of project supervision and work overload 32–8; estimated earnings and expenses 38–9, 180–81; continental travel 40, 163–5, 172–3, 179; move to Truro 41–2; visit to North America 45–6; post card collection 46, 149, 170; imperial politics 47; Harbour of Refuge campaign 47–9; feud with Pendarves Vivian 53–5; Liberal politics 55–6; vendetta with Town Clerk 57–61; member Society of Architects 62; unsuccessful projects 67–8; defeated as Truro Councillor, elected County Councillor 69; poor railway links to Cornwall 72–3; Assistant Surveyor Newquay 73;

Cornish Hotels Company 75–6;
campaigns for Truro as seat of
County Council and centre for
agricultural education 79–82; public
health crusade as Truro Councillor
and Chairman of County Council
Sanitation Committee 83–6; Great
Western Railway and North
Cornwall Railway 87–9; member of
Technical Instruction Committee
90–91; prime mover of holiday trade
98–104; Mayor of Truro 105; quarrels
with Henry Buck 106; Mayoral
Banquets 107; Chairman Sanitary
Committee 107; interest in selling
whisky, drying guano, quarrying
granite 113–13; Passmore Edwards
commissions 124–137; opposition to
hotel at Tintagel 138–40 'Newquay
Riots', obstruction by Newquay
Council 140–44; tourist slump,
bankruptcy of hotel company 150–51
sanitary reform in Truro and County
Councils 152–3; asylum architect
153–5; personal health problems
162–4; President of Society of
Architects, FRIBA, 165; London
newspapers report speeches 166;
advocate of Town Planning 166, 167;
death of mother 167–8; presidential
entertainments 167–70; deaths of
father and George Hicks 171; final
depression 174; inquest on death 175;
funeral 174; professional problems
176–8; political disappointments
178–9; possible symptoms of manic-
depression 180–82; Trevail's legacy
183–5

Trevelyan, Sir George (MP): 92

Treverbyn: school 22; schoolmaster's
house by Hancock 30

Trood, T P (Mayor of Launceston): 129

Trounson, John W (architect): 30

Truro: agricultural education centre 81;
art gallery 45, 68; St Andrew's
Mission Church 159; Blackford's
premises 123, 178; Boscawen Street
house 42; British School (Bosvigo)
159; Buckingham's shop (proposed)
123; Burton's shop 50, 120, 127;
Cabmen 107; Cathedral 44, 169, 173,
174; Cathedral Lane shop 123;
Central Technical Schools for
Cornwall 130–33, 162, 169, 176;
Chyvelah School, Threemilestone
158; Corn Exchange 49, 50, 120;
Cornish Bank 113; County Council
seat 79, 80; Debating Society 46;
Devon and Cornwall Bank by Rice
29, by Trevail 50, 113; Ferris Bequest
125; Fisheries Exhibition 90; Free
Library 107, 126, 169; Gill's
warehouse 123; Harrison Terrace 95;
High School for Girls 159; housing
by Whiteley and Hicks 42; St John's
vicarage (proposed) 67; Kenwyn
Church 169; Kenwyn housing
accounts 61; Kenwyn School Board
158; Lemon Street residence 169,
170; Liberal Club 55; Library
Reading room 46–7, 62; Mansion
House 58; Martin's stores & stables
62, 120; St Mary's Wesleyan Church
62–4, 169; St Mary's Wesleyan
School 97; Mercantile Association 80,
88; Methodist Conference 107;
Nankivell's shop 120; Mitchell Hill
house (proposed) 160; North
Cornwall Railway 88; St Piran's R C
Chapel & presbytery 62, 64; planning
disputes 57–8; Polkinhorne
warehouse 57–8, 120; Polwhele
Mansion by Scott 29; population and
institutions 42; Post Office 49–50,
120, 127; Prince's House, Princes
Street 58, 93; Prince's dining rooms
120; Public Baths 56, 111, 112; Public

Benefit Boot Company 121, 123; public health 83–5, 152, 178; Railway Rates Conference 87; Railway Station staff 107; Ratepayers Association 173, 179; Red Lion Hotel 62, 76, 88, 104, 114; Royal Hotel 149; Royal Institution of Cornwall 40, 42, 45, 68, 81, 169, 174; Triumphal Arches 42–5; Truro Council election 58; Wesleyan College hospital 97; West End Stores 123; William Street Chapel (Lemon Chapel) 64

Tunbridge Wells: Harrington Hotel Company 145; Mayoral Dinner 107

Tweedy: family 60; Robert 76

Tyringham, William Backwell: 145

Tywardreath: church by Coad 29; Masonic Chapter 40; reservoir 28; Trenython 94, 97; Trevail's residence 40

United States of America: 46; President of 180

Upton Cross: Board School 21, 32; Church 65; Sunday school 65

Veale & Company: 121

Veale, J E: 140, 151, 156

Vivian, Arthur (JP, MP, later Sir Arthur) Pendarves (CA): 53, 54

Vivian, Rev Charles W G (of Lapford): 160

Vivian, James Francis: 121

Vivian, John (JP): 103, 121

Wadebridge: schools 25, 34, 35, 38; GWR 88; public health 154

Washaway Infant School: 35

Watts, Francis (builder): 136

Watts, George Frederick: 137

Watts, W H (Lord Mayor of Liverpool): 109, family 46

Webb and Pearce (architects): 38

Webber, Thomas (Falmouth Alderman, CC): 20

Wells, Alec (architect): 182

Wendron: see Edgcumbe

St Wenn School; 21, 25

West Penwith: public health 153

Wharncliffe, Lord: 138, 140

Whetter, Dr James: 175

Whiskey suppliers: 112

White, Henry (architect): 28, 30

White, William (architect): 25, 111

Whiteley Nicholas (architect): 42

Whitford, Henry (solicitor): 27, 114

Wickett, James and Charles (brothers, brewers): 99

Williams, John Charles (CC, MP): 89, 90, 132

Williams, J M (MP): 53

Williams, Michael Henry (DL, JP, Newquay Councillor, CA): 76, 81, 83, 143

Wills, George: 134

Wise, C P (architect): 29

Wise, L C P: 129

Wright, W H K: 108, 126

Wyatt, Matthew Digby (architect): 17

Yorke-Davies, Dr W E: 163